böhlau

APPEAR

Participative knowledge production through transnational and transcultural academic cooperation

Edited by Andreas J. Obrecht

2015
BÖHLAU VERLAG WIEN KÖLN WEIMAR

The publication of this book was made possible by financial support from APPEAR. APPEAR is a programme of the Austrian Development Cooperation. The opinions expressed in this book are those of the authors and do not necessarily reflect the views of the editor, the APPEAR team or the Austrian Development Cooperation (ADC).

All printed photos have been made in the context of the described APPEAR projects, therefore individual authorships are not listed separately.

Deutsche Nationalbibliothek Cataloging-in-publication data:
http://dnb.d-nb.de

© 2015 by Böhlau Verlag GmbH & Co. KG, Wien Köln Weimar
Wiesingerstraße 1, A-1010 Wien, www.boehlau-verlag.com
All Rights Reserved. No part of this publication may be reproduced or transmitted in any form or by any means, electronic or mechanical, including photocopy, recording, or any other information storage or retrieval system, without prior permission in writing from the publisher.

Translation: Mag. Irmgard Schmoll (OeAD GmbH), Mag. Sylvi Rennert
Proof-reading and copy-editing: Dr. Anthony Ross-Hellauer
Cover design: Michael Haderer, Wien,
Typesetting: Bettina Waringer, Wien
Printing and binding: Theiss, St. Stefan im Lavanttal
Printed on acid-free and chlorine-free bleached paper
Printed in the EU

ISBN 978-3-205-79690-9

CONTENT

INTRODUCTION AND ACKNOWLEDGEMENT — 9

1 HIGHER EDUCATION DRIVES DEVELOPMENT — 11

2 APPEAR – CREATING TRANSNATIONAL AND TRANSCULTURAL SPACES OF KNOWLEDGE — 16

3 THE CENTRAL AMERICAN CONTEXT — 30
  3.1 Desarrollo Participativo Integral Rural - The growing involvement of the National Agricultural University with rural communities — 30
    3.1.1 The project - DEPARTIR — 30
    3.1.2 Changing minds and structures: Evolution or revolution? — 33
    3.1.3 So what are we going to do about gender?! — 37
    3.1.4 Enumeration of results — 40
  3.2 Improvement of Social Work Education to Foster Social Development and Poverty Reduction: An Academic Exchange of Theory, Methodology and Practice — 44
    3.2.1 The project - Trabajo Social – Educación y Cambio Social — 44
    3.2.2 Public space, safety and security — 47
    3.2.3 Social work and gender aspects: Why can social work not be considered gender blind? — 50
    3.2.4 Enumeration of results — 55
  3.3 Bioremediation of Contaminated Sites: Research and Education — 60
    3.3.1 The project - BIOREM — 60
    3.3.2 BIOREM and its people – researchers and beneficiaries — 62
    3.3.3 Gender monitoring — 66
    3.3.4 Enumeration of results — 71
  3.4 An Interdisciplinary Approach for the Sustainable Development of Spontaneous Human Settlements in the Central Urban Area of Managua — 77
    3.4.1 The project - Urban Managua — 77
    3.4.2 Seeking partnership between academics and practitioners — 79
    3.4.3 Transforming city: The challenge of developing the centre of Managua — 83
    3.4.4 Enumeration of results — 92

4 THE CONTEXT OF THE PALESTINIAN TERRITORIES — 95
  4.1 Capacity Building for Rural Development in Occupied Palestinian Territory — 95
    4.1.1 The project – RURAL DEV — 95
    4.1.2 The project's importance — 97

	4.1.3 Cross-cultural exchange and teamwork	100
	4.1.4 Enumeration of results	101
4.2	Conflict, Participation and Development in Palestine	106
	4.2.1 The project – CPDP	106
	4.2.2 Emancipatory knowledge production under occupation	107
	4.2.3 Ethics in conducting fieldwork in conflict areas – Occupied Palestinian Territory	110
	4.2.4 Enumeration of results	112

5 THE NEPALESE CONTEXT — 118

- 5.1 Development of an Academic Programme on Energy Systems Planning and Analysis in Nepal — 118
  - 5.1.1 The project – ENERGY — 118
  - 5.1.2 Energy as a crucial element for sustainable development — 119
  - 5.1.3 How to see technical problems from a different point of view — 122
  - 5.1.4 Enumeration of results — 126

6 THE CONTEXT OF MOZAMBIQUE — 133

- 6.1 Strengthening Universities' Capacities for Improved Access, Use and Application of ICTs for Social Development and Economic Growth in Mozambique — 133
  - 6.1.1 The project – ICT4D — 133
  - 6.1.2 The project's importance — 135
  - 6.1.3 Between high expectations and daily routine — 138
  - 6.1.4 Enumeration of results — 142

7 THE EAST AFRICAN CONTEXT — 146

- 7.1 Master's Programme in Medical Anthropology and International Health — 146
  - 7.1.1 The project – MA-MEDANIH — 146
  - 7.1.2 The Southern perspective — 147
  - 7.1.3 The Northern perspective — 151
  - 7.1.4 Enumeration of results — 153
- 7.2 Strengthening Universities' Capacities for Mitigating Climate Change Induced Water Vulnerabilities in East Africa — 158
  - 7.2.1 The project – WATERCAP — 158
  - 7.2.2 Enhancing the relevance of partnerships between higher education institutions and development partners — 160
  - 7.2.3 Does knowledge really emerge when knowledge is needed? — 165
  - 7.2.4 Enumeration of results — 167
- 7.3 Promoting Gender Responsive Budgeting and Gender Mainstreaming — 172
  - 7.3.1 The project – GENDER — 172
  - 7.3.2 To hear and to be heard: Reflecting on power relations and knowledge production from a postcolonial perspective — 174

	7.3.3 The prospects of and constraints upon gender budgeting and mainstreaming in Uganda	179
	7.3.4 Enumeration of results	183
7.4	Promotion of Professional Social Work towards Social Development and Poverty Reduction in East Africa	189
	7.4.1 The project – PROSOWO	189
	7.4.2 Making cross-national academic partnerships work	191
	7.4.3 "Mzungu, how are you?" Reflections on the human element of North-South partnerships	197
	7.4.4 Enumeration of results	203

8 THE CONTEXT OF BURKINA FASO   208

8.1	Elements for a Burkina Faso National Pharmacopoeia: Monographs Redaction and Quality Control of Endangered Antimalarial Medicinal Plants	208
	8.1.1 The project - MEAMP	208
	8.1.2 The project`s importance	210
	8.1.3 Complexities of implementation and dissemination challenges	212
	8.1.4 Enumeration of results	213
8.2	Sustainable Management of Water and Fish Resources in Burkina Faso	217
	8.2.1 The project – SUSFISH	217
	8.2.2 A transdisciplinary approach to the integration of people, fisheries, socio-economic factors and higher education	219
	8.2.3 Joint research and scientific exchange for higher education	225
	8.2.4 Enumeration of results	229

9 THE ETHIOPIAN CONTEXT   240

9.1	Academic Partnership on Legal and Human Rights Education	240
	9.1.1 The project – APLHRE	240
	9.1.2 The project and its people	241
	9.1.3 The importance of the cooperation	244
	9.1.4 Enumeration of results	247
9.2	Strengthening Rural Transformation Competences of Higher Education and Research Institutions in the Amhara Region, Ethiopia	250
	9.2.1 The project - TRANSACT	250
	9.2.2 Ensuring sustainable agricultural development, enhancing transdisciplinary skills and developing interdisciplinary competences	252
	9.2.3 Transforming research? A critical reflection	256
	9.2.4 Enumeration of results	258
9.3	Responding to Poverty and Disability through Higher Education and Research	264
	9.3.1 The project – RESPOND-HER	264
	9.3.2 Reflections on mutual learning experiences	265
	9.3.3 Lessons learnt from the Austrian perspective	267

| 9.3.4 Enumeration of results | 270 |

10 STUDENT MOBILITY — 275

10.1 The Second Component of APPEAR — 275
10.1.1 Scholarships within the new framework — 275

10.2 Perspectives from Students and a Supervisor — 291
10.2.1 Experiences of scholarship holders — 291
10.2.2 From Kenya to Austria – key lessons learnt — 293
10.2.3 Gains, deeds and suggestions: A personal reflection on PhD study — 296
10.2.4 What does it mean to be a scientific supervisor within the APPEAR Scholarship Programme? — 297
10.2.5 Of PhD, beer and Redbull: My student life — 300

AUTHORS — 303

INTRODUCTION AND ACKNOWLEDGEMENT

Five years have passed since APPEAR – the "Austrian Partnership Programme in Higher Education and Research for Development" – first saw the academic light of day. Five years in which we have written, researched, designed, thought and taught together, all whilst generating knowledge relevant to development-policy that has altered social realities and strengthened the individual, institutional and scientific capacities of all partners. Five labour-intensive, stimulating and lightning-fast years in which 17 cooperative projects between Austrian higher education institutions and scientific institutions in partner countries have been successfully implemented across national, cultural and linguistic borders.

This book presents these projects and their results – the fruits of APPEAR's first phase. On the one hand, the book is a summary of the projects' differing research areas, with their distinct methodologies and results; on the other hand it is a self-reflexive analysis of the different participatory and communicative processes that have led to the generation of transnational and transcultural spaces of knowledge. In each project presentation, two contributions are to be found – one each from the perspectives of the southern and the Austrian partners – which deal with cross-sectional topics and, so to speak, address the "inner logics" of the academic partnership. It has been essential to the editor to allow the authors ample freedom, and that they also discuss where possible those aspects of cooperative research projects usually neglected by purely scientific reports. Student mobility, a crucial capacity development component in APPEAR, is presented to round off the collection.

The result is a series of 17 remarkable portraits of oft-unconventional higher education projects which all derive from a common understanding: Scientific inquiry, participatory knowledge-generation and capacity development in the development policy context must focus upon effecting sustainable change and improving the quality of social realities. Those who dwell in the countries studied count above all else. The scientific findings presented here open to them new and constructive vistas on life.

With this in mind, the editor would like to thank first and foremost the book's 80 authors – 32 of whom are female and 48 male – and the many committed people who have contributed operationally to making these APPEAR projects reality. Special thanks go to the Austrian Development Cooperation (ADC) and the Austrian Development Agency (ADA) for initiating and financing such an ambitious programme in the first place. As head of the programme, the editor also especially wishes to thank the APPEAR team, who have conducted the high-quality professional management and administration of the programme with boundless enthusiasm, great expertise and unrelenting personal idealism. Finally, the editor would like to thank the Austrian Agency for International Cooperation in Education and Research (OeAD GmbH), the APPEAR programme's administrative base, for its tremendous institutional support, which has played an essential role in the programme's success.

Andreas J. Obrecht
Editor, Head of the APPEAR Programme
August 2015

1 HIGHER EDUCATION DRIVES DEVELOPMENT

by Gertraud Findl and Robert Zeiner

2015 constitutes a crucial year for development policy and cooperation. Following the achievements and experiences of the Millennium Development Goals (MDG), the post-2015 agenda is being prepared. One of MDG's main findings will form part of this agenda: Sustainable development is impossible without higher education and scientific research. Well-educated people are the driving force behind sustainable social and economic development. Optimally equipped to meet the needs of a global knowledge society, they provide a country with the highly qualified workforce it needs. Hence an efficient higher education system plays a key role in the development process. Consequently, one of the main goals of the Austrian Development Cooperation (ADC) since 2009 has been to strengthen partner countries' educational institutions and science and research capacities. APPEAR, an ADC programme, is one of the cornerstones of this strategic approach.

Education has always been one of ADC's foremost priorities. This is manifest in Article 2 of the Austrian Federal Act on Development Cooperation[1]. The basic right to education is also firmly established by Article 26 of the United Nation's Universal Declaration of Human Rights. Against this background, ADC particularly supports the availability of technical and professional education and meritocratic access to higher education. Approximately 10 to 15 percent of ADC's annual working programme and project budget is allocated to education. Measures focus on higher education, including research, followed by vocational training and to a minor extent primary education.

For many years, scholarship programmes were the main modality of ADCs cooperation in post-secondary education. Nearly two thirds of the higher education budget was spent on longstanding programmes whose focus was the capacity-building of individuals. In 2007, an evaluation of ADC's education sector was carried out and reported two key findings.[2] Firstly, ADC development funding was widely dispersed as a result of the high proportion of NGO projects in the education sector. Secondly, the primary instrument used to that point had been scholarships for foreign university students in Austria, which were open to students from developing countries around the globe. This approach demonstrably resulted in a situation where support had little structural impact or worked to increase brain drain. In addition, it was stressed that scholarship programmes alone could not improve the quality and efficiency of educational and research institutions in the target countries. Therefore the 2007

---

1 Bundesgesetz über die Entwicklungszusammenarbeit (EZA-Gesetz), Bundesgesetzblatt vom 29.3.2002
2 Evaluation of the Education Sector of Austrian Development Cooperation and Cooperation with South-East Europe, 2007

evaluation recommended a moratorium on all scholarship programmes financed by ADC and a profound change in the approach taken towards institutional capacity development in the partner countries.

The Austrian Development Cooperation took this central recommendation to heart and initiated the development of a multi-dimensional capacity development approach, sharpening its profile with clear thematic and geographical focuses, which were laid down in a new strategic framework. The key conclusions and recommendations of the evaluation offered an excellent set of innovative ideas for this framework. In addition, the strategy also responds to the prominent international development objectives put forward in the Millennium Development Goals and in the targets and principles for aid effectiveness and effective development cooperation.

As a first step towards implementing this new approach, in 2008 the Federal Ministry for Europe, Integration and International Affairs described in the "Higher education and scientific cooperation" section of its "Three-Year Programme on Austrian Development Policy (2008-2010)" the policy framework's profile as follows:

- ADC prioritizes the strengthening of post-secondary educational structures, as well as science and research in the partner countries.
- ADC concentrates future programmes on institutions in its partner countries.
- Emphasis is placed on institutional cooperation and regional networking between Austria and its partner countries and between partner countries.
- To focus on specific regions and themes is a precondition for improving effectiveness and impact especially in the light of limited resources.
- In general the programmes should be more relevant in terms of poverty reduction and contribute significantly to the sustainability of development processes.

The second step followed in 2009 with the formulation of a strategy paper on Higher Education and Scientific Cooperation[3], which serves as an important midterm navigator for the Austrian Development Agency (ADA), the operational unit of Austrian Development Cooperation. The document encompasses key measures, including a new partnership programme on higher education and research.

"Strategy on Higher Education and Scientific Cooperation"

The Austrian Development Cooperation has always understood higher education to be a vital instrument to help attain the Millennium Development Goals, and thus contribute to poverty reduction. The social and economic development of a country or a region is based on increasing the population's levels of education and qualifications. An efficient and effective system of higher education is regarded as an indispensable requirement for people's empowerment, enhancing their capacity to participate in political, societal, economic pro-

---

3   ADC: Strategy on Higher Education and Scientific Cooperation, 2009

cesses and decisions and helping shape their future. Therefore, ADC argues in its strategy paper that education cannot be exclusively limited to Millennium Development Goal number 2, universal primary education. Moreover, higher education has served to achieve the MDGs on several levels:

- Improving the education system (related to MDG 2 and 3).
- Supplying the necessary skilled workforce (related to MDG 4 to 7) and assuring the professional development of human resources.
- Contributing to the creation of partner countries' organizational and institutional capacities. Improving the absorption capacity of partner countries' systems and creating the conditions for the use of the increasing aid flows needed to attain all MDGs.
- Generating knowledge and participation in global knowledge production (related to MDG 8).
- And, in more general terms, improving human resources, knowledge and technology in order to stimulate economic growth and thereby reduce poverty and hunger – all of which relate to the overall goal of development cooperation.

The Millennium Development Goals in general, and the reduction of global poverty more specifically, are guiding elements for the goals and principles described as main objectives of the Austrian Development Cooperation in the respective law. ADC-funded activities for higher education and development-related applied research should relate to partner countries' development policies and plans. Improving these countries' higher education and academic research systems can make a major contribution towards the efficient implementation of national policies, strategies and programmes aimed at reducing poverty and achieving national and international development goals. ADC helps elaborate educational strategies and measures for reform in those partner countries which lack such strategies.

The central methodological approach for ADC as described in the strategy paper is capacity development.[4] All educational activities in priority countries and key regions revolve around capacity development in public universities and research institutions. Structures are comprehensively strengthened from human resource, institutional, and systemic points of view. Programmes with lasting effects promote capacity development not only in terms of teaching and research, but also on the levels of planning, governance, organization, management, and policy-making. Against this background, the traditional ADC funding of scholarship programmes based on the principle of individual financial support has been relativized. Now, scholarships must be demonstrably integrated into a comprehensive institutional capacity development programme. The risk of brain drain is reduced if colleges and universities are managed in an efficient and transparent manner, an open atmosphere prevails,

---

4 Capacity development is an umbrella concept that relates to the elaboration of international development co-operation activities. "Capacity" is understood as the ability of people, organizations and society as a whole to manage their affairs successfully; in contrast to the traditional concept of capacity building, "capacity development" is a process of internal change whereby people, organizations and society as a whole unleash, strengthen, create, adapt and maintain capacity over time.

curricula have strong links to the country's current needs and demands, and students have sufficient opportunities to apply their acquired experience and competencies.

Austrian universities and research institutions as well as their partner organizations in ADC partner countries already collaborate in many different ways. With the "Strategy on Higher Education and Scientific Cooperation", ADC underlined the strength of its support for research and higher education and potential to foster structured institutional cooperation. Clearly, without the commitment of our scientific partners in Austria, ADC could not succeed in assisting the capacity development process of our partners in the South. North-South and South-South cooperation, as well as knowledge networks, allow for systematic scientific knowledge sharing at the regional and international levels. They constitute a key instrument for institutional capacity development. Longstanding partnerships can engender a cooperative mind-set that is based on the respective strengths of all participating partners and is mutually beneficial both culturally and scientifically. Such partnerships are also an efficient instrument for the promotion of "brain circulation". APPEAR, as the key programme for ADC's implementation of the "Strategy on Higher Education and Scientific Cooperation" has furnished evidence for the importance of such cooperation for the Austrian partners.

APPEAR

The Austrian Partnership Programme in Higher Education and Research for Development (APPEAR) was initiated, tendered and commissioned by the Austrian Development Agency in 2009. The programme replaces a diverse range of scholarship schemes without thematic or geographical focus, which were phased out or integrated into the new institutional higher education cooperation programme. One well-known example was the North-South Dialogue scholarship programme. The design and principles of APPEAR are based on the cornerstones outlined in the strategy paper and include the strategy's defined specifications and standards. But they also are steered by lessons learnt and best practices from comparable international programmes. Special emphasis is placed on:
- Strengthening institutional capacities in higher education, research and management in most of the key regions of Austrian Development Cooperation.
- Building up partnerships between academic and/or research institutions in these regions and Austrian universities and facilitating these partnerships via Master's and PhD grants.
- Improving the quality of teaching and research, and enhancing the efficiency and effectiveness of management and administration within the institutions involved.
- Strengthening scientific dialogue and creating an enabling environment for it both nationally and internationally.

In 2009, the success of APPEAR certainly could not have been anticipated. After decades of funding mainly individuals, the paradigm shift to structural and institutional support for universities and research bodies in the global South was a big challenge not only for ADC, but also necessitated significant upheavals in approach and processes on its partners' sides. For example, for most of the Austrian universities involved, it has turned out to be difficult to provide evidence for their commitment to, and interest in, development policy due to the absence of development goals in their institutional profiles and the narrow results-oriented nature of their financing.

However, working together, the Austrian Development Agency, Austrian universities and scientific partner institutions in the Global South have realized a veritable success story. At the end of 2012, a mid-term evaluation of APPEAR was commissioned to assess the first phase of the programme [5]. Overall, the evaluation team concluded that APPEAR has indeed been a success. Its conception, design, implementation and levels of participation are considered to be state-of-the-art internationally. The transition from a disparate range of untargeted scholarships driven by largely academic goals to a coherent, international higher education cooperation programme with explicit developmental goals was stated to be a considerable achievement.

The next chapter of APPEAR commenced at the end of 2014. Based on the evaluation, lessons learnt, the setting of the Post 2015 agenda (including higher education) and the principles of the global partnership for effective development cooperation, the Austrian Development Agency tendered and commissioned the second phase of APPEAR. With a duration of six years from 2015 to 2020 and a direct programme budget of 12 million Euros, APPEAR leaves no doubt about the strong and continuous commitment of Austrian Development Cooperation to higher education and scientific cooperation.

---

5   Mid-term evaluation of the Austrian Partnership Programme in Higher Education and Research for Development (APPEAR), 2013, www.appear.at/application

2 APPEAR – CREATING TRANSNATIONAL AND TRANSCULTURAL SPACES OF KNOWLEDGE

by Andreas J. Obrecht

From experiment to successfully institutionalised cooperation programme

APPEAR began as an experiment in academic research and teaching cooperation and capacity development, undertaken with great enthusiasm by all involved. Over time, with boundless commitment and expertise, it has become something more – an institutionally established higher education cooperation programme. APPEAR is a new type of cooperative venture between higher education institutions in Austria and research institutions, universities and scientific institutions in priority countries from the Global South, whose programmatic basics and thematic criteria build upon the "Strategy: Higher Education and Scientific Cooperation", published by the Austrian Development Agency (ADA) in 2009. This was an important, long-term setting of the course in development policy practice and also a new challenge for the Austrian tertiary education sector.

Austria had been criticised by the OECD for the fact that the percentage of science, research and teaching in development contexts in its Official Development Assistance (ODA) was too low. Based on a new strategy, the higher education cooperation programme was put out to tender in 2009. The "Education and Research for International Development Cooperation" team of the "Austrian Agency for International Cooperation in Education and Research" (OeAD GmbH) successfully took part in the bidding process. What followed were hectic months in which all the essential characteristics of APPEAR were elaborated, from the name of the programme, to its "guidelines" (which were also elaborated in international workshops), thematic criteria for selection procedures and the formal framework conditions of the first call.

APPEAR also began as an experiment simply because nobody knew how Austrian higher education institutions would accept this new programme, if at all. Cooperative projects between Austrian universities and developing countries had always existed, but APPEAR was the first systematically elaborated programme of its size which was oriented thematically towards the focus areas of the Austrian Development Cooperation and in which the countries were predefined (the priority countries and regions of the Austrian Development Cooperation).

However, it soon became apparent that there was (and remains) extremely high interest in and demand for such a programme from Austrian higher education institutions and many academic institutions in the partner countries. By the end of 2014, 134 applications for preparatory funding had been submitted through four calls for applications, of which 44 had been approved. A further 109 applications for the funding of an academic partnership had led to 21 approved projects. Moreover, 19 master's and 41 PhD scholarships had been financed to colleagues from the partner countries. 68 scholarships from the expiring North-South-Dialogue Scholarship Programme were also taken over by APPEAR.

18 of the 21 Austrian universities took part in the calls, with the universities of applied sciences also taking very enthusiastic part. In addition to this appeal from across the broad institutional spectrum, priorities in social and natural sciences have also remained balanced, and inter- or transdisciplinary methodical approaches were favoured in most of the project designs. Allowing higher education institutions in the partner countries to also be able to assume full responsibility for the project and its financial aspects, not a matter of course with comparable European programmes, proved to be the right decision to guarantee a true "partnership of equals". One third academic partnerships have been successfully implemented by colleagues from the priority countries, a fact which received particular praise in an external evaluation of the programme by the British agency "Education for Change" in 2013. This evaluation also gave a very favourable assessment of the ADA's preliminary work towards the programme goals, the cooperation between ADA and OeAD-GmbH, the administration and management of the programme by the APPEAR team and, especially, APPEAR's intensive public relations measures.

Goal, Structure and Instruments

In the first half of the programme, 2009–2015, higher education institutions and scientific institutions from 13 countries in the "South" were invited to cooperate with Austrian higher education institutions; in the second half – 2015 to 2020 – there will be 16 countries in total.[6]

The superordinate goal of APPEAR in its first five years has been: *Strengthening institutional capacities in education, research and management in the key regions in the South identified by the Austrian Development Cooperation (ADC) through academic partnerships with Austrian academic institutions and Master's and PhD programmes.*

This goal was to be achieved by means of cooperation in the following thematic focus areas: *Higher education and research for development, water supply and sanitation, rural development, energy, private sector development, governance and human rights, poverty reduction, environment and natural resources, peace building and conflict prevention, gender equality, and the strengthening of skills in social sciences as an instrument to systematically analyse the reasons of poverty and to empower capacities in social science research.*

The instruments for achieving this goal were the following:

Preparatory Funding: For university and non-university teaching and research institutions

---

6 As of the 5th call in spring 2015, Moldova, Armenia and Georgia are also included in the programme. All countries that were eligible up to then remain so: Ethiopia, Uganda, Kenya, Mozambique, Cape Verde, Burkina Faso, Senegal, Nicaragua, El Salvador, Guatemala, Bhutan, Nepal and the Palestinian Territories. Moreover, other countries can be included in the Academic Partnerships in the framework of "regional networks" – with a share in the budget of up to 20% of the total volume – provided that coherent and conclusive reasons can be given for this.

in the "South" as well as Austrian higher education institutions wishing to prepare mutual cooperation projects. This instrument is intended for researchers who are in the initial stages of jointly formulating research questions and planning to develop these ideas into a full application within APPEAR.

Academic Partnerships: For university and non-university teaching and research institutions in the "South", as well as Austrian higher education institutions cooperating in the framework of an academic partnership with a higher education institution in the "South". This stream is intended for researchers and lecturers at relevant departments and scientific institutions as well as the management and students of higher education institutions. It especially aims at curricula development and the use of scientific content in courses. Moreover, an *Advanced Academic Partnership* will be funded in the second half of the programme, from spring 2015. On the basis of successfully completed projects, further proposals (based on new ideas, research questions and concepts) can be submitted for a continuation of a maximum period of three years.

Academic Partnerships strive to develop capacity in the fields of teaching, research and management in higher education, in order to contribute to national poverty reduction and the implementation of other relevant development policy goals. In addition to these general programmatic provisions, the partnerships must be expounded in such a way that it becomes clearly visible which social groups will benefit, in which ways and by which means (e.g., administrative, logistic, financial) from the expected results, in terms of poverty reduction and the Millennium Development Goals (MDGs). In many cases these are regionally, ethnically, economically or politically marginalised groups; special emphasis is also put on gender.

The selection procedure for the academic partnerships, which are conceived for a maximum of three years in the first half of the programme, is highly competitive. In addition to project submissions' ranking via the framework of an international peer review procedure, the selection board thoroughly deliberates upon the submissions' relevance with regard to regional and national development strategies. Innovative scientific ideas and concepts should orient themselves to development policy-relevant results and practices. The methods and the expected results of each partnership must be reflected by the relevant social reality. The "development sociology" approach – where knowledge is generated together in order to change the social reality – must be taken into account from the very conception of the project and not only fundamentally influence empirical research approaches but also the ways in which research results are disseminated. Due to this approach, each partnership will have target groups and beneficiaries in a societal-social area which goes beyond the tertiary education sector – whether they be slum inhabitants, economically marginalised population groups, groups with specific disadvantages or gender-specific problems, for example. The clear definition of these target groups is an important criterion for the positive evaluation and eventual award of academic partnerships.

An important instrument for achieving the superordinate goal of strengthening institutional capacities are also the *master's and PhD scholarships*, which crucially combine APPEAR's scientific and educational aims. Preference is given to students already involved in current higher education cooperative projects, who thus have the required institutional anchoring. In this way – following an international trend – "brain drain" is prevented while capacity development at the partner institutions is supported. APPEAR also supports "individual scholarships", provided that these can be well justified in their specific regional and scientific contexts.

Principles

APPEAR's goals are based on five basic principles, which illustrate both its development philosophy and epistemological approach. These principles are by no means hierarchically super- or subordinated but rather reflect a new understanding of participatory knowledge-production,which is application-oriented and aims to reduce poverty in terms of sustainable resolution. These principles demonstrate a scientific stance which fundamentally rejects the paternalism that can manifest itself through "knowledge" and "technological superiority". They are further an appeal to academic communities – across national, linguistic and cultural boundaries – to challenge themselves in a self-reflexive and participatory way with urgent "global challenges" by engaging in emancipatory forms of knowledge generation.

Participation: The implementation of the projects follows the principle of the equal status and equal treatment of everybody involved, the cooperative elaboration and implementation of the project activities on a partnership basis and joint exploitation of the outcomes. Students are regarded as cooperative partners who are assisted organisationally and as regards contents. They also constitute an enrichment for the Austrian higher education landscape and participate in the cooperative generation and dissemination of knowledge.

Cultural open-mindedness: Interest and respect for different approaches in the generation of knowledge and problem resolution are seen as a prerequisite for cooperative project implementation. This methodological approach, which is based on the plurality of knowledge, deliberately refrains from one-sided knowledge and technology transfer, which was for a long time characteristic of the relationship between "North" and "South". This approach, moreover, proceeds on the assumption that cooperation based on partnership enables learning experiences for all involved.

Practical and empirical approaches: It is possible to include research and teaching outcomes in project designs, research questions and empirical approaches from the very beginning. This should be done in a target-specific way. Beneficiaries of the cooperative activities, and especially also of the exploitation of the results, are to be identified, especially also with a view to poverty reduction.

Gender sensitivity: The promotion and empowerment of women are aims inherent to the programme's implementation at every level of organisation and content. Moreover, gender constitutes an analytical category for the analysis of social and scientific institutions, as well as socio-economic situations and problems. It can serve as a resolution-oriented approach to dealing with issues of the unequal distribution of the various forms of power, including social, economic and political power. With particular focus on APPEAR's superordinate goal of poverty reduction, the problem resolution-oriented analysis of the feminisation of poverty is especially emphasised.

Bottom-up and demand-driven approaches: The demand for the resolution of specific scientific questions or capacity problems on the part of the southern partner institutions primarily determines the content of each project. The relevant specific interests and expectations of all involved parties are outlined and communicated in a transparent way in the preparatory phases.

Transcultural production of knowledge and new modes of interaction

Through the implementation of the five principles described above, APPEAR endeavours to create a new space of transnational and transcultural interaction, communication and knowledge-generation that is highly relevant to development policy, in which new modes of communication between "North" and "South" can also develop. This attempt was not only positively cited in the above-mentioned external evaluation but has also led to an increasingly positive external perception of the programme, far beyond national borders. APPEAR was, for example, invited to present at the global "Future Earth" initiative in New York in 2013 and in Johannesburg in 2014.[7] APPEAR is also acknowledged in a critical European study on higher education cooperative projects as a committed programme which actively endeavours to implement cooperation on an equal footing: "The 'Appear' programme of the Austrian Development Cooperation provides an attempt to reverse the power relationship from the outset: the funding call is open to southern institutions which then have to select suitable northern partners."[8]

This positive external perception has been especially driven by the possibility that partner institutions from the south can assume full responsibility for a project. For this simple administrative rule reflects APPEAR's content-related and methodological principles, which can – almost fully – be summarised in one sentence: *APPEAR is not interested in one-sided knowledge transfer!* The days when "western" researchers dictated the scientific programmes of non-European countries are not yet gone, but they are nearing a fundamental transformation: The dawning realisation that the consequences of modern, rationalist knowledge have brought the world's ecosystems and thus its people to the brink of global collapse is making us more sensitive to alternative knowledge systems and epistemologies.

It is high time that we begin once again to learn from each other, and not merely to "teach". This approach is reflected in APPEAR's understanding of science. The "western" scientific approach to the world and its people is a momentous yet quite new "innovation" – no older than 500 years. In this half millennium world-views and methods of knowledge-generation have been created which have unleashed untold productive power while also making the exploitation of man, nature, capital and society the major motor of a quite dubious "progress". In constructive terms, APPEAR supports positions that take a critical approach to science and

---

7 www.futureearth.org
8 Carbonnier, G./Kontinen, T. (2014): North-South-Partnerships. Academia Meets Development? EADI (European Association of Development Research and Training Institutes) Policy Papers, p. 62

condemns the paternalistic position which has traditionally been based on an assumption of the superiority of "western" knowledge and exercised this "superiority" first through colonialism and later via unequal and unfair relationships between "North" and "South".

Basically APPEAR espouses a new "knowledge practice", which fundamentally foregoes paternalism and exclusive access to knowledge, which gives preference to participatory approaches to knowledge-generation and which puts knowledge and science at the service of humanity in a programmatic way. The participatory generation of knowledge to reduce poverty is a superordinate goal. This new "knowledge practice" establishes a new social contract between science and society. For in it, science is no longer an end in itself, but serves people and their societies in terms of a sustainable progress that can meet humanity's needs.

Why APPEAR is highly relevant to development policy

APPEAR addresses the central problem of fundamentally weak infrastructures in the tertiary education sector in "less" and "least developed countries", which affects research, teaching and management alike. For some time now, international development policy has identified and implemented cooperative strategies for strengthening the science, teaching and infrastructure capacities of higher education institutions in economically weak or marginalised countries, recognising this to be an effective development policy tool that helps reduce poverty and raise living standards. Hence, in line with international trends, APPEAR also supports new "markets of knowledge" – including employment, further project cooperation and integration into international research programmes – from which the partner institutions in the "South" and their wider societies can benefit, but which also allow Austrian scientists to implement new approaches to interesting, participatory and development-relevant activities in research, teaching and institutional cooperation.

Cooperative research and teaching projects with institutions in "less" and "least developed countries" address problems which can be localised regionally in the relevant societies. At the same time, however, the rising global appreciation of the problem of resource-limitation and thus life opportunities means that research issues can no longer be examined in isolation. Through new media technologies they can attract worldwide attention and so demand international resolution efforts. As Austria's former Federal Minister Univ.-Prof. Dr. Karlheinz Töchterle has said:

> Especially in the context of the pressing worldwide challenges, development research is an important and continuously expanding research field. For not only scientific working has been internationalised in transnational, and often transdisciplinary, networks but many scientific fields have globalised: Desertification and soil erosion in Sub-Saharan Africa are as relevant for us today as the melting of the alpine glaciers for the inhabitants of the islands of the South Pacific. [9]

---

9   In: Obrecht, A. J. (ed. 2012): Wissen und Entwicklung. Studien Verlag Innsbruck, p.7

A programme such as APPEAR strengthens development research capacities and contributes to the resolution of local problems, integrating southern tertiary education sector partner institutions into a new global knowledge discourse which transcends the boundaries of nation states. This discourse also alters the actors involved. No longer strait-jacketed by the roles of "givers" and "takers", the actors are now free to engage in the participatory identification of new spaces of knowledge, to be explored together. In this respect, a cooperation programme such as APPEAR goes far beyond the traditional bilateral development policy perspective. This can also be seen in particular in the international and transnational dissemination of results. The strengthening of capacities in the tertiary education sector is also expressed by this possibility to cooperate creatively in new global knowledge and problem resolution discourses.

Due to the specific social, economic and political problems in its priority countries, APPEAR's knowledge discourse focusses on practice-oriented research, the results of which are also to be included in academic teaching. Due to worldwide (especially digital) connectivity, "local" problem resolution strategies which aim at promoting development and enabling acceptable life-chances tend to become "globalised". In this way, the use of research and teaching to achieve development policy goals among specific target groups has become embedded in a worldwide discourse which strives for a better social and economic balance of the interests of "poor" and "industrialised" countries, according to the MDGs and eventually the "Sustainable Development Goals" (SDGs). Here the importance of APPEAR also shows itself. By international comparison a small yet well-run programme, APPEAR proactively participates in transnational knowledge discourses, whether in the form of transnational public relations activities, programme presentations or conference participation.

From the Millennium Development Goals to the Sustainable Development Goals

The MDGs, defined in 2000, and the "Paris Declaration on Aid Effectiveness", adopted in 2005, still play an important role in the programmatic orientation of development policy intervention and the general transnational discourse about the efficient use of ODA funds. These two consensual guidelines are also of great importance for understanding scientific and educational cooperation: The MDGs state that tertiary education sector capacities should be developed in order to support poverty reduction, while the Paris Declaration calls for the enhancement of personal responsibility for and transparency within and between development policy interventions. The partner countries should themselves be responsible for development processes (ownership), existing (scientific) infrastructures and institutions are to be engaged and supported (alignment), the "benefactors" should endeavour to coordinate the measures in the tertiary education sector (harmonisation), the focus should be on the results of research and teaching projects and these should also be measurable and available for auditing purposes (results) and, finally, as much accountability as possible between benefactor and beneficiary countries and partners should be developed (mutual accountability).

The relevance of scientific, research and teaching projects in the tertiary education sector has increased in the last few years, despite decreasing ODA due to the worldwide recession in 2009 and its consequences. This may also be due to the fact that the transnational discourse about the post-MDG, post-2015 era is also in full swing with a view to global ecological questions. How will development be defined according to determined development indicators in terms of the SDGs? And what implications will this have for a programme such as APPEAR?

The international trend, in any case, is moving in the direction of a holistic reflection on global disparities and ecological crises. In this perspective, the strict division between "poor" and "rich", "developed" or "underdeveloped" countries is altered. Development research and its funding agencies already satisfy these changed paradigmatic ideas in the relationship between the "North" and "South" and are increasingly orienting their policies and initiatives on "global challenges".

The stagnation which emerged after the UN conference Rio+20 (2012) at the interface between science and development is to be overcome. The central challenge is quick and resolute action so that the human habitat is not further jeopardised. On 6th June 2013, the "Sustainable Development Solutions Network", a collective of outstanding scientists and scientific institutions, submitted the report "An Action Agenda for Sustainable Development – Report for the UN Secretary-General" to the secretary-general of the UN, Ban Ki-Moon. This document set out the "Sustainable Development Goals (SDGs)", which succinctly address the most important factors (global challenges) which make global transformation essential. The SDGs define goals as guidelines for the post-2015 era, where (in contradistinction to the MDGs) not only "poor countries" but all the world's nations, with their varied economic, ecological, cultural and political interdependences, must be addressed.

The Sustainable Development Goals (SDGs), which are to be adopted by UN member nations in September 2015, have been developed on the basis of economic, social, ecological and government-specific dimensions. The latter especially also take into account the maintenance of peace and security under democratic conditions. What is emphasised is the underlying normative concept that every country has the same right to sustainable development and that no new "winners" or "losers" should result from the new goals; that human rights and social inclusion are inherent to the achievement of the goals; that a convergence principle should lead to the fact that the improvement of the standard of living in "poor countries" should be explicitly desirable whereas "richer countries" will grow comparatively less so in economic terms, which in the medium term will result in global living standards converging; and that global responsibilities and possibilities will be shared, meaning in particular that the "poorest countries" will get more bilateral development funds (ODA) in order to initiate sustainable development and that countries which have escaped the spiral of poverty should contribute to helping the marginalised regions. These dimensions of sustainability and the normative criteria which underpin them, form the foundations for the "Sustainable Development Goals (SDGs)":[10]

---

10 Source: Proposal for Sustainable Development Goals (SDGs), June 22nd, 2015; https://sustainabledevelopment.un-
.org/sdgsproposal

- *End poverty in all its forms everywhere.*
- *End hunger, achieve food security and improved nutrition and promote sustainable agriculture.*
- *Ensure healthy lives and promote well-being for all at all ages.*
- *Ensure inclusive and equitable quality education and promote lifelong learning opportunities for all.*
- *Achieve gender equality and empower all women and girls.*
- *Ensure availability and sustainable management of water and sanitation for all.*
- *Ensure access to affordable, reliable, sustainable and modern energy for all.*
- *Promote sustained, inclusive and sustainable economic growth, full and productive employment and decent work for all.*
- *Build resilient infrastructure, promote inclusive and sustainable industrialisation and foster innovation.*
- *Reduce inequality within and among countries.*
- *Make cities and human settlements inclusive, safe, resilient and sustainable.*
- *Ensure sustainable consumption and production patterns.*
- *Take urgent action to combat climate change and its impacts.*
- *Conserve and sustainably use the oceans, seas and marine resources for sustainable development.*
- *Protect, restore and promote sustainable use of terrestrial ecosystems, sustainably manage forests, combat desertification, and halt and reverse land degradation and halt biodiversity loss.*
- *Promote peaceful and inclusive societies for sustainable development, provide access to justice for all and build effective, accountable and inclusive institutions at all levels.*
- *Strengthen the means of implementation and revitalize the global partnership for sustainable development.*

The international discourse about "development" is integrated directly into the discourse about the SDGs. "Enhancing collaboration between the development aid and the global environmental change communities to achieve development goals in Africa" was the title of a meeting of the initiative group "Future Earth" in May 2014 which, as far as personnel is concerned, is closely linked to the "Sustainable Development Solutions Network". APPEAR was invited to present the key principles of the programme at this event, which took place in Johannesburg, South Africa. APPEAR's research goals reflect the central concerns of these global discourses and their implications for development policy. Given the content and stated goals of the SDGs, APPEAR is fundamentally in tune with global trends in development policy and thus well-placed to enable the Austrian Development Cooperation to meet its post-2015 international obligations. The positioning of APPEAR in transnational discourses is not only a challenge for the programme's management but also for project participants: the fact that this challenge has been successfully met in many ways is confirmed by the significance of APPEAR's results and their many channels of dissemination, all of which are described in this book.

Transnational framework conditions and empirical development research

The transnational framework conditions for a higher education cooperation programme, such as APPEAR, which is highly relevant for development policy are changing continuously. This is especially true this year, 2015, following the expiry of the MDGs. It is in this evolving context that the setting of political direction occurs and that globally effective discourses regarding knowledge and problem-resolution skills take place. In the "globalised world", regional and national research and teaching are integrated *per se* in a worldwide network that enables the generation of scientific results oriented to resolving real-world; civic commitment towards the use and implementation of these results is essential.

The development policy implications of the SDGs mean that APPEAR, too, is at the centre of a global discourse the aim of which is an ecologically, socially, economically, culturally and geopolitically more agreeable world. In this struggle to find sustainable models for a future which affords those born in the future no fewer life chances than we now enjoy, development research plays an essential role. Our efforts to create habitable living spaces in the future can only work on the basis of evidence-based and ultimately scientific research.

Empirical development research has been massively revalued as a monitoring and auditing instrument, especially since the establishment of the MDGs which specify indicators for achieving the relevant goals. Moreover, practice-oriented development research directly contributes to evidence-based development cooperation. In the discourse about the post-MDG era, the "Sustainable Development Goals" mark the emergence of a perspective which fundamentally accommodates transnational higher education cooperative ventures. For, unlike the MDGs, the SDGs are not only a matter of the social, economic and ecological (amongst other factors) situation in the "developing countries" but of the interdependence between economically rich and economically poor countries and an economic balancing of interests between these spheres, which enables an ecological transformation of worldwide cohabitation and economic activity. With this programmatic direction from the United Nations, a common field of learning, especially also in the tertiary education sector, is opened which really impacts researchers equally – both intellectually and existentially – no matter whether they live and work in "rich" Europe or in "poor" East Africa. From this point of view, reciprocity and the expansion of ideas for problem-resolution as equal partners is made manifest.

The SDGs will not only deal with the interdependence of the social, ecological, economic or political realities, but also increasingly with the interdependence of the results of scientific research in a global context. In the transnational discourse about the generation and exploitation of scientific knowledge, it becomes ever more self-evident that in the future, priority must be given to the interlinking of scientific results rather than to the generation of individual scientific data and that for this interlinking and the meta-analyses that support it, scientific cooperation will definitely become more important than scientific competition. In this way, APPEAR's participatory, cooperative organisation and content follow a strong worldwide trend which propagates the idea of an all-encompassing knowledge society – as a prerequisite for the implementation of sustainable forms of human cohabitation – on a transnational level.

The changing global knowledge architecture

Digital technologies and the World Wide Web have changed the organisation of and access to knowledge in a fundamental way. An enormous amount of data in all scientific areas must be organised and aggregated according to new criteria and standards. Orientational knowledge – knowledge which answers questions such as "what is to be known?" "to what end?" and "by whom?" in order to cope with specific tasks – has become more important than ever due to the enormous amount of factual knowledge. What knowledge should be generated for which purpose is not a sterile, neutral consequence of a purely rationalist consideration but a deliberate decision which is of an implicitly normative character. "Science" has changed our world significantly; due to it we substantially define the ecological, social, technological and economic framework conditions of human cohabitation. Thus "science" also has an enormous responsibility for the resolution of the most urgent global problems, which are becoming equally visible everywhere. Whether or not "science" will be able to cope with this responsibility also depends to a significant degree on the way in which science will be practised in the future. Science for profit or political hegemony, or science for the people and for the preservation of the habitat in which these people – we – live.

The global knowledge architecture is changing, the European/Anglo-American hegemony of knowledge which has ruled since the beginning of the Enlightenment – and which has defined the relationship between "North" and "South" – is showing signs of waning. Especially in Asian countries, centres of excellence in, for example, nanotechnology, computer and energy sciences, cybernetics and genetic engineering, are emerging. In some disciplines, the "brain drain" from "East" to "West" is already starting to reverse. Significantly, the People's Republic of China has started initiatives for scientific cooperation and education outside its own national borders. These are exceptional in terms of both quality and quantity. African countries, in particular, are the "beneficiaries" of such schemes. Chinese investments in the tertiary education sector accompany their enormous investments in the real economy, developing those local capacities which will support these investments in the long run. Due to its own economic and social problems, at present "Europe" can do little more then give passive acknowledgement, whether it be critically concerned or cautiously affirmative.

The APPEAR programme clearly locates science as an instrument of a sustainable development that can meet the needs of humanity. With this, the above-mentioned normative question is answered in a programmatic way: It refers to the development policy goals of poverty reduction, improvement of the living conditions of people in "poor" countries and regions and new forms of participatory interaction, communication and cooperation in the area of generation and dissemination of knowledge. A dedicated funding programme such as APPEAR finds itself in the midst of change as regards the global knowledge architecture and must also consider this at every programmatic stage. Besides the scientific cooperation of "new" geopolitical players, which ensures economic expansion by means of extensive investment in the tertiary education sector, there is also a new worldwide "scientific community" which regards itself as at the forefront of a new conception of knowledge that rejects the idea of knowledge-generation as an instrument for securing or maintaining political power. On the contrary, people themselves and their ability to organise themselves in a sustainable way on this planet should benefit from the cooperative generation and dissemination of knowledge. This endeavour can only be accomplished via transnational agreements, cooperation and initiatives. The normative direction of the APPEAR programme complies with this concept of the egalitarian distribution of knowledge and transnational cooperation. In this respect it is important that the role of APPEAR as an agent of change in the global knowledge architecture is also communicated.

Aggravation of social differences and its implications on the countries addressed by APPEAR

Social inequalities are increasing all over the world – neither "industrialised" nor "developing" countries are exempt. For the last twenty-five years, the global neoliberal economic system has converted almost all areas of human life into "markets" in which decisions are taken according to the monetary criteria of supply and demand. As a result of the first worldwide recession since World War II, 2008/2009, we can now clearly see just how shrivelled the political scope of action has become due to the primacy of economy and business. And "Europe" still suffers from the "social faults" which systemic economic crises periodically bring.

For the "developing" countries and their socio-cultural realities, this means two things: Firstly, poverty and marginalisation have been heightened – something especially true since profits from the exploitation of resources are often systematically skimmed off without flowing back to the local real economy. Secondly, a new, usually urban or semi-urban, middle class has emerged in all the countries addressed by APPEAR, which has been able to benefit from new access to markets and technological developments. Development policy discourse often regards these new middle classes as carriers of a new civil society; however, the question of whether such discourse is too fixed on a European/American democratic model remains open.

The countries that APPEAR addresses may differ very much from one another. However, the socio-economic dimensions which aggravate social differences are very similar:

- *Migration to cities and towns, and thus exponential urbanisation, which entails fundamental issues such as the creation of settlement structures which are fit for human living, access to public services, water, hygiene, preventive healthcare and so on.*
- *Feminisation of poverty: This migration favours men, for whom urban areas and their labour markets (including newly emerging labour markets) are more favourable. Economically marginalised areas are characterised by an enormous rural exodus; those who remain are usually women, children and old people.*
- *Small economic and thus also political scope of action due to weak economic output or non-existent "trickle-down" effects in the systemic exploitation of resources.*
- *A trend towards economic dependence – price fluctuations of goods that are traded at international stock exchanges – due to mineral or agrarian "monocultures".*

- *Partial political instabilities and problematic human rights situations due to weak state and civil society institutions.*
- *Economic pressure due to unstable state refinancing models, political pressure due to geopolitical power and "greed".*

APPEAR wants to help curb these growing social inequalities by hypothesising that empirical development research and capacity development in the tertiary education sector help to reduce poverty in the medium- and long-term and advance social developments in a broad positive sense. In this context it is particularly important to deal with those contradictions which tend to prevent these developments. APPEAR does not follow this programmatic principle in a singular way but in discourse and in accordance with worldwide trends, which no longer revere division and competition in the generation of knowledge, but rather the possibility of a collective response to problems which affect – in differing ways and with differing levels of intensity – all of us.

The "new practice" of knowledge – and what APPEAR can contribute to it

Competition and cooperation are synergetic, mutually-dependent principles which cumulatively accompany development. This is true not only in biological evolution but also in the acquisition and dissemination of knowledge. Knowledge opens up competitive opportunities and can lead to unequal distributions of power and powerlessness within a society. But it can also equalise, democratise and make a society fairer and more worth living in as a whole. It depends on how knowledge is generated and for which purposes it is used. Moreover, it depends on whether individual and collective action focusses on competition or cooperation. In historical terms, the acquisition and exploitation of knowledge were for a long time subject to national competition. Globalisation, the increasing complexity of knowledge systems and the new possibilities for the digital distribution of knowledge have abolished such borders for both the acquisition and dissemination of knowledge.

Generation of knowledge nowadays takes place in "epistemic" and "scientific communities" which operate and identify themselves on a transnational level, even where the individuals are linked to national economic infrastructures. Moreover, the "global challenges" – from climate change and food security to the fostering of democratically legitimised social systems which enable human rights and peace – require transnational cooperation and resolution approaches. Due to the necessarily-intertwining nature of such issues, as well as the quantitatively and qualitatively exponential growth of knowledge, the unification and metaanalysis of scientific findings across individual disciplines gains ever increasing importance. This new scientific challenge, though, can only be dealt with on the basis of transnational and transdisciplinary cooperation, which also means that the stakeholders of knowledge generation, especially those who are affected by the exploitation of the results, should be involved in these processes from the beginning. Associatedly, scientific work should function with maximum transparency and present its goals and tasks in straightforward, unpretentious terms.

APPEAR's participatory and cooperative approach promotes and supports this new emancipatory knowledge culture and its far-reaching socio-cultural implications. For in this context, science is not practised for itself – which has for too long been the case – but is rather regarded as an instrument for the improvement of social and ecological living conditions. This concept finds concrete realisation in cooperative activities with those countries formerly excluded from the generation of scientific knowledge simply for lack of suitable infrastructure. With such cooperation, national scientific institutions are enabled to take part in transnational knowledge discourses and problem resolution scenarios – for in a globalised, cross-linked, extremely interdependent world, there are no longer any strictly "local" problems without greater global ramifications, or whose resolutions will not also contribute to problem resolution in other local contexts.

APPEAR understands itself as a promoter of this "new practice" of knowledge, especially to its domestic "scientific community". The autonomy of science can stretch only so far given that its funding derives from the public purse. Publically-financed research and teaching must demonstrate its purpose and "added value" for the society which enables it. The "added value" of APPEAR lies not only in the capacity-building, action on poverty reduction and securing of basic needs which is taking place under its name in its partner countries, but also within Austrian research institutions for whom participatory engagement with non-European knowledge cultures also represents enrichment. This is why APPEAR also attaches such special importance to public relations and media relations: Through the many international events, items in print media and web fora, as well as through its own radio cooperation with the Austrian broadcasting company (ORF-Ö1-Campus), essential programme outcomes, including its participatory methods and partnership results have been presented to the general public both in Austria and abroad.

The contributions from programme participants that make up this book demonstrate that in the concrete, quotidian world of research, the tension between scientific cooperation and competition remains ever present. Some projects have struggled to find balance: was it about excellent results which can be published "well" or about unfulfilled expectations because certain methodological ideas could not be asserted towards the relevant institutional partners, or was it maybe about common learning and focusing on the social consequences of the common activities?

APPEAR, although now a successfully institutionalised cooperation programme, nonetheless continues to be an experiment, a "work in progress". Critical reflection upon our own actions and results – at both on a programme and a project level – remains immanent within APPEAR. Immanent, too, is reflection regarding the axioms and framework conditions required in order to facilitate the reunification of knowledge and development, where knowledge can enable optimal development. All stakeholders are invited to take active part in this reflection in the coming years, to engage with reflection about a new knowledge culture and the socio-cultural changes resulting from it.

3 THE CENTRAL AMERICAN CONTEXT

3.1 Desarrollo Participativo Integral Rural - The growing involvement of the National Agricultural University with rural communities

Project Coordinator: Daniel Querol
Coordinating Institution: Universidad Nacional Agraria (UNA), Faculty of Agriculture (FAGRO), Managua
Partner Institutions: University of Natural Resources and Life Sciences, Vienna (BOKU), Quality Management; Fundación Casa de los Tres Mundos, Instituto de Estudios Interdisciplinarios (IEI), Granada
Partner Country: Nicaragua
Project Duration: 1 February 2011 - 31 January 2014
Project Website: www. departir.net

3.1.1 The project - DEPARTIR

In order for the National Agricultural University (UNA) to further its development of the poor rural communities which form the backbone of Nicaragua's population, it was seen to be necessary to change minds and university structures in relation to teaching and research. The DEPARTIR (Desarrollo Participativo Integral Rural) project therefore sought to identify and confront the underlying causes of the heretofore restricted interaction between the rural world and the academic environment.

Academically, students make the transition from school to university still needing improvement, but find themselves in educational programmes which need to adopt a more hands-on approach if they are to produce skills that go beyond specialization in one career. Furthermore, the theoretical focus of academic staff means that university structures themselves can paradoxically prevent students from getting closer to the complexities of rural life. This situation may be set to change as around half of all present professors are set to be replaced by a new generation. However, the process of curricular change remains pending, as it has done for the last ten years.

From an administrative point of view, the university maintains a rigid structure well-suited to the control of state-allocated resources, but not well-adapted to the dynamic processes of research and agricultural production. At an institutional level, the achievement of an interdisciplinary approach is rendered problematic by the differing structures of specialized and autonomous departments with independent teaching and research facilities. All of this is in turn further complicated by the endemic scarcity of resources for research and development activities.

Within this context, three UNA professors formed a research and development team to teach a theoretical and practical course that connected the university to the rural population. Unfortunately, the course was extra-curricular, lacked resources and was not officially part of the UNA. Hence, the team were tasked with developing a strategy to ensure the long-term continuity of their work which also maintained the flexibility essential for effective field work:

First we contacted and reached an agreement with three professors from the University of Natural Resources and Life Sciences (BOKU) in Austria, who were willing to provide scientific and technological support, especially in soil analysis, animal husbandry and geographic information systems. The goal was to establish a link between academia and the rural sector, while simultaneously providing support in curricular reform and interdisciplinarity. A second alliance was then established with the Casa de los Tres Mundos (C3M), an NGO devoted to culture and development processes, with whom we had been working successfully for three years and who provided support in the form of analysis and advice that helped optimize the administrative processes. Through their Institute for Interdisciplinary Studies (IEI), they provided follow-up support and made proposals to improve the course methodology, particularly in sociological and anthropological areas.

While we were developing the methodology for cooperation, the APPEAR programme issued a funding call with goals that corresponded to our own. We were able to extend most of our expectations by three and a half years and adapt all our objectives with minimal changes in order to fit into their call.

The central objective of the project was to validate and institutionalize a series of participatory, educational, research and extension tools within the UNA in order to enhance the training of future professionals, while responding to the demands and needs of rural families and the urgent challenges they face.

We set three specific objectives:

- Iterative validation of the participatory diagnosis and development of a methodology with families and students in the field.
- Consolidation, systematization and dissemination of the methodology
- Incorporation of the methodology into institutional and curricular development

To meet objective one, the project organized four courses in different communities (see map). Based on the methodology we applied during each course, professors from the BOKU and researchers from the IEI accompanied us, to observe, participate and finally make suggestions which would improve the scientific, technical and methodological quality of interventions in the field as well as aid their systematization and subsequent use. Together with farming families and students we tested and evaluated new procedures that aimed to enhance the development of students' abilities and generate information useful for the rural families. At the end of each course, at a community meeting with the families, we presented our results, discussing the most important problems identified in the diagnosis and their possible solutions.
Families voted to prioritize alternative solutions, and based on the outcome of this democratic process, a series of specific projects were developed and tackled with the support of

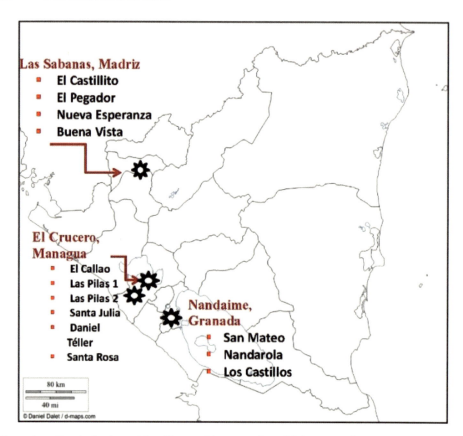

the university, students and families working together. Of the more than seventy proposals presented in the communities, the project participants selected, and with our support executed, 27 projects which ranged from technology for drilling wells and pumping water, through to photovoltaic systems and more traditional processes such as vegetable production in yards and biological management of pests and diseases in basic grains and coffee.

To consolidate, systematize and disseminate the developed methodology we used a number of strategies in parallel:

- Manuals and technical guides explaining procedures and methodologies.
- Posters and banners to elucidate and disseminate select community experiences.
- A web page (www.departir.net) that includes links to Facebook and Twitter and where all documents, reports, manuals, scientific papers and other results are made available to the general public. Students, farmers, researchers and extension workers have already downloaded over 25,000 copies of documents from this site.
- Audio-visual presentation of DEPARTIR activities in 13 videos, various television presentations and via a YouTube channel.
- Finally, we detailed the experiences of the course and methodology in a book that was published and distributed.

To fulfill our third goal of incorporating the methodology into institutional and curricular development, multiple alternative proposals were drafted, both for the curriculum and for the structure, operation and rules of procedure of DEPARTIR. The University Council, in two separate sessions, first approved the establishment of the Programme for Participatory Integrated Rural Development as an Institutional Programme and, even though the needed institutional curricular transformation within the UNA has not yet taken place, approved the two DEPARTIR courses, validating them for all study plans in the four faculties.

3.1.2 Changing minds and structures: Evolution or revolution?

by Daniel Querol

Few people can doubt that universities must change significantly if they are to fully integrate into the societies that support them. This is necessary not only in order to train future professionals in a way that ensures their usefulness to society, but because in addition to contributing their capacity for analysis, synthesis and critical reflection, universities must also interact with the real world.

We are, however, confronted by two questions:

Given that society is not a homogeneous entity, whom should the university serve? In most European and North American universities, the political composition of society has determined that the entrepreneurial sector be the prime beneficiary of academic skills. This serves as the starting point for growth, thereby benefiting society as a whole. In the case of Nicaragua, with an incipient entrepreneuriat, there is general consensus that we must engage with the problems of the poorest and largest segment of the population.

The second question, which we analyze herewith, concerns our own institutional limitations and the possible changes that the UNA can undertake to better contribute to this part of society. As examples we will use some of the changes effected during our project, named *Changing Minds and Structures: the growing involvement of the UNA in rural communities,* as implemented through DEPARTIR (Comprehensive Rural Participatory Development). More specifically, we will discuss a course in which students are first trained at the UNA, then live with families in rural communities and prepare a diagnosis of the situation jointly with them.

The academic staff

DEPARTIR wanted to build up a core team of young, academically-competent professors with a vision for the future and the will to serve. Unfortunately, most of the UNA's professors are nearing retirement and have a somewhat inflexible vision of their role and functions, so any change in their general approach is not a realistic expectation. However, this project seemed to present an opportunity to open the door to young candidates with fresh energy and vision. Therefore, over the last seven years, more than forty professors from four faculties have contributed to training and research through DEPARTIR, in addition to the core group.

The students

There are more than 400 students in their final year of study at the UNA, so it was self-evident that a team of just three professors could not possibly undertake the project on their own. While the university is limited in its selection processes, we suggested the academic requirements and opened a dialogue with the students, stressing the serious nature of their involvement with the rural population. In July 2014 the University Council approved a better solution which takes into account prior academic requirements and divides the course and diagnosis into two segments:

- A first course in the academic semester involving theory and practice, where in addition to acquiring inter-disciplinary skills, the students are assessed in key-competencies relative to field work, including the basic capacity to work in a team, the will, flexibility and availability to adapt to changing situations, and solidarity.
- A second practical course, open to all students who have completed the first course, but restricted due to the limited staff and financial resources available.

Support staff

The administration of UNA depends essentially on the budget allocated to it by the state, and consequently its function and approach is determined by the Court of Auditors, while its objective is to comply with the requirements for the delivery of funds. Unfortunately, the strict budgetary rules regarding expenses and the attendant complex paperwork are not conducive to research and development processes in the field. As a result of this situation, DEPARTIR had to create an administrative "appendix" which was accepted by the UNA and in certain cases speeded up internal procedures, but which often had to also look for alternative shortcuts.

Structure and operation of the UNA

Whilst the UNA's organizational and operational structure is manifested in hundreds of official documents, it is so rigid that the academic community must often be creative in avoiding its self-imposed hurdles. By law, the UNA is structured into faculties which each have specialized, totally autonomous departments. Spontaneous interdisciplinary action is impossible, since any interaction between professors from different departments, much less different faculties, needs to be justified and negotiated in great detail. This means that when students in one specialized field go into communities and are confronted with the complex trans-disciplinary nature of reality, they have to deny this complexity and concentrate exclusively on their area of specialty.

As it would be necessary to redraft the University Law in order to open up the departmental structure and make it more flexible, the University Council instead opted to convert the Research and Development group, part of the Department of Plant Production, which in turn is a part of the Faculty of Agronomy, into the university-wide programme for Comprehensive Participatory Rural Development, even though its staff continues to operate within the same departmental niche. At the same time, by agreement of the Council, its status places it above the faculties, with an ensuing organizational chaos.

What we teach and what we learn

Due to the gulf between reality and what is taught, the university has for the past twelve years been examining the need for curricular change. Additionally, its new curriculum needs to be geared not only to the accumulation of knowledge but to the development of competencies. While waiting for this curricular transformation to take place, partial reforms go unaccepted, since specific changes would affect the whole and possibly unbalance the curriculum even more seriously. In the meantime, however, the necessary change of mentality in the academic community has not occurred and so the curricular transformation remains pending.

Initially DEPARTIR was only able to provide its students with a certification, since its course contents were not considered part of their mandatory training, but after seven years of offering the course in an academic limbo, we are the first to have submitted a curriculum for the creation of competencies. Having reached this impasse, the UNA's University Council has simply ruled that DEPARTIR's interdisciplinary course will now be valid for all the university's careers.

Our contribution to research and development

Given that the limited state budget is basically channeled towards teaching activities, essentially all research, extension activities and development support are financed from external sources. Unfortunately most of the research is conditioned by the priorities of those who administer the funds, and although usually altruistic, they also tend to be divorced from actual needs. The UNA's staff then becomes involved and conducts these projects despite knowing that the corresponding research and development frequently do not coincide with local or even national priorities.

Our first step consisted of establishing a dialogue with local communities on what they considered their chief weaknesses and problems. We then developed a practical course, which initially established a diagnosis of each of the participating "fincas" (usually most of those in the community). The end result was a community-sanctioned list of proposals, ordered according to their perceived priority, as to what the UNA could do with and for the individual farmers. We thus took the population's concrete needs as our point of departure for the research guidelines, limited only by the skills and interests of the researching professors and students.

The second step was to look for sources of financing sympathetic to our priorities and flexible enough to adapt to a research project that never presupposes the priorities of the population, given that the initial objective of every intervention in the field is to listen and only act after there has been agreement in the community about the actions to be taken. After four years of variable and varied financing sources, we were able to obtain APPEAR's support for a three-and-a-half year period, enabling us to concentrate our activities on diagnosis, research and development. To date we have worked with 197 students and 865 families in 17 communities, and have launched 44 productive alternatives.

This entire process has also served to ease one of the university's most serious problems, namely that of finding ways to increase the number of graduating students. During this period and through the research work, 28 students have graduated and two of them have completed a master's degree. In the coming years, other students will be able to submit similar research work involving the systematized implementation of alternatives as an end-of-studies dissertation.

Limitations and pending issues

We still don't know how we can more organically involve professors and students from all the university faculties in either the courses or the development of projects. Further, there is no detailed procedure for ensuring compliance with the requirements of quality and pertinence in the work performed for graduation.

We have received statements of interest from other universities that would like more information about this structure. Within our university, the possibility of developing a specialization course has been raised which would strengthen the capacities of our graduates. At the same time we know full well that the UNA cannot devote an important part of its budget to development activities, since this is not its main function. We are currently setting up a methodology which will permit the financing of 30 microprojects a year with the communities, and which would simultaneously serve as material for a minimum of 60 graduation papers.

Conclusion

Ultimately, many of these small changes give us a feeling of concrete progress even though they constitute processes outside the existing structure. The doubt therefore remains as to whether they represent an evolution or no more than an agreement to turn a blind eye to a breaking of the rules.

Thus we can see two parallel situations:

- Where a deep change of paradigm is required, we are frequently paralyzed; we wait for a revolution to take place while putting off the small modifications which would bring us closer to the necessary change.
- Where a university system lacks flexibility, either change shall have to be incremental or alternative options shall have to be pursued. When these alternative paths are repeated, their integration becomes the basis for major change.

Universities are currently rigidly structured and managed institutions that exist within a framework of external rules, and are unchanged by internal voices. A project that modifies this is merely a single step in the desired direction, since the transformation of minds and structures cannot be seen as an isolated revolutionary event but as a process of continued evolution which will culminate in the yearned-for revolution.

3.1.3 So what are we going to do about gender?!

by Verena Pflug

I was assigned the task of designing a gender strategy for DEPARTIR. I failed. Here I discuss why this was, but also why I think that we nonetheless succeeded in gendering our project.

The role of a so-called "gender-expert" was handed to me right at the very beginning. I think it was on my first or second day of working for DEPARTIR that I was told that high hopes were set on me solving "the gender problem". Incorporating gender at all levels of the project was one of our main requirements and so far no project team members in either Nicaragua or Austria knew exactly how this was to be done, or even exactly what the requirement was. Someone, an expert on gender issues, had to come and help, so when I joined the project team I was asked to become familiar with the topic and figure out how we could achieve said requirement. From then on I was the gender expert.

The only problem was: I was not at all an expert on gender. The most likely reason for my being asked to become DEPARTIR's gender person was the simple fact that I was a woman and did not know much about agriculture. So my field of expertise was to be gender. I did have my doubts about this role in the team, and especially the reasons for which I was chosen, but as I was generally interested in the topic, I naively accepted the task of dedicating a part of my work to gendering DEPARTIR.

The first task in my career as gender expert seemed easy: I was to present BOKU's gender plan, the university's approach to achieving gender equality on all levels. At our first partner meeting in Managua, in May 2011, I was due to present my findings. I had found out about "daughter's day" and about several scholarships for women and particular measures to support women. Like many other public institutions, BOKU has struggled and still struggles with phenomena like the leaky pipeline or glass ceiling – structural barriers which prevent women from climbing the ladder and obtaining higher and thus better-paid and more reputable positions. I also researched student statistics and found female students to be still underrepresented in technical fields of study. All of this wasn't exactly new to me, although the numbers – for example the very low number of female professors – did startle me. A few weeks later, in the DEPARTIR office at the Universidad Nacional Agraria in Managua, we sat down to talk about gender. I was the only woman in the meeting. Our colleagues listened to what we had to say about BOKU's gender strategy and then told us about gender at UNA: about the low numbers of female students who graduate, about the difficulties women have returning to their jobs after giving birth because of the lack of day-care for their small children, about how the DEPARTIR team tried to specifically support female students and encourage them to actively take part in the courses. This first discussion was fruitful and lively, and everyone was engaged and aware of the importance of the topic. I was highly motivated to contribute what I could, so (again naively) I accepted the task of designing a gender strategy for DEPARTIR. And like I said, I failed.

The first step was to compare the two universities' approaches to achieving gender equality. I was to write a report which we would then sit down and discuss. But what then? I started reading and thinking, and very soon the whole matter seemed far too complex for me to transform into a simple strategy for a three year project. I realized that our first discussion was far too limited and that we couldn't reduce the issue of gender to just a comparison of universities or even to the discrimination of women – it was far more complicated. And even if we reduced it to that: How could we achieve gender equality in our DEPARTIR classes, let alone the whole university, when there just weren't enough female students? And if we couldn't even manage to achieve equality in numbers, which seemed to be the easiest problem to solve, what could we do?

I felt overwhelmed by the complexity of the matter and did not know where to start. Although I managed to complete the report on gender in BOKU and send it to Nicaragua, all the while I was writing it I doubted its meaningfulness and questioned if anyone would ever read it. Our first approach of comparing the universities suddenly seemed one-dimensional and unnecessary to me; what difference would it make if we knew that we were still far from gender equality on both sides of the Atlantic? It wouldn't benefit anyone, and nor would we gain any actual additional knowledge from it. I felt that we were heading in the wrong direction and that we needed to add many more dimensions to our gender approach. The word "gender strategy" next to my name on our to-do lists started to annoy me.

"So what are we going to do about gender?" I would be asked in meetings, the other team members looking at me expectantly. And I could just shrug and list all my doubts, explain how complex it all was, and how we needed to decide at which level of the project we would start our gendering process. There where so many project levels where gender mattered: the university level which we had already started to discuss and compare, then the DEPARTIR team itself, the students, the farmers (who were they, who had which function, who decided and who didn't?, etc.) and so on. There was gender on a practical, operational level, usually limited to counting numbers of males and females, as opposed to the possibility of thinking about gender theoretically and studying gender roles at the university, on farms and among the students in order to find out more, for example, about the reasons for those low numbers of women in the university or among graduates. In short: I felt I had failed in my attempt to solve the gender problem and that we were no wiser than before.

And then the deadline for submission of the annual project drew near. Of course, I was asked to summarize our efforts and activities in the area of gender. My first thought was that unfortunately this section of the report would have to remain blank. But after sitting in the office for some hours, struggling to transform confused thoughts into logical sentences and a more or less structured text, I noticed that I had actually written something. And this was when I suddenly realized two things:

Firstly, that even though I had failed at designing a gender strategy, we, as a team, were actually already in the middle of the process of implementing one. We had been constantly discussing gender, having new ideas, ditching old ones, discussing them again and getting confused. Simply by its status as a topic we knew we could not just ignore, gender had become an important topic for the project and – even if only in our thought-processes – had become an issue at almost every level of the project.

Secondly, I realized that the overwhelming number of ways we could tackle the issue of gender in our project was not necessarily a problem. We could do different things, tackle gender from diverse angles, on various levels and in different ways. We did not have to solve the problem of gender inequality in our universities, among student groups or in the rural communities with which we worked. Such results were obviously unachievable in the project's three years duration, and in any case this were not what had been asked of us. We could talk about gender roles in our project team, and we could try to change them. We could also study gender and perceptions of gender and gender inequalities among students, or in the field.

This was when we went from thinking and discussing to acting and implementing our ideas. First, we decided that we wanted to find a master's student willing to contribute to our project by writing a master's thesis on a topic related to gender and DEPARTIR. A person who was not involved in the project team and who had sufficient time to conduct such a study would add more to the project than any member of the project staff could. We did not have to search for long. A student soon approached us and asked if she could write her thesis within the framework of the project. She did, and conducted a very interesting study on gender relations on farms in the communities where one of the DEPARTIR courses took place. The outcomes of her thesis added to the project just as much as did her presence in the DEPARTIR course and the many discussions on gender and gender roles in agriculture she had with students, professors, project team members. She was much more of a gender expert than I was. Her thesis was supervised by an Austrian professor, but in Nicaragua she also worked together with another student from UNA and this student's supervisor, a female professor from UNA who had some stories to tell about her own struggles as a female scientist in a male dominated field of study.

This other supervisor helped to plan and implement another activity. She supported the Nicaraguan project team in conducting a study on gender at UNA. Together with the project team members from the Instituto de Estudios Interdisciplinarios, our colleagues from UNA conducted a survey on gender among students, professors and general staff at their university. They interviewed students, teachers and other staff about their perception of gender, about their opinion of the discrimination of women and about the importance of discussing gender equality in general. At UNA, gender was not a commonplace topic, so this survey aimed not only at gaining information, but was also regarded as an awareness-raising activity.

So, in spite of our initial confusion, my failure to design a gender strategy and many long discussions which had seemingly been going nowhere, I think I can say that our project ended up being quite gendered. When I finally sat down to write my parts of the final project report, and was again forced to transform the answer to the question: "so, what did we do about gender?" into a coherent and structured text, I was pleased to find that we had managed to bring gender to various levels of the project. Although we had not managed to change the number of women graduating from UNA or the low number of female professors at BOKU or female students in technical fields of study in general, or the fact that poverty still affects more women than men, we had achieved something: we had studied gender on farms, discussed it in classrooms as well as project meetings, had done a survey at the university and had compared the universities' gender policies. Gender equality among the project team had been a lively topic and, although there were still more men than women involved, more women were actively participating at the end than in the beginning.

Throughout the three years of DEPARTIR, the question "So, what are we going to do about gender?" confused me, gave me doubts, annoyed me and made me anxious, but it also helped me to see that without realizing it at the time, we had been doing something about gender all along. And even though what we did about gender might not have changed structures, I am convinced it did change some minds, including my own.

3.1.4 Enumeration of results

- Systematization and publication of the methodology for the Comprehensive Participative Rural Diagnosis (CPRD) course.
- Training of human resources required to implement the CPRD course.
- Establishment of the DEPARTIR University-wide Programme by agreement of UNA`s University Council.
- Validation as credit courses for all UNA careers of the optional courses DEPARTIR I: Methodology for CPRD and of the DEPARTIR II: CPRD practical module, by agreement of UNA`s University Council.
- Successful participation of 143 students from UNA`s four faculties in four CPRD courses.
- Positive acceptance of the academic activities of UNA students and instructors on the part of the rural communities.
- Twenty-seven options agreed on with the population and implemented in the areas of agronomy, engineering and irrigation facing climate change, renewable energy and rural development in general.
- Establishment of a solid base for complementary work with other university sectors including the laboratories for soils and microbiology, the public information department and the offices for information and communication technologies.
- Successful transfer and installation of soil laboratory equipment from BOKU to UNA and subsequent training.
- Establishment of the technical base for the use of renewable energy and water harvesting and management for the development of a sustainable agriculture.
- Definition and construction of an operational online geographical information system.
- Availability of equipment and instruments required for the development of the course and support of the pertinent research.
- Development and publication of six technical guides and six manuals.
- Ten theses within the framework of the project, including two master's theses.
- Publication of nine scientific articles and production of thirteen videos for television.
- Development of a web page and DEPARTIR YouTube channel.
- Production of a Dossier on development concepts and theories.
- Completed institutional gender diagnosis of UNA.

Additional project results include:
- Three annual DEPARTIR field days on the central campus of UNA, in cooperation with C3M, with over 300 participants.
- Participation of 4 BOKU students in CPRD training courses
- Successful implementation of the concept of a joint master's thesis between a UNA and a BOKU student
- Elaboration of an instruction video on Soil Monoliths in Spanish
- Training of Prof. Juan Carlos Moran Centeno (2013, 2014) and Prof. Felix Humberto Nieto Reyes (20014) at BOKU, Vienna.
- Building lasting cooperation possibilities between the universities and with the Casa de los Tres Mundos.

Families developing their diagnostics

Basic soil analysis by students and local families in Nandarola

Community meeting in Santa Julia

DEPARTIR field team, Granada 2012

Students with local families

Methodological tool development with rural families in Buena Vista

Meeting in the Nandarola community

Transect by students, community members and professors in the Buena Vista community

Repairing soil laboratory spectrophotometer

DEPARTIR project coordinator Daniel Querol is preparing the well drilling equipment in Apacunca Chinandega

Poster and advertisement for solar pumping system developed by DEPARTIR

Tonkua, production project with Nandarola families

3.2 Improvement of Social Work Education to Foster Social Development and Poverty Reduction: An Academic Exchange of Theory, Methodology and Practice

Project Coordinator: Eva Klawatsch-Treitl
Coordinating Institution: University of Applied Sciences Vienna (FH Campus Wien)
Partner Institution: Universidad Luterana Salvadoreña
Partner Country: El Salvador
Project Duration: 1 August 2012 – 31 July 2014

3.2.1 The project - Trabajo Social – Educación y Cambio Social

The academic partnership "Trabajo Social – Educación y Cambio Social (TECS)" between the Departments of Social Work of Universidad Luterana Salvadoreña (ULS), El Salvador and FH Campus Wien (FHCW), Austria aimed at enriching and improving the education of social workers and strengthening the role of social workers as drivers of social change in Austria and in El Salvador. Social workers are important actors in the promotion of public welfare, gender equality and sustainable development. Social work as a profession is a public good and *per se* the backbone of social services in a country. The overall objective of the TECS project reflects this view by embracing the notion that all cooperation activities should enrich and improve social work education to strengthen the profession's role as a driver of social change, especially in El Salvador. Partners from both institutions assume that initiatives in the areas of conflict mediation, poverty reduction, distribution of resources, good governance, as well as the development of a socially-oriented public sector, enriching of political participation and the reduction of domestic violence are important drivers for the social betterment of a country.

Social work's above mentioned "role as a driver of social change" must always be viewed and evaluated in a broad and political sense. In the final documentation of the earlier ULS/FHCS project "Trabajo Social y su contribución para un desarrollo equitativo e inclusivo", the participants came to the conclusion that the reflection on social work *per se* must also analyze the role of social work stakeholders in the contexts of individual and structural socio-politics, existing structures of community empowerment, and the operability of social work in the realities of capitalistic market structures. Following this reasoning, social work cannot be classified as a "craft" but rather as a scientific discipline that relies on scientific reflection on professional social work within the fields of socio-economic realities, state action, the history of the social work profession, power relations and specific specialist knowledge. Therefore, a scientific approach must take into consideration the various competences in social work theory, an appropriate scientific methodology, and a thorough analysis of cultural and gender related implications of social work studies. Further, it is crucial for a country's professional social work policies to reflect on the social challenges for an appropriate theory of social work and on how to improve the educational sector that leads to adequate social work qualifications.

During their particular histories, both Austria and El Salvador have experienced important developments in social work policies and in the education of social workers. These changes correlate with the social and political developments in the second half of the 20th century, especially after World War Two in Austria, and the civil war in El Salvador from 1979 to 1992. Since the end of the Salvadorian civil war and World War Two, huge efforts have been made to further social work policies and to integrate social work education into the university curricula (El Salvador, 1991) and universities of applied science (Austria, 2001). Between 1953 and 1960, in El Salvador the first period of social work policies embraced the idea of social work as psychological assistance. During the 1960s, the Salvadorian notion of social work evolved toward a better integration of sociological insights and the macro-social context into concepts of social work. In the 1970s, social work policies in El Salvador experienced a period of revision by adding the new approaches of the "Movimiento de Reconceptualización promovido en Sur América" (Movement of Reconceptualization promoted in South America). The latter opened the way to modern social work strategies in El Salvador, which suffered a bitter blow when the Salvadorian civil war started in 1979.

The Austrian history of social work differs in many ways not only from that of El Salvador but also the histories of other European countries. In Austria, at the beginning of the 20th century, social work policies were youth welfare strategies that neglected poverty alleviation measures. During this first phase of Austrian social work policies it was the state rather than civil society that engaged in such strategies. The history of social work policies in Austria must necessarily also be discussed in the light of the horrific social work ideas of the "Third Reich". Following World War Two, it would not be until the end of the 1960s and into the early 1970s that Austrian social work notions embraced a more modern and professional conception of social work. Further, Austrian policy makers integrated international social work theories and methodologies into educational curricula and practice later than did policy makers in most other European countries. Social work education is "applied education" and thus differs from other studies in various significant ways. State-of-the-art social work education must integrate the lessons of best-practice projects, modern theory and methodology. Social work education must update its perceptions of social realities and foster dialogue with social work institutions, including civil society and governmental stakeholders. Such a multidimensional educational approach is the best way to meet the needs of a professional social work policy. Further, social work education must embrace adequate didactic methods and offer undergraduate and graduate educational curricula which integrate the expertise of professors from different disciplines.

With regard to the participating academic institutions and individuals in Austria and El Salvador, this project focussed on the following goals:

- Amplifying theoretical and methodological knowledge in the field of social work by working with communities and groups in the fields of conflict prevention, the handling of domestic violence, establishing gender equality and social welfare in Austria and in El Salvador.
- Capacity building for a sensitive and holistic perception of realities and regular coop-

erative discourse between the practice of social work institutions and individual social workers and educational institutions.
- Revaluating social work as an important public good by promoting discourse about social work as "paid care-work" and as a traditionally female profession.
- Improving academic teaching regarding its content, didactic proposals and supervision of student research activities and internships.

This cooperation was mainly driven by the two country coordinators: Eneyda Arteaga de Valle for the Department of Social Work at ULS and Eva Klawatsch-Treitl for the Department of Social Work at FHCW. The work of both coordinators would not have been possible without the help of support teams at both institutions. The teams engaged in an interesting exchange of thoughts that led to a multifaceted outcome. The results of this intellectual exchange created a rich foundation of new ideas that have the potential to lead to new teaching manuals, conferences and practical implementations. During the project, the Austrian and Salvadorian core teams met twice in Vienna (October 2013 and May 2014) and once in San Salvador (January 2014). The members of both teams used the meetings to exchange their particular ideas of social work and social work education, in order to better understand the different realities, challenges and diverse approaches of both institutions. In addition to managing the group processes between the two teams, both groups also used the meetings to get to know their respective partner institutions, to talk with colleagues from particular departments and to participate in workshops and an international conference at ULS. The three visits enabled lively exchange and worthwhile discourse between academic personnel, civil society stakeholders, and social workers from all relevant institutions. The international conference "Trabajo Social – Educación y Cambio Social" at ULS was a great success, with more than 100 participants from Austria, Canada, Cuba, El Salvador, Honduras, Nicaragua and the United States, as well as a live stream for the public. A video summary can be found at: http://uls.edu.sv/trabajosocial.

During the entire project, students from ULS and FHCW participated in research in the areas of community work practices, social work teaching methodology, domestic violence protection, leadership strategies and social work strategies with homeless people. The experience of members of both groups led to the conclusion that the valuable insights learnt from social work practices in Central America can also be used in an innovative social work approach in Austria. The development of a workshop on the topic of social work as "paid care-work" was a big success. In both countries most social workers and social work students are women. Engendered discourse about the role of social work promises to enrich policy debate at the respective departments in Austria and El Salvador. A total of 130 persons participated in these workshops. As a result a manual was published in El Salvador. Additionally, the topic "social work and gender" was addressed in the project final publication as well as in different courses at ULS.

Both partner institutions aim to integrate newly acquired knowledge from the project into their respective educational curricula. ULS will begin an overhaul of its curriculum in social work in 2015, while the social work studies curriculum at FHCW will integrate the topics of global learning, development policies and international social work on an ongoing basis. The interested reader can read about the methods and results of this project in more detail in the final project report "Trabajo Social y su contribución para un desarrollo equitativo e inclusivo", published in August 2014.

3.2.2 Public space, safety and security

by Eneyda Arteaga de Valle, Elfriede Fröschl, Eva Klawatsch-Treitl, Maritza Rivas de Romero, Christoph Stoik, Angelika Widowitz

Introduction
by Eneyda Arteaga de Valle, Eva Klawatsch-Treitl

The TECS project – English title: "Improvement of social work education to foster social development and poverty reduction. An academic exchange of theory, methodology and practice" – aimed at "enriching and improving social work education to strengthen the profession's role as a driver of social change". This shows the focus of our approach: We consider social work a profession that seeks to promote human development and the participation and empowerment of individuals, enabling them to become the agents of the change they want to see in their lives, their families, the groups they belong to, the communities in which they live, and society in general. Our collaboration and all its results (meetings, analyses, publications, seminars, and trips) were characterised by a mutual learning process that focussed on different approaches to and methods of teaching social work at both universities and the ways in which the profession is practised in our countries. This process is still ongoing. Our topics included, among others, different social work methodologies, social work as a "women's profession" and the guidance of students' research and internships. There was one topic that we had not included in our programme during the planning phase, but which inserted itself onto our agenda: safety and security. These are words with many different meanings and we encounter them in a wide range of areas. Safety and unsafeness can be a subjective feeling or a real situation – particularly in El Salvador, with its history of civil war and criminal gangs. In the context of social work, systems of social security are naturally important. Safety and security mean different things to women and men. During our collaboration, we kept discovering connections to different aspects of safety and security. We, the TECS team, believe that reflecting on the issue from different perspectives shows interesting contrasts in how it is addressed in both our countries and reflects the differences in its meaning for women and men. This may be interesting to others as well, including other APPEAR project members who may have had similar experiences.

Reflections on safety
by Angelika Widowitz

Safety is a word that means different things to different people. Safety is a place where we feel safe and secure and can live free of violence. Safety is a colour that surrounded us in good times and now calms us. Safety is an object that has an emotional significance to us because it was a gift from a loved one. Safety is an animal that was our trusted companion in childhood. Safety is a plant we made bloom with our care and nurturing. Safety is a photograph that recalls pleasant memories. Safety is family that supports us all our lives. Safety is friends who share our laughter during the good times and our sorrow during the bad. Safety is a person in whom we can confide our most intimate troubles and worries. Safety is a basic need that every human being seeks to satisfy. Safety is a feeling that we ache for when we lose it. Safety is a vacation where we can leave our everyday life behind and engage in self-reflection. Safety is an embrace you can lean into. Safety gives us time that we can use to take care of ourselves. Safety is honesty from the people around us. Safety is a touch that gives us new strength. Safety is a song that helps us cope with the past and prepare for the future. Safety is a picture that captures our imagination. Safety is a gesture that gives us new hope. Safety is enjoying life because we have energy to spend on other things. Safety is important because it gives us space to breathe. Safety is a word at the right moment. Safety is an irreplaceable good. Safety is everything and nothing. Safety is a word that means different things to different people.

Uncertainties about being made to feel unsafe in the public space
by Christoph Stoik

Talking about "subjective security" and "promoting a sense of security in the public space" in Europe, and particularly in Vienna, feels very different after our trip to El Salvador in January 2014. Even though literature on the matter and my own reflections had made it clear to me before this trip that these discussions have little to do with any actual "dangerous situations in the public space" in Vienna, they now seem nothing but absurd, even cynical, since my return. I was aware that discussions about security in the public space are social phenomena that make people feel less safe and secure, related to increasing social inequalities, social uncertainty, and the dismantling of social security systems. They have to do with neoliberal uncertainty, with societal processes of transformation, the transferral of political responsibility to citizens, and symbolic politics trying to demonstrate that security is being protected in the public space while in reality the political scope of action regarding the causes of subjective lack of safety and security is (apparently) shrinking.

The trip to El Salvador showed me two things. The first was that in both El Salvador and Austria, this "lack of security in the public space" is used for political purposes, to demonstrate the political capacity to act, which makes people in El Salvador feel even less secure. The second was that I began to see what a lack of safety and security in the public space can truly mean when people are affected by great poverty, when systems of social security hardly exist, when the pressure to survive makes people turn to illegal means of securing their livelihoods, and when criminal gang structures begin to manage public security in parallel with official systems of the state.

Public space in El Salvador was completely different from what I was familiar with in Europe. Even the locals cannot move freely in all parts of San Salvador. Nightlife is only found in the rich districts, which resemble gated communities. We, as European guests, were particularly urged not to move freely in the public space. Our colleagues from ULS were very concerned about our safety. They would always pick us up by car and drive us around. We moved around with a large group of students to be able to see the city centre of San Salvador. Only through this experience, this visit to El Salvador, did I begin to comprehend why our Salvadoran guests had initially been so reluctant to explore Vienna on their own when they were visiting.

But it was also very impressive to experience what "public" can really mean in the public space: At the final rally of an election campaign, which we were able to attend, thousands of Salvadorans gathered in the street. I had never felt this safe and secure in the streets of San Salvador. The public space was created by the people expressing their political interests. This made me realise how precious a good public space is and how important it is to preserve and protect its qualities in Austria – also against the fear-mongering instrumentalisation of a supposed lack of security in the public space.

Waking the soul in a garden in Vienna
by Maritza Rivas de Romero

In Vienna, it is easy to just pick up a book, find a bench to sit on and read for a while in calm and safe surroundings. You can breathe in the smell of the trees and the grass, and watch people pass by in the afternoon.

It is pleasant to watch them amble along unhurried, walking their dogs. It is when fear, uncertainty and stress give way to tranquillity and enjoyment of life that the soul is nourished. Regardless of your social status or wealth, no matter whether you are a thinker or a dreamer, alone or in company – this calm fills you with bliss and satisfaction and allows you to enjoy that inner peace for which we all yearn. For is not easy to let go of the social problems in Central American countries, particularly El Salvador, where the majority of people are faced with the barred windows and doors of their houses every day, the security bars that imprison the inhabitants. Their spirits are not free either, incarcerated as they are by political turmoil, social inequality and a lack of opportunities.

This contrast with the constant fear in which we live in El Salvador allows us to enjoy a park – such a normal, everyday thing for the Viennese – to relax peacefully, to drift along with the wind, walk safely along the paths without watchful glances, to have a cup of tea and some apple strudel, to enjoy life and organise your thoughts, to feel free in a country that is not yours, to enjoy it to the fullest. That is when your fears dissipate, and in this environment of sublime security, the soul begins to shine.

Safety, security, and gender
by Elfriede Fröschl

Safety and security mean different things to women than to men. Women have only recently gained the right to make decisions about their own bodies, so it is not something they take for granted. This is linked to the unsafe feeling many women have as they move around in public space, especially at night. They do not feel safe until they are home, although even that is a place fraught with danger for many women in Austria and El Salvador. This has been confirmed by numerous empirical studies that show that one in five women is a victim of domestic violence. (Young) men, however, who are most at risk in the public space, act as if nothing could harm them. Discussions about "public order and security" also contribute to this subjective sense of safety. In these discussions, the perpetrators of violence are mostly strangers, so the public space is being placed under increasing control.

Curiously, the threat to women in the so-called private space is simultaneously ignored. Social workers should contribute to making power dynamics in "private" space a subject of public discussion. Speaking openly about domestic violence should also be used to empower communities to become more involved in planning safety measures for women who are victims of violence. People are given more freedom to act by the open discussion of security and safety and the lack thereof, violence and non-violence and individual and communal safety measures, and by reclaiming the public space. It is empowerment won without the addition of new forms of control cloaked in terms of public security policy, such as new security measures with cameras, security guards, or the expulsion of vulnerable groups of society.

3.2.3 Social work and gender aspects: Why can social work not be considered gender blind?[11]

by Eneyda Arteaga de Valle, Eva Klawatsch-Treitl

In our academic cooperation (TECS), the process allowed us to heighten our awareness of gender perspectives and their application in the frame of the theory, methodology and practice of social work, but it also led us to a process of internal analysis of the profession. At the beginning of our academic exchange process, when we were first defining our concept, it was very important to the whole team to include the aim of fostering appreciative discourse between social work practice and theory and to organise discourse about gender issues in social work. We combined both of these aspects in special activities, organising, as an important first step, a pilot workshop in Vienna (May 2013), followed by a second pilot

---

11   This article is an adaptation of the two articles by Eneyda Arteaga (Trabajo Social y perspectiva de género) and Eva Klawatsch-Treitl (Soziale Arbeit und Entwicklungspolitik – Plädoyer für eine diskursive Praxis) in the final publication of TECS: ULS (2014)(ed.): Trabajo Social y su contribución para un desarrollo equitativo e inclusivo / Soziale Arbeit und ihr Beitrag zu einer gerechten und inklusiven Entwicklung. ULS Editores. San Salvador – Vienna.

workshop in San Salvador (January 2014) on the issue of social work as care work.[12] The second workshop was facilitated by Eneyda Arteaga and Eva Klawatsch-Treitl and was the first opportunity to really cooperate in a workshop. Its concept included as didactical focus a participatory methodology (psychodrama) and the idea of the common generation of knowledge about social work as care work, as a public good, as employment, as a profession, and as a so-called women´s profession (a term that has a highly dubious definition). In Vienna, 13 primarily young female social workers (graduates of the department) attended the workshop and expressed their pleasure about the space for reflection beyond being students. In El Salvador, about 120 participants (female and later also male) attended the pilot workshop and the five further workshops on this topic.

We all know that both in El Salvador and in Austria, the majority of students and professionals of social work are female, and males the minority. Although the dual-topic of professional social work and aspects of gender is very important for the further development of social work in all countries, we see the topics of gender and development of the profession being addressed separately by different groups of authors. Only very rarely are both questions combined. The very abstract and gender-blind discourse of the profession bears the danger of discussing theoretical concepts without recognizing the realities of social work. Our workshops allowed us to reflect on this situation from a holistic perspective and with a gender-sensitive approach, as well as to generate spaces of reflection, discussion and analysis of the implications that this situation has with respect to the status of social work as a profession, a discipline and a course of studies, and its forms of organisation, such as trade unions and professional associations. The interest of the workshop participants showed the possibilities and need for further discourse. This allowed us to focus very specifically on the gender issue in social work. Although we had not planned it, the topic was present throughout. Our activities provided a frame within which we were able to discuss working conditions, the theory and methodology of social work, the structure of our teams, departments and universities (of applied sciences), the development and further development of the profession. Therefore, we decided to use this article to address these different aspects rather than further explain the concept of our workshops[13]. Please read our theoretical considerations as reflection and insights on the topic. We really hope to open the space for further discourse in an appreciative, interdisciplinary way.

The history of how social work became a (women's) profession can be told in different ways. It is important to highlight that the tradition of modern social work is directly linked to the Industrial Revolution and the institutionalisation of social welfare services and social policy, i.e., the period of transformation that Karl Polanyi (1997[1944]) refers to as the "Great Transformation", which originated in England. In the late 18th century, the developments that had begun in the 16th century (proto-industrialisation, creation of trading companies, found-

---

12 The German title was: Soziale Arbeit – Was für eine Arbeit? Eine psychodramatische Reflexion der Praxis sozialer Arbeit. The Spanish title was: Trabajo social – profesión de mujeres?

13 As an example see the following page: https://docs.google.com/a/uls.edu.sv/file/d/0B8YEZE_eO8NKeTVMcm-Q0UjZ6ekU/edit?pli=1 [23 Oct. 2014]

ing of colonies, etc.) finally resulted in previously unimaginable socioeconomic changes (cf. Bachinger/Matis, 2009: 16). Before this transformation, domestic economy (the household in its entirety) was the dominant economic principle, characterised by reciprocity and redistribution (cf. Polanyi, 1997[1944]: 224).

When discussing the history of the social work profession, the narrative usually begins before the Great Transformation, which means that the context in which these analyses discuss poor relief is completely different from current approaches to poverty and many other social problems (illness, addiction, marginalisation, domestic violence, unemployment, etc.). Considering that professional social work in most countries has its roots in poor relief, this seems perfectly logical. Nevertheless, we believe the developments since industrialisation to be more relevant for professional discourse today. Catrin Heite (2011: 28) interprets the emergence of social work as a concept of social reformers aimed at "integrating the working class into the emerging bourgeois society" (ibid., own translation). She comes to the conclusion that "social work [...] became a social institution when the bourgeois public began to see the *social issue* as worthy of discussion" (ibid., own translation). Her assumption is that the emergence of social policy as the "active shaping of social structures and class relations based on political ideas" also brought about a new understanding of the problems, so that supporting the poor was no longer considered "purely charitable relief for the poor as an act of good will" (ibid., own translation).

At the same time, this means that social work as an institution of governmental social policy was linked to normalisation processes brought about by the capitalist system and market economy. In the 19th century, "productive labour [...] becomes paid labour" (Bachinger/Matis, 2009: 78). Male labourers were paid wages just above subsistence levels, women and children usually worked as well, and it was not uncommon for the working day to last 16 hours or longer (cf. ibid.). These are the realities that Europeans tend to consider in a historical context. However, they are not only memories of a past long gone but remain the bitter reality of capitalist economy worldwide. The origins of social work as a profession are very diverse, but they are often linked to civil society. The Swiss social work scientist Silvia Staub Bernasconi (1995: 58, own translation) writes that professional social work "originated in social movements with their self-defined needs, objectives, demands, rights and responsibilities, i.e. the women's, peace, and the reformist social settlement movements, and not legal or governmental prescriptions or administrative decrees and mandates".

Catrin Heite (2011: 27) describes that it was a clearly political strategy of the bourgeois women's movement to take over welfare activities by attributing them to a "maternal spirit". This allowed women to do charity work outside their homes. "We see a hegemonic overlap between the structural categories of class and sex: Equals in their bourgeois class, but different in their sex, these women present measures of social policy against poverty, illness and human misery as solidarity of the bourgeois with the lower classes"(ibid: 27f., own translation). At the same time, this strategy led to the creation of a "little appreciated and therefore poorly remunerated profession" (ibid: 28, own translation). The first female social work theorists emerged in the late 19th century. These include: Jane Addams (1860-1935), who, inspired by the settlement movement, moved to a Chicago slum to study the living conditions of the residents; Alice Salomon (1872-1948), who was active in the German bourgeois women's movement, founded one of the first Social Schools for Women in Germany and also collected (economic) data through participant observation; and the Austrian Ilse Arlt (1876-1960), who founded the first school for welfare in Vienna and has since been considered synonymous with research-guided welfare (cf. Engelke 2002). All of these women were concerned with the practice and theory of social work, but it would take decades for social work to become a regular academic subject.

Therefore, it is important to examine stereotypes concerning women and men that have a strong impact on the definition of social work as a profession. Gender stereotypes are "culturally shared beliefs concerning psychosocial characteristics that are considered prototypical for men and women" (Monreal Gimeno 2010: 44f., own translation), while gender roles are "functions that are considered appropriate for each sex" (Vásquez 2005: 55). Both gender stereotypes and roles tend to postulate opposites, i.e., what is considered "appropriate" for women is not considered "appropriate" for men, and vice versa. This opposition is construed in four steps (ibid: 60f., quotes own translation):

- Being a man or being a woman is "naturally" associated with certain activities, potentials, limitations and attitudes.
- Certain activities and expressions are classified as masculine or feminine, again "naturally".
- The same activity is ascribed different value depending on the sex of the person performing it. Although all people do some type of work during their life, the social value of this work depends on whether it is performed by a woman or a man. "Women's entry onto the labour market is supported when their professions correspond to their 'natural calling' – education, administration and health care professions, where they are given tasks associated with the emotional, individual and subjective – while professions that have to do with knowledge, thinking and science, things associated with the rational, universal and objective" are reserved for men.
- Activities considered typically male and typically female are valued differently. There are "male" and "female" professions. "Men's professions" require characteristics considered typically male (strength, intelligence, rational thinking), while "women's professions" require character traits considered typically female (selflessness, friendliness, dedication, commitment and sensibility).

Social work is considered a strongly female profession in many countries. Tomasa Báñez Tello considers this to be due to two factors: "First, the socially legitimising function of the profession itself – social control over the most disadvantaged groups of society – needed women, who already contribute to social reproduction in their families by raising the children. Second, professional social work assumes a number of tasks in a formal and institutionalised manner that were traditionally performed by women in the family" (Bañez Tello 2013: 161, own translation). Generally speaking, a profession – as specialised work – has the following characteristics:

- *Theoretical knowledge:* In order to understand the relationship between social work and scientific knowledge, we have to consider the history of the profession, which was originally institutionalised in order to train suitable staff for the provision of social care and assistance. "It was not recognised as a legitimate profession because its theoretical foundations were recognised, but because it had a mandate from the state" (Genolet et al. 2005: 148, own translation). In order to incorporate social work training into the university setting, it was necessary to organise the accumulated experience from previous social welfare and care services from an empirical and pragmatic point of view and utilise theoretical and methodological foundations of other disciplines. Therefore, social work is given less scientific weight than other professions in the traditional areas of intervention, such as the studies of medicine and law.
- *Autonomy in exercising the profession:* Where the autonomous exercise of the profession is concerned, professionals generally form associations that set standards for their work and usually have a code of ethics and conduct. The challenge of strengthening the organisation of associations is particularly difficult for women, as active participation in the governing bodies of an association or trade union would burden even more work upon people already struggling with their paid employment and their workload at home. Participation in governing bodies is also considered typically male, and men are more likely to be chosen for such positions, even by women. This challenge shows how necessary individual and collective empowerment are.
- *Authority over the users or clients of the professional service:* Generally, this kind of authority is wielded through theoretical knowledge. This is in contrast to the traditional association of social work as the "natural calling of women" with innate – not acquired, and therefore less meritorious – characteristics, such as sensibility, dedication, and altruism. These characteristics are also related to the original vision of the profession as providing relief and care. Another challenge in the exercise of the profession is moving from a micro-social intervention (through administration at the operational level and provision of direct services for case work at the group and community level) to a meso-social level (administrative and social management at the institutional and community level) and to macro-level action (development, administration and monitoring of social policies).This requires the incorporation of appropriate subjects into the curricula of graduate social work courses as well as the promotion of Master's and postgraduate studies in order to provide professional social workers with the theoretical, methodological and practical knowledge required for effective intervention at these higher levels.

In conclusion, the challenges of the social work profession in El Salvador are doubly challenging for female social workers, and the situation is similar in Austria. This is because the profession encroaches upon areas traditionally considered male, including the academy, science and committee work, as well as focussing on individual and collective empowerment. Social workers in El Salvador and Austria alike must analyse their situations as women and professionals in order to deconstruct and redefine gender roles and stereotypes taught by a patriarchal and sexist society. They should ask themselves the following questions: Is there awareness of the feminisation of social work? Is it hidden or accepted as normal? How does this situation impact the working conditions of social workers? Is there room for reflection and debate in academic and associative contexts? What should our contribution be to consolidating the scientific and academic status of social work in El Salvador and Austria?

Bibliography

Bachinger, K./Matis, H. (2009): Entwicklungsdimensionen des Kapitalismus. Klassische sozioökonomische Konzeptionen und Analysen. Böhlau Verlag, Wien, Köln, Weimar.

Bañez Tello, T. (1997): Género y Trabajo Social. p. 161. Online source: http://dialnet.unirioja.es/servlet/articulo?código=170226(last access 10 February 2013)

Engelke, E. (2002): Theorien der Sozialen Arbeit. Eine Einführung. Freiburg im Breisgau.

Genolet, A. et al. (2005): La profesión del Trabajo Social cosa de mujeres? First edition. Espacio Editorial. Buenos Aires, Argentina.

Heite, C. (2011): Geschlechterpolitik als Sozialpolitik. In: Böllert, K./Heite, C. (Eds.): Sozialpolitik als Geschlechterpolitik. VS-Verlag. Wiesbaden.

Melano, M. C. (2001): Un Trabajo Social para los nuevos tiempos. La Construcción de la ciudadanía, Buenos Aires, Ed. Lumen

Monreal Gimeno, M. d. C./Amador Muñoz, L. V. (2010): Intervención social y género. Madrid, Ed. Narcea.

Polanyi, K. (1997[1944]): The Great Transformation. Politische und ökonomische Ursprünge von Gesellschaften und Wirtschaftssystemen. Frankfurt am Main.

Staub-Bernasconi, S. (1995): Das fachliche Selbstverständnis Sozialer Arbeit – Wege aus der Bescheidenheit. Soziale Arbeit als „Human Rights Profession". In: Wendt, W. R. (Ed.): Soziale Arbeit im Wandel ihres Selbstverständnisses. Beruf und Identität. Freiburg im Breisgau, 57-99.

Vásquez, N. (2005): El ABC del Género. Second edition. Equipo Maíz.

3.2.4 Enumeration of results

Final publication
- ULS (2014) (Hg.): Trabajo Social y su contribución para un desarrollo equitativo e inclusivo/Soziale Arbeit und ihr Beitrag zu einergerechten inklusiven Entwicklung. ULS Editors: El Salvador CentroAmérica.

Presentation of publication
- ULS presented the final publication twice – 28th and 29th of August 2014 to the academic public and social work actors. Approximately 90 people participated live, as well as many guests at Cabañas (branche) and at home via video conference and live stream.

International conference
- Seminario Internacional "Trabajo Social – Educación y Cambio Social", ULS – San Salvador, January 22. 24 2014. 70 participants attended directly and about 30 participants

attended via video conference (using equipment financed by APPEAR) at Cabañas – the branch of ULS. International experts tackled relevant topics and enabled an important and interesting discourse between academics, practical social workers and students. The conference can be seen as a big achievement – as this was the first conference of social work experts (academics and social worker) in El Salvador for decades. Participants included lecturers, social workers, students and experts from Austria, Canada, Cuba, El Salvador, Honduras, Nicaragua and the United States.

Research social work theory, methodology and methods: Presentation
- The activities linked to this research resulted in an article in the final publication, contact to other social work departments in San Salvador, student theses and a lecture at the conference (systematization done by Eneyda Arteaga) but also in a very interesting presentation from the students who carried out the research work (TECS&meeting, January 2014).

Workshop 1 – TECS:
- Workshop German/Spanish: Soziale Arbeit in El Salvador. Herausforderungen & Ansätze. 10th October 2013.

Workshop 2 – TECS:
- Workshop German/Spanish: Soziale Arbeit in El Salvador & Österreich. Methoden & Praxis Sozialer Arbeit im internationalen Austausch. 14th May 2014.

Manual 1 – Proyectos Locales:
- *Manual para la construcción de Proyectos de Vida. Con personas en situación de vulnerabilidad.* Didactic tool for the guidance of local projects (special design for internships of social work students– research, social work activities, impact, and development of profesional social work approaches). Published in August 2014 (print).

Six Proyectos Locales:
- Six "Proyectos locales" took place. This is a special internment scheme for social work students. Within their internship 47 students (extra-occupational students who usually face difficulties in finding ordinary work placements) were supervised by Eneyda Arteaga and other colleagues of ULS. They could combine research (social diagnosis), preparation of social work intervention, and reflection on a personal & professional level and on the basis of potential further developments within social work. The topics were: leadership – working with young men and women of grassroots organizations; leadership – working with women of grass-roots organizations; adult education for youth and young adults; working with adolescents to prevent conflict; promotion of the rights of elderly people; and social work with homeless people in the centre of San Salvador. The improved guidance of students during their applied research activities will have great impact on their future work.

Manual 2:
- *Trabajo Social – Profesión de Mujeres? Manual para la reflexión,discusión* y análisis del trabajo social como proceso de trabajo. Didactic tool for workshops with professional social workers, students and lecturers on the issue of social work as paid care-work, important social service and public good. Published in August 2014 (print).

Article:
- Klawatsch-Treitl, E. (2013): Dienstleistung und Care. In: Bakic, J./Diebäcker, M./Hammer, E. (Hg.): Aktuelle Leitbegriffe der Sozialen Arbeit. Ein kritisches Handbuch 2. 46-61

Workshops – Social work as paid care-work:
- Seven workshops took place, two pilot workshops (May 2014 –Vienna/FHCW and January 2014 – San Salvador/ULS). A total of approximately 130 women and men participated in these workshops.

Suggestion for the further development of the curricula (new courses starting 2015) at ULS and FHCW:
- List of recommendations and discussions with the authorities of ULS. New courses at ULS. New courses (optional subjects) introduced at FHCW – 2014/2015: Development policy and dimensions of international social work.

Participants of the workshop "Social work as female profession" using psychodrama methods

Closing ceremony of the FLMN in the centre of San Salvador on February 1st 2014, the eve of the presidential election

A visit to WIDE – Women in Development Europa

Eneyda and Maritza

Seminario Internacionál

Land of volcanoes

Care workshop, January 2014

3.2 Improvement of Social Work Education to Foster Social Development and Poverty Reduction

Local project with old people

Local project with children

Seminario Internaciónal

3.3 Bioremediation of Contaminated Sites: Research and Education

Project Coordinator: Irene Lichtscheidl
Coordinating Institution: University of Vienna, Faculty of Life Sciences, Cell Imaging & Ultrastructure Research (CIUS)
Partner Institutions: Universidad Nacional Autonóma de Nicaragua, UNAN - Laboratorios de Microbiología; Universidad Nacional Santiago Antunez de Mayolo, Facultad de Ciencias del Ambiente
Partner Countries: Nicaragua, Peru
Project Duration: 1 August 2011 – 31 July 2014
Project Website: www.biorem.univie.ac.at

3.3.1 The project - BIOREM

Past and present mining activities due to the high demand for metals from industry have created huge areas of mine wastes and tailings. These places are often highly toxic for most organisms, including plants. They are barren or only sparsely vegetated, so that fine toxic sand erodes and is transported by wind and water to the surrounding environment. This can be inhibited or reduced by the formation of a closed vegetation cover. In Europe, there have been intensive mining activities for centuries, and mining dumps still represent a considerable danger for local populations, especially in Eastern European countries such as Slovakia, Hungary and Romania. In Nicaragua and Peru, reckless exploitation of metal mining sites has left large contaminated areas that not only constitute a serious hazard to the health of their populations, but waste land and water which could otherwise be used for agriculture. Several studies have shown that more than 10% of plantation land world-wide is contaminated by Cadmium, Arsenic, Chromium and Lead; in Western Europe over 1,400,000 sites are affected.

Rehabilitation of contaminated soil should therefore be of paramount importance for people, their environment and their agriculture. Bioremediation using plants and microbes has proven to be the most adequate and efficient method of such rehabilitation, especially in developing countries. It requires expertise in the fields of biology (mainly botany), microbiology, geology, biochemistry and environmental engineering. In the BIOREM project, we therefore built an interdisciplinary team of members with expertise in these fields; partners from the University of UNAN-Managua (Nicaragua) are specialists in geology, hydrology and soil microbiology, partners from UNASAM-Huaraz (Peru) have long-standing experience in ecology, geochemistry and social interactions and are a leading centre for bioremediation, the University of Vienna (Austria) investigates plants of heavy metal soil and their growth promotion, and the environmental company BLP-Geo (Austria) of Gerhard Kreitner is dedicated to waste management and has established cooperation with UNASAM-Peru. They all involve their colleagues and students in their common research.

Our research aimed to develop knowledge and solutions that are directly useful to a diversity of stakeholders including international mining companies, small farmers, business entrepreneurs, local government authorities, resource-based user groups and community-based organizations. Different individuals and groups of individuals brought different perspectives, experiences, knowledge and interests to the management of resources and to our associated research and development initiatives. The communities affected by contaminated sites took an active role in directing our research. For example, people suffering from acid rock drainage in Pastoruri, Peru, asked for bioremediation of their contaminated water and the community of La Libertad, Nicaragua, asked for expertise about the risks posed to their drinking water resources by a projected mine drilling. Further, mining companies are themselves now participating in interactive research and learning processes. For instance B2Gold in Nicaragua and Baia Mare in Romania have been involved in our research about plant growth promotion in contaminated soil, and its rehabilitation. For artisanal miners, it was very important that BIOREM afforded the means to inform them about the risks of mercury that they use regularly for the amalgamation of gold and how they could reduce its ecotoxicology.

The project's scientific exchange and participative research work was focused on developing efficient strategies and methods for bioremediation of heavy metal contaminated sites in Nicaragua, Peru, Austria and Romania. In year one, partners selected experimental model sites and identified their level of toxicity, their geological situation and their vegetation and microbial potential. In year two, we visited the selected places in network-wide excursions and started multidisciplinary fieldwork with regard to geology, mining history, mineralogy, soil properties, hydrology, plant diversity, vegetation patterns and animal diversity. This was followed in year three by laboratory experiments under controlled conditions, growing plants on untreated or altered mine waste and identifying their reactions.

One of our research foci was the identification of candidate plant species for the revegetation, phytostabilisation or phytoextraction of mine waste: we focused on plants that occur spontaneously on the experimental sites and studied their ecological amplitude and their ability to absorb and translocate metals, such as *Phragmitesaustralis* (common reed), *Plantago* spp. (plantain) and *Rumexacetosella*, which all occur in heavy metal places world-wide. Bryophtes, or "mosses", unlike vascular plants, can colonize mine waste sites in great abundance and diversity, and lichens may tolerate metal contamination even better than bryophytes, especially if metal rich substrates combine with high irradiation and intense draught. Accordingly we investigated their behaviour towards heavy metals. Metal rich habitats are usually believed to be poor, too poor for a functioning ecosystem, in microorganisms but we found the blue-green alga *Phormidium* sp. in biofilms with a thickness of up to 20 cm, covering great parts of the bed of several copper contaminated creeks. The most remarkable feature of this biofilm is its constant accumulation of copper from the running water of the creeks, thereby reducing the water's copper content and remediating the water quality over a course of not more than 300 m. Soil fungi were tested for their potential to mobilize heavy metals in soil so that leaching could be more efficient for *ex situ* soil remediation.

Bioremediation is a slow process needing many years. In order to ascertain the continuation of the remediation measures that were started during BIOREM, we therefore had to create groups of experts who will proceed and expand soil rehabilitation beyond this programme. Accordingly, we involved students in all steps of our common work. Research and education often went hand-in-hand, since most valuable research was accomplished by students in the frame of bachelor, master and PhD theses as hands-on training. In addition, we designed lectures, practica and excursions for students and invited them on excursions and to seminars and conferences. Teaching materials were provided for mutual exchange on our BIOREM homepage. In UNAN-Managua, a post-graduate curriculum was provided, a Diplomado about „Environmental Contamination and Remediation". In UNASAM, two postgraduate programmes, for a Master and a Doctor in Science and Engineering about „Environmental Management", were improved by placing special emphasis on the bioremediation of polluted places.

Communication was another major goal of BIOREM. Knowledge-exchange was at its most intensive during our common fieldwork and excursions in Peru, Nicaragua, Austria, Romania, Hungary and Poland, and during network-wide meetings (kick-off, mid-term and final). Additional expertise came from the involvement of external partners. Our special thanks go to Katarzyna Turnau (University of Krakow, Poland), Maria Roman and her group (Polytechnical University of Bucharest, Romania), Alfredo Grijalva (Central University of Managua, Nicaragua), Monica Marian (University of Baia Mare, Romania) and Valer Micle (University of Cluj, Romania). Jose Mostacero from the University of Lima became a BIOREM partner.

Concerning the socio-economic aspects of our research, cooperation with communities, environmental protection agencies and NGOs as well as propagation of our results to artisanal miners and large mining companies is of pivotal importance. They attended our BIOREM seminars, where they defined their problems and we together developed measures for improving the situation.

The successful collaboration of our BIOREM network and the students graduating from our programmes make us confident that the established cooperation between universities and stake holders in Nicaragua, Peru, Austria and Romania will continue beyond the timeframe of our BIOREM project, so that the risks from heavy metal contaminated environments will be reduced and new information about the ecology of heavy metal areas and their organisms will be achieved.

3.3.2 BIOREM and its people – researchers and beneficiaries

by Gerhard Kreitner

As BIOREM undertook a large number of quite different activities over the last few years, many of them still continuing, it is difficult to make reference to all of the involved groups and persons, but it is worth trying to pay respect to all the highly motivated people who have given their efforts to the project, mostly unpaid, and with great enthusiasm for the project goals. The aim of naming those involved should not be just to list them, but to give appreciation to their capabilities and their voluntary contributions to the project.

The main problem BIOREM confronted was soil and water contaminated by mining activities in Nicaragua, Peru and Europe. In Nicaragua the most serious problem is uncontrolled use of mercury and cyanide acid by thousands of clandestine miners, causing health damage and environmental disasters. In Peru the main problem is the huge contaminated areas of mine waste left by big companies, mostly causing damage to water resources. In Austria the age of big mining activities is past, but large contaminated areas like Arnoldstein can serve like examples for bioremediation. In Romania, Slovakia, Hungary and Poland, meanwhile, we investigated sites quite similar to our Peruvian project areas.

The original project idea for BIOREM was a result of long term cooperation and relationships between Austrian and Peruvian universities and other institutions in the field of environmental sciences. The team of Prof. Julio Palomino at UNASAM, as well as the CIUS-researchers of Prof. Irene Lichtscheidl, already had a lot of field experience investigating plants and micro-organisms for bioremediation of soil and water, and wanted to extend their research and education activities internationally. Together with Gerhard Kreitner from GeoRisk-team Vienna (who was also a visiting professor at UNASAM) they built a consortium with two Nicaraguan institutes from UNAN-Managua, the CIGEO-team of Prof. Dionisio Rodriguez and the Laboratory of Microbiology with its director Prof. Martha Lacayo, which are presently the only institutes in Central America (except Mexico) with any experience in bioremediation.

These five teams developed the project idea and prepared the BIOREM project-proposal for submission to the APPEAR programme. From the beginning one of the overall goals was to build up a network and strengthen the international cooperation of researchers in the field of bioremediation, although this aspect was not expressed in the proposal, but seen as self-evident by all partners. Therefore it was typical for the project that already during the kick-off meeting in Vienna, a colleague from a Hungarian university took part who would one year later organize some very interesting excursions in his country.

The percentage of female staff members among UNAN-Biorem team members at laboratories of microbiology reached 75%, which is remarkably high. CIGEO's level of female participation, at only about 42%, is nevertheless high for this subject area when compared with Austrian participation levels. Within the CIUS-team of the University of Vienna, the female proportion amounts to nearly 69%. The UNASAM team within the project under the direction of dean of faculty Julio Palomino reached a female quota of 75%. The overall percentage of female team members of all partner organizations amounts to 58%.

After our kick-off meeting, all partners started their cooperative research and education, fieldwork and social work, networking and dissemination activities. During these manifold activities a large number of people and institutions became involved and were integrated into the project.

In Nicaragua the fieldwork began after a phase of preparation with information campaigns and awareness training for communities, illegal gold searchers and their families, teachers and local authorities, especially in the two project regions of Santo Domingo and La Libertad in the department of Chontales, to face the challenge of uncontrolled mercury, cyanide and heavy metal contamination of soil, rivers and groundwater as result of mining activities. The international mining company B2GOLD was also involved in this important process, which reached all stakeholders. This work was carried out by social experts and scientists managed by Dionisio Rodriguez and Martha Lacayo, including five UNAN students. Here too, female team members were in the majority. The UNAN team received excellent support and encouragement from the municipality of La Libertad local authorities. In the municipality of Santo Domingo, the support was even greater than at La Libertad because of concerns about drinking water contamination problems.

At the same time, the UNASAM team in Huaraz prepared the fieldwork and BIOREM conference in Peru. They established many contacts and relations to rural communities, local authorities, governmental institutions, and the big mining companies Barrick and Antamina. Catac is home not only to the experimental plant for bioremediation of UNASAM at the mining heap of Mesapata, but also the disappearing glacier of Pastoruri, which became an interesting focus of BIOREM activities on natural acid drainage remediation.

In Austria, CIUS started research work, among whose results was the discovery of a consortia of symbiosis between mosses, bacteria and micro-organisms able to remediate acid mine drainage in the mountains of Salzburg. The project website was designed by another team led by Gregor Eder, Lukas Nebel and Georg Beretits. The BIOREM database for heavy metal sites was established by Lukas Nebel together with the website team.

The project's first big collective activity was the meeting in Peru, with field research at five contaminated sites, laboratory work and the UNASAM conference. In addition to our partner institutes, we welcomed Prof. Dr. Katarzyna Turnau and her team from Jagellonian University Krakow, Poland, especially Prof. Dr. Przemyslaw Ryszka, who joined BIOREM as an associated partner and gave excellent lectures in plant investigation and laboratory work in Huaraz. The conference benefitted from the participation of many UNASAM colleagues and their rector. Also taking part and joining us on some excursions were a group of 28 students and professors of environmental science from the University of Tingo Maria, Peru, as well as colleagues from Trujillo University, La Molina University, Cayetano Heredia University and the Catholic University, all of them from Lima. In particular, Prof. Jose Mostacero, dean of the biology faculty at the University of Trujillo, enthusiastically joined our field work and excursions as an expert on plant identification and later became an associated partner of BIOREM. At Universidad Nacional de San Antonio Abad del Cusco, the BIOREM team was hosted by the dean of Faculty of Biology, Prof. Mgt. Luciano Julian Cruz Miranda and his team, who are cooperating with UNASAM in the field of bioremediation of plants and also became part of our Peruvian BIOREM network. At Peru's oldest and largest herbarium, we were hosted by Blgo. Pascual Paccori Álvarez. In Lima we visited Cayetano Heredia University. This collective research work in Peru initiated a bioremediation network of Peruvian scientists at different universities, with strong international relations.

Another group within the project collected and developed teaching material and scientific literature about bioremediation, to be made available via the BIOREM website. The CIUS team coordinated by Gregor Eder produced scientific video clips for plant and soil sampling, analysis and investigation, also for the project website.

Meanwhile, at the University of Vienna, Amadea Horvath investigated cytoplasmic metal tolerance of plants from the spoil heap in Knappenberg, Lower Austria, Sebastian Antreich conducted a comparison of the model moss Physcomitrella with the copper mosses Mielichhoferia and Pohlia, Isabella Meyer studied Phragmitesaustralis and its potential for phytoremediation, Lisa Vrbecki Plantagos as a candidate for revegetating heavy metal soil, and Rebecca Steinhard investigated the structure and functions of biofilms formed by Phormidium in copper contaminated soil. Stefan Sassmann (Vienna) researched heavy metals in mosses and Anna Burger Uran and the radionuclides Strontium and Caesium in plants. Thanks to BIOREM funding, a group of young researchers coordinated by Wolfram Adlassnig investigated a very interesting and unique habitat of a biofilm consortium at Schwarzwand in Salzburg, which is able to remediate extremely acidic drainage water from an old mining site.

At UNAN some theses were developed within the context of our project, while at UNASAM in Peru, 19 junior researchers and thesis students investigated bioremediation.

After a BIOREM meeting in Vienna in July 2012, the excursions and field research in Austria, Hungary and Romania brought some interesting new partners into the project to join the scientific work. In Austria, Othmar Horak from the Austrian Institute of Technology, Seibersdorf, Austria's most experienced expert in heavy metal soil bioremediation, guided our tour to some heavy metal and experimental sites. The Hungarian part of our fieldwork was organized by Erika Mühlmann, Szoltan Verrasztó and his team from Budapest University and led us to the heavy metal disaster site of Kolontar, some mining districts and contaminated sites at Gyöngyösoroszi, where we made contact with many Hungarian experts, local authorities, public organizations and private rehabilitation companies. The Romanian part of the excursion led us to Baia Mare, where we undertook some research work together with our Romanian colleagues, among them Maria Roman from Bucharest University, who also joined our BIOREM network. We had consultations and discussions with Compagni Spataru, a mining company aiming to recycle the large and dangerous mine tailings in Baia Mare, Romania.

The Midterm Meeting in Managua with a symposium at CIGEO-UNAN was a great opportunity to disseminate information about our research topics and results to the Nicaraguan government, politicians and authorities involved in environmental affairs, as well as other universities and research institutes. Nicaragua's Vice President Omar Halleslevens opened the symposium, explaining the national strategy for biotechnological investigation, which became the most important priority of the Nicaraguan research policy. During the symposium Daniel Corrales MSc from National University of Mexico and Prof. Alfredo Grijalva MSc from UCA (Central American University) Managua joined our cooperation as associated partners. Our Polish partners from Krakow University, Prof. Katarzyna Turnau and Prof. Dr. Przemyslaw Ryszka took part in the symposium and the field research in Nicaragua, as well as a group of University of Vienna students.

Prof. Grijalva and his team from UCA elaborated a taxonomic analysis and field study about the biodiversity of herbaceous plants in our two project areas of Santo Domingo and La Libertad, in cooperation with the National Herbarium, contracted by the BIOREM project. The social and environmental impact studies for our project regions were worked out by the UNAN-team of Jilma Romero and 5 students.

Our postgraduate curriculum for bioremediation and biotechnology was developed by the UNAN-team of Lester Rocha, Francisco Picado, Martha Lacayo, Katia Montenegro, Manuel Enrique Pedroza, Jorge Pitty and Marlene Muñoz. The first graduation year was passed by 28 students, with a female quota of 50%. Most of our graduates were sent by national environmental authorities and ministries. Here too the majority was represented by female researchers.

In Peru the analysis of soil and plants were conducted by the team of Prof. Mario Leyva, Percy Armando Cano Carbajal, Beatriz Coral, Yeidy Montano and others at the UNASAM laboratories of the Faculty of Environmental Sciences. Here the total and extractable metal and metalloid content of soils and herbaceous plants was analyzed in order to understand metalloid uptake by plants.

From May to August 2013, the UNASAM young researchers Katy Medina, Yeidy Montano and Patricia Barretos stayed at the University of Vienna to receive special training in bioremediation technology. We took this opportunity make contact with Austrian companies working in the field of biotechnology, and received great feedback and support for our project, organizing excursions, lectures and seminars and practical training sessions. Our UNASAM researchers took part in the Summer University at Southern Bohemian University, field research in Romania and training at the University of Vienna.

In October 2013, after the BIOREM meeting in Vienna, the whole team was invited by Katarzyna Turnau to the EUROBIOTECH congress in Krakow, Poland, which was an excellent opportunity to meet the world's most reputable biotechnologists and to extend our network. There we also organized a side event to present our project results. The papers by members of BIOREM were summarized and collected by Wolfram Adlassnig in a publication.

Prof. Katarzyna Turnau and Prof. Dr. Przemyslaw Ryszka also invited us for interesting field research and excursions to contaminated mining sites and remediation experimental sites in Poland.

The final meeting in Managua also included a BIOREM conference with more than 100 participants and many representatives of national authorities and ministries and mayors of our project areas. Also Vice President Hallerslevens held another interesting lecture about Nicaraguan efforts in environmental science.

In conclusion, it can be said that all participants were both researchers and beneficiaries at the same time, as the project followed, as a matter of principle, a participatory approach to research and education, which has been especially valuable in developing countries.

3.3.3 Gender monitoring

by Claudia M. Gonzalez and Angelika Kreitner

BIOREM is an academic partnership between the Universities of Vienna, Huaraz (Peru) and Managua (Nicaragua) within the APPEAR Programme, focused on developing applications of bioremediation for contaminated sites, establishing academic curricula and supporting local populations in the remediation of contaminated areas.

As an APPEAR project, from its inception BIOREM incorporated gender mainstreaming as a central issue on both the structural, as well as on the content level. For example, women were well represented at senior and junior levels. This perspective was also applied in the selection process for postgraduate students, as well as in the study area, where possible given that the majority of people involved in mining activities (e.g. artisanal miners) are men.

The BIOREM gender monitoring process provided updated information on the situation of gender equality at every stage of the project. It focused not only on core data regarding the people working in the project, but also on those who have participated in all information dissemination activities. The gender of the BIOREM team is evenly split, with 50% women and 50% men. Whereas there was observed a slight gender gap in management, with 40% women and 60% men involved in management activities, in the research area there were more women involved in the project (55%). Compared to the general levels of gender distribution in research at University of Vienna, the gender structure of BIOREM at the research level was more equal.

Introduction
Monitoring is the regular collection, analysis and distribution of information and data on the progress of implemented activities and programmes (Walters, 1995). The information produced can help to identify gender differences in opportunities and access to resources and decision making.

The strategy for implementing the aim of gender equality and empowerment of women is called "gender mainstreaming", which is generally defined as the planning, organization, improvement, development and evaluation of policy processes so that a gender equality perspective is incorporated in all development policies, strategies and interventions, at all levels and at all stages by the actors normally involved therein.

This report aims to ascertain the level of gender equality in BIOREM Project, assessing whether the APPEAR programme's Gender Strategy targets have been met. In order to monitor the project, input indicators (percentages) will be used to measure which resources have been allocated, and to what extent, to ensure that the project contributes towards gender equality.

Methodology
For the documentation, measurement and evaluation of all efforts and results towards gender perspectives within the BIOREM project, a gender monitoring process was instigated, which included the chronologic development during the project period of three years, separate evaluations of the different project partners and countries and investigations about gender perspectives in decision making structures within the project.

To date, all activities of BIOREM have been empirically registered, documented and analyzed with descriptive statistics in respect of gender perspectives. To do so, the following approach was taken:
- Establishment of the nature of gender relations in spheres relevant to the project (management, research, teaching and support)
- Establishment of project activities that would have a potential impact on gender relations
- Establishment of the information required and design of the appropriate indicators
- Collection and analysis of the data

Results

The analysis of the data was divided into two groups: "Project Team" and "Project Activities". The project team group consists of those working in the project who have a direct influence on the decisions and results (active participation). The project activities (passive participation) group, meanwhile, are those who have been influenced by the project while participating in different activities (symposiums, excursions, community meetings, etc.).

The management level was defined as the part of the project where important decisions were made. Teaching included the lecturers involved in BIOREM activities. The research sphere is comprised of the people directly involved in the project's scientific tasks. The support level was defined as technical and administrative support, as well as homepage and database elaboration and accounting.

People external to the project are included in the project activities group. This is important because information from the project is shared and exchanged with students, miners, politicians, the general public, as well as the scientific community taking part in lectures and symposiums. Students from Austria have participated in the project at university lectures that aimed to support exchange. Project activities included, for example, three symposiums, field research and excursions or community meetings.

Project team

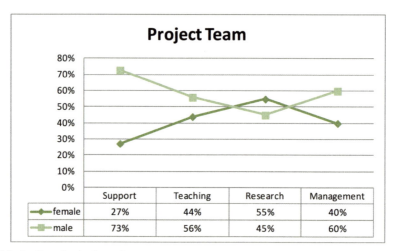

Graph 1: Project Team Gender Proportions

Graph 1 shows the variation in percentages of gender distribution in the different project areas (management, research, teaching and support). Management and Teaching were observed to have a slight bias towards men (20% and 12% respectively). Although almost three quarters of support staff were men, there were only few people involved in such tasks. In total, 88 people worked in different areas of the project. The gap between gender in research shows only 10% more women.

A comparison was made between the number and proportion of active participants in the BIOREM Project Team by country. Research, in general, had the largest proportion of staff (61%). Peru had the largest number of workers because of the junior researchers working on their Master Theses in connection with the BIOREM project. However, the proportion of women is almost equal in all countries, except in Nicaragua where 40% more women were involved. The amount of people working in teaching and management is very similar in all of the project countries. The management area is quite evenly distributed in terms of gender. But looking at the percentages of men and women working in teaching, the results show differences. Less than 20% of females are working in the teaching area of the project in Austria and Peru, while in Nicaragua they form more than 75%. The support area includes 11 active participants, where more men are involved.

Research team

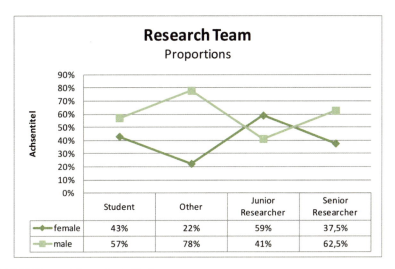

Graph2: BIOREM Research Stages: Leaky Pipeline

Graph 2 shows the distribution of gender at the different research stages of the BIOREM project. Senior researchers are the professors engaged in the project. Junior researchers are the assistant professors and PhD/Master students working on their theses in connection with BIOREM. Others are administrative and support functions related to research. Students participated in the project during excursions and university courses.

On the senior research level, 25% more male professors were involved. The difference on the junior researcher level amounts to 18%, with a majority of female researchers. At the support level (others), there are 56% more men engaged in the project, which in reality is not a big difference if we take into account the relatively small number of persons working at this level. At the student level there are 14% more male students.

To assess whether the gender structures of the universities engaged in BIOREM affect the gender structures of the project itself, a short look at the gender structures of University of

Vienna shall be taken. Unfortunately, not enough information about the universities' gender structures was available for Nicaragua's UNAN and Peru's UNASAM. At the University of Vienna, the gap between male and female professors amounts to almost 50%.[14] The gender structure of BIOREM at the research level tends to be more equal. When compared to the "Leaky Pipeline" at the University of Vienna Faculties engaged in BIOREM, the gap between male and female senior researchers becomes even larger. At the University of Vienna's Faculty of Life Sciences, the gap between male and female professors amounts to 66.6%, with a majority of male professors. At the Faculty of Earth Sciences, Geography and Astronomy, there are 82.6% more male professors. Junior researchers, others and students at BIOREM shall not be compared directly to University of Vienna's gender structures, because of differences in categorization.

Project activities

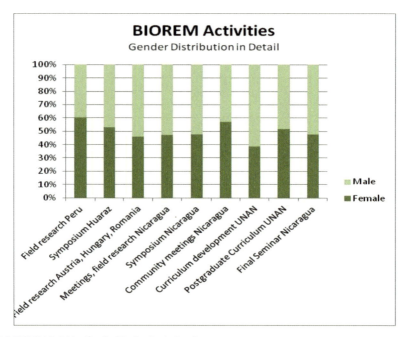

Graph 3: BIOREM Activities Gender Distribution in Detail

In Graph 3, the proportion of women in the different BIOREM activities is compared to that of men. It shows that on average, female participation accounts for 50% of the total, with the area of curriculum development being that where fewest women were involved (39%).

---

14 See „Gender im Fokus. Frauen und Männer an der Universität Wien" (2013) www.gleichstellung.univie.ac.at

An important aspect of BIOREM activities, and of the project itself, is the community meetings which, as shown in Graph 3, had a strong level of female participation (57%) even though mining activity is dominated by men.

Conclusion

Gender mainstreaming was a central issue of the BIOREM project from the very beginning. The topic was implemented into the project's personnel choices at both the management and the research level.

As a conclusion, the number of women and men seemed to be evenly distributed with 50% women and 50% men in the project team. Whereas there were slightly more men working at the management level, in the research area there were more women involved in the project. Compared to the gender distribution in research at all involved universities, the gender structure of BIOREM regarding the research levels tends to be more equally distributed between women and men.

3.3.4 Enumeration of results

Research about the chemical, biological and geological situation of polluted areas

Our research was partly done by individual groups and partly during our four common network-wide excursions and fieldwork expeditions. Publications have appeared in the form of articles in international scientific journals, as well as student theses. It should be noted that the European system of Bachelor Thesis (after 3 years) and Master Thesis (after 2 additional years) is not directly comparable to the American system; in Peru and Nicaragua, 5 years of study are required to finish with a Bachelor Thesis. Accordingly, the American Bachelor Thesis, in its volume and content, more closely resembles the European Master Thesis than the European Bachelor Thesis.

- At UNAN, 4 Bachelor Theses were finished
- At UNASAM, 10 Bachelor Theses, 5 Master Theses and 5 Doctoral Theses were accomplished and partly still ongoing
- At the University of Vienna, 2 Bachelor Theses and 6 Master Thesis were finished, and 4 Master Theses and 2 Doctoral Theses are ongoing
- 5 articles about our research results were published in international scientific journals, 2 of them co-authored by partners from both the University of Vienna and UNASAM

Dissemination

Our research results were presented to the scientific community at eight international conferences as a total of 18 lectures and poster presentations. Concerning BIOREM specific conferences, one was held in Huaraz, Peru, two were held in Managua, Nicaragua, and one was held as a satellite meeting to the Eurobiotec in Poland with considerable international participation. Altogether, 25 contributions were presented by the consortium.

For further dissemination of our results, a global database BIOREM (http://www.univie.ac.at/biorem/) was developed. It is a repository for the accumulation of data about heavy metal locations, their mineralogy and their vegetation. It serves as a tool for information about heavy metal tolerant plants and their application for the re-vegetation of heavy metal contaminated soil.

Education
Lectures, practical instruction, fieldwork and seminars were offered to students by all partner institutions. Teaching material in the form of videos and PowerPoint slides was produced and technical protocols were developed and made available via the BIOREM website. Protocols about best practice of practical work in bioremediation were also developed. A review of the environmental risks of cyanide was written. In addition, literature relevant to the topic was gathered and is made available on the website. For wider dissemination, the University of Vienna also contributed several topics to the International Summer School in NoveHrady, CZ, attended by undergraduates from 11 different countries.

In Nicaragua a post-graduate "Diplomaed in Remediation of Contaminated Sites" was developed. It started in May 2014 with students from government institutions and UNAN-Managua. There has been a satisfactory participation of young researchers and students in fieldwork and seminars at UNAN-Managua.

In Huaraz the UNASAM adapted two postgraduate programmes for a Master and a Doctorate in Science and Engineering with specific focus on Environmental Management. The Master's programme includes courses such as bioremediation of polluted places (microbial and phyto remediation), as well as water and soil remediation.

Cooperation
BIOREM partners have cooperated with a total of 10 other universities

- Peru: Universities of Trujillo, Cusco and Lima
- Austria: University of Agricultural and Life Sciences (BOKU)
- Romania: Universities of Bucharest, Baia Mare and Cluj
- Poland: University of Krakow
- Slovakia: Universities of Bratilava and Kosice

Concerning the socio-economic aspects of our research, cooperation with communities, environmental protection agencies and NGOs as well as dissemination of our results to artisanal miners and large mining companies is of pivotal importance. They attended our BIOREM seminars, they defined their problems and together, we developed measures to improve the situation.

- 3 Environmental Protection Agencies and NGOs
- Small and large mining companies
- The Municipaities of Santo Domingo in Nicaragua, Catac in Peru and Baia Mare in Romania

The successful collaboration of our BIOREM network and the students graduating from our programmes make us confident that the established cooperation between universities and stake holders in Nicaragua, Peru, Austria and Romania will continue beyond the timeframe of our BIOREM project, so that the risks from heavy metal contaminated environments will be reduced and new information about the ecology of heavy metal areas and their organisms will be achieved.

Mine heap on the slopes of the mountain Obir in Carinthia/Austria containing mainly zinc and lead: the toxic soil carries sparse vegetation which is specifically tolerant for the metals and was named "Galmei flora"

Gyöngyösoroszi/Hungary: Excursion and field work of the BIOREM team, together with the colleagues from Hungary, Prof. Dr. Zoltán Verrasztó and his team

Biorremediación de Sitios Contaminados, Managua, Nicaragua. Seminar at the Universidad Nacional Autónoma de Nicaragua in July 2014

An international seminar was held at the University of Nicaragua in Managua about Bioremediation of heavy metal-contaminated sites. It was attended by national stakeholders and national and international researchers

Project coordinator Irene Lichtscheidl gives a presentation

3.3 Bioremediation of Contaminated Sites

Melida Schliz gives a talk, which is translated into English

Cooperativa la Estrella in Santo Domingo/Chontales in Nicaragua: water flowing out of the gold mill

Cooperativa La Estrella: a student takes water samples from the river that takes up the wastes of the mining company

The BIOREM team at the mine tailing of the B2gold Company in La Libertad

Waste of an active mine in Boleslaw/Poland: excursion and field work together with our Polish partners from the team of Prof. Dr. Katarzyna Turnau

The zinc-tolerant metallophyte *Arabidopsis arenosa* on the zinc mine waste of Boleslaw in Poland

The polymetallic mine waste dump of Ticapampa in Peru, at the banks of Rio Santo, the main river of the region

The National Park of Pastoruri in the Andes of Peru: ten years ago, the glaciers reached down to the lake. They have melted, and one rich rock is exposed to melting waters

The National Park of Pastoruri in the Andes of Peru: Because of acid mine drainage, plants have difficulties to grow

3.4 An Interdisciplinary Approach for the Sustainable Development of Spontaneous Human Settlements in the Central Urban Area of Managua

Project Coordinator: Romer Altamarino
Coordinating Institution: Universidad Centroamericana, Faculty of Science, Technology and Environment
Partner Institutions: Fundación Casa de los Tres Mundos, Instituto de Estudios Interdisciplinarios; Vienna University of Technology, Institute of Urban Design and Landscape Architecture
Partner Country: Nicaragua
Project Duration: 1 October 2012 – 30 September 2014
Project Website: www.urban-managua.org

3.4.1 The project - Urban Managua

Urban_Managua was conceived as an academic cooperation project with an interdisciplinary approach, which sought to contribute creative tools to study and work in Spontaneous Human Settlements (SHS). Structures in such settlements usually result from processes that are based on land occupation and social exclusion. In many cases, the population lacks basic services such as drinking water, electricity and sanitation, as well as suffering deficiencies in road infrastructure, health services, education, culture, recreation and housing.

The three project partners, Universidad Centroamericana (UCA), Instituto de Estudios Interdisciplinarios (IEI) of Casa de los Tres Mundos of Granada, Nicaragua, and the Institute of Urban Design and Landscape Architecture at Vienna University of Technology, worked for two years to introduce creative urban design tools and innovative methodologies in urban studies, such as urban sociology and history, into the curricula of architecture and other related disciplines at Universidad Centroamericana,. A major objective was to integrate academic, practical and socio-cultural approaches and responses to the needs and demands for the improvement of living conditions in Spontaneous Human Settlements (SHS) in the central urban area of Managua.

The project, which began in October 2012 and ended in November 2014, was guided by three interrelated objectives:

- To strengthen educational and applied research skills in the academic curriculum of urban planners and researchers through an interdisciplinary partnership between the UCA, IEI, UT Vienna and other primary stakeholders in this field. Integrated Urban Development Studies (IUDS) will be introduced and institutionalised in UCA's urban studies discipline and will allow an integrated and interdisciplinary urban planning approach that is demand/needs-driven and community-based.
- To foster a permanent dialogue between academics and practitioners to strengthen the relation and cooperation between Nicaraguan and other Latin American urban planning academics ("know why") and practitioners ("know how") by creating spaces where national and international professionals act as guest lecturers in classes and give

expert critiques on practical works.
- To help to improve the local living conditions of the families of Barrio Candelaria, where cultural activities and accompanying academic research took place throughout the project. Key to this was the Participatory Development Approach (PDA) that was adopted at a local level throughout the project, to implement cultural activities to promote the local community's inclusion in the planning and research processes, thereby strengthening their sense of project ownership.

To achieve these objectives, the project comprised seven interrelated components:

1. *Preparatory Studies.* From its inception, the project was intended to compile management processes through the presentation and analysis of urban plans that have contributed to the expansion of the City of Managua to its current status. This was done in order to recognize the influence of such processes over time, as well as their relationship with Barrio Candelaria, located in the central area of Managua and defined as an urban space for the activities of the Urban_Managua project. This led to a review of prevailing spatial regulations, to be used as supporting material for the International Urban Design Laboratory.
2. *International Urban Design Laboratory.* Ever since the International Urban Design Laboratory (UDL) was held in April 2013, students and professors from the UCA and UT Vienna have been working together with IEI on an interdisciplinary urban design concept for the improvement of the SHS of Barrio Candelaria in Managua. The first phase was based on a reconnaissance of the site and definition of a thematic design for Barrio Candelaria. The second phase is the core methodology. After a diagnosis and field study, an outline of the urban design project was prepared. In the third phase, a more detailed project was developed over a period of 8-10 weeks. In the fourth and final phase of the project, the results of the project were shared with the two schools of architecture and the population of Barrio Candelaria within the framework of the International Urban Design Symposium.
3. *International Symposium on Integrated Urban Design Studies.* The objective of this symposium, held in September 2014, was to strengthen relations and cooperation between urban planning academics and practitioners on a national and regional level, where Latin American experts could share "best practice". It also served as a platform for disseminating the results of the International Urban Design Laboratory. The Symposium was an appropriate space for establishing a regional network between urban planning and design practitioners.
4. *Urbanist_Xchange.* Urbanist_Xchange brings Nicaraguan urban planners and architects together with Latin American colleagues by providing grants for study trips to successful projects to learn about innovative practices in the improvement of SMS. It is targeted at university professors in the disciplines of architecture and social science, NGOs and public institutions. Internships lasted up to 10 days in the months of June and July.

5. *Central American Forum of Integrated Urban Development Studies.* This event, held in September 2014, made it possible to disseminate and share experiences, specifically local innovations, between civil society representatives and practitioners. Following the presentation of the results of the Urbanist_Xchange programme, case studies and field visits, the Central American Forum was prepared as a scenario for the discussion of urban planning and urban studies in Managua, which evolved around the challenges faced by the city and potential solutions.
6. *Research component.* Accompanying research activities were carried out by IEI throughout the project, using innovative methods and social research techniques to facilitate a better contextualization that enabled us to get closer to the complexity of this social phenomena with gender-based and interdisciplinary approaches. A core objective was to build specific knowledge, information and local capacities, in collaboration with the community, in order to provide sustainable solutions that would help the public administration to deal with the constant challenges of SHS.
7. *Socio-cultural activities.* The project's cultural component proposed a series of courses and other cultural and artistic activities for Barrio Candelaria, defining the objectives, activities and expected results, and involving various artists, groups and institutions of Managua. Diverse cultural activities were promoted through music, dance, rap and musical instrument workshops (guitars and flutes), as well as sports activities to promote the social integration of children and youth of Barrio Candelaria.

To close the project, a Memory Book was prepared, which compiles all the activities developed, the methodology applied and the results achieved, as well as the presentations made by invited lecturers and project collaborators during these two years.

3.4.2 Seeking partnership between academics and practitioners

by Veronica Mora

A major challenge in urban studies is to link academia and professional activity. Lack of engagement, as first effect, prohibits meaningful cooperation. Professionals miss everything that has been created, investigated and innovated by students and teachers in the classroom, while the wealth of practice of the professionals who face daily the complexity of the reality of our cities is missing from the classroom. As a second consequence, this situation obstructs the realization of appropriate new urban interventions, with a lack of new methodologies that take the populations to be the main actors within such settlements.

Despite their status as main actors, the inhabitants of Spontaneous Human Settlements (SHS) in cities such as Managua remain totally divorced from both theory and practice. They struggle to construct place, territory and life-systems, with very little technical support from decision makers or researchers. Such a disconnect can lead to feelings of helplessness, hopelessness and conformity.

Urban_Managua recognised this lack of dialogue between these three main actors who study (researchers), make high-level decisions about (professionals) and transform (inhabitants) these urban areas. The project sought to strengthen links between these parties and so included among its aims the fostering of new modes of inter- and multidisciplinarity .

Therefore, the project chose to study the Barrio Candelaria, one of Managua's traditional neighbourhoods, located near the historical centre. The area is vulnerable to natural disasters and has suffered a high degree of social degradation. Hence the area represented a favourable setting for this project "pilot", where work was convened around the actors, from whom consensus was sought regarding their needs and in choosing from potential solutions that might bring improvements to these types of settlements and their inhabitants.

Meeting the Barrio Candelaria

The Barrio Candelaria is located in the central area of Managua. Its northern side is enclosed by the shores of the polluted Lake Managua, while its south is delimited by the large road that connects the city to the north of the country. On the east is the Mercado Oriental, the Central America's largest informal market, as well as settlements similar to Candelaria. In close proximity are commercial, educational, historical, governmental and cultural buildings. This makes it a very busy and dynamic area, but despite this very few people know about or visit the Barrio Candelaria.

Candelaria was destroyed by an earthquake in December 1972, which is evident even now, as the ruins of buildings and houses belonging to the old centre of Managua persist – some even with families still living in them. There are also many poorly constructed informal homes. Residents of Candelaria are endangered not only by the poor conditions of the buildings they inhabit and the presence of active seismic faults in this area, but also due to the proximity of Lake Managua which has a propensity to flood and whose rainy season currents can produce high runoff in the streets. Finally, there is a lack of sanitation, many streets are untarmacked, there are large concentrations of garbage and the only recreational space, Park La Candelaria, suffers similar neglect.

Candelaria's population is mainly young and lacks opportunities because of low levels of education, with the majority not completing basic education. There is a high rate of unemployment and informal employment, due to the proximity to the Mercado Oriental, which is a major source of income for families. This includes dealing in drugs and alcohol, which in themselves represent latent threats to young people and the population in general.

From its inception, the project stressed the importance of contact with representatives of the community. Therefore, a first priority in 2012 was to establish such relationships. This first activity enabled a physical approach to the built environment and a link to the district authorities. In the preliminary stages it was demonstrated that this approach could illustrate existing environmental problems to Urban_Managua researchers. The preparatory meetings were also essential to the construction and shaping of the methodology used to study the informal settlements.

Creating spaces for the consultation
The roles for each project partner were defined according to the needs of the interdisciplinary approach, with the strengths of each institution helping fulfill project objectives.

- The *Technical University of Vienna (UTV)* was established as the academic support professionals due to their experience in intervention in urban projects. They were also responsible for initial contact with specialists in the improvement of SHSs in other South American countries, who shared their successful practices in intervention projects with methodologies that accounted for all actors.
- *The Institute for Interdisciplinary Studies (IEI)* at Casa de los Tres Mundos in Granada contributed social and participatory methodologies for the identification of the population's needs. The Casa de los Tres Mundos also led the cultural contribution, promoting the capacities of children and young adolescents from La Candelaria by offering educational courses specially developed for the Urban_Managua project. Similarly, the project established links between national artists and La Candelaria, organizing a programme of events centred around integration and diversity.
- *The Central American University (UCA)*, as project coordinator, also served as the project headquarters by facilitating events, links, equipment, personnel, spaces of disclosure and prestige and experience at the university level. In turn, it played host to a great part of the activities and their results.

First dialogue space: The Barrio Candelaria
The first link in the participatory methodology, the planning of cultural activities, involved a series of community meetings with community leaders and the general population. These meetings served as a decentralized platform for decision-making, with community residents and leaders coming together with institutional actors such as the Ministry of Education, National Police, pastors and religious leaders to agree upon activities within Candelaria.

The research process was also strengthened in these meetings through the disclosure of vital information about the community's needs, structure and stakeholders, as well as by developing the empathy, understanding and mutual-confidence needed for such a research approach. This reduced suspicion and dispelled perceptions of the researchers as being foreign actors. Participatory processes were well integrated, with the employment of bottom-up methods for decision-making and residents skills being strengthened via occasional training.

The methodology developed from this first contact allowed students and teachers of the UCA, as well as students and teachers from the Vienna University of Technology, to appreciate the importance of focusing significant efforts on deepening our knowledge of the Barrio, most importantly from the point of view of its residents. Hence, activities such as field visits were conducted that were based on observation, listening and written and photographic documentation. This led to rich dialogue between academics and residents.

Integration was enabled by communal activities, such as undertaking tours side-by-side with residents, conducting interviews, being invited into the company of families during lunch time, as well as playing sports and making music at the Park La Candelaria. This was especially successful among students and the youth and children of Candelaria, but the whole community's support for the project was evident from the first activities.

The strategy for the project's cultural component was to develop tools adapted to the local situation, which would help develop the capacities of Barrio Candelaria's children and young people. Courses were designed by the IEI in collaboration with the invited artists, but always respecting the interests and needs of the people and keeping in mind the spaces available. The courses we offered focussed on the diversity of cultural and artistic expression, which led to the establishment of theatre and music (guitar, flute) courses. To more fully involve Candelaria's youth, rap was included as part of the music courses.

An important point to note is that the cultural component made it possible for the young people of Candelaria to visit various cultural centres for the first time. Without the intervention of the project this would not have happened. Among these sites were the Ruben Dario National Theatre, the National Palace of Culture, the Spanish Cultural Centre in Nicaragua, Universidad Centroamericana, the National University of Engineering UNI and the American Cultural Centre.

This academic approach enabled significant learning. For the students, the reality of spontaneous human settlements, forgotten within the urban fabric of Managua, was made manifest. Students were also made to realize the challenges that they will face as future professionals to try to bridge the gap between technological and methodological realities and the hopes of the people.

From the point of view of teaching, lessons were learnt regarding the importance of implementing long-term processes, meaningful involvement in the identification of problems from community-members themselves, the need to implement new research approaches and the need to work collaboratively to develop responses.

Second dialogue space: The university

The pupils and teachers at the UCA School of Architecture managed the spaces for the project exchanges. Students of the Vienna University of Technology were among the first to undertake such exchanges, which were highly participatory and creative. Interdisciplinarity was in evidence as work groups were formed by students from different specialties from the two universities. Likewise, the opportunity to interact with graduate students from Vienna University of Technology was of great importance for the undergraduate students of Architecture and Sociology at the UCA, as they were not only able to learn from the greater experience of their colleagues, but were also able to communicate their own skills and abilities.

The workshops ensured a collaborative learning context. An abundance of participants and opinions resulted in rich debate that tested students' skills in teamwork, interdisciplinarity and consensus-building, leading from an initial diagnosis of the problems of Candelaria to the preparation of proposals. The final workshop presented the project ideas to a significant number of residents and community leaders, as well as various professionals, NGOs and the mayor of Managua. Such events were of great importance in enabling frank discussion about interventions in Candelaria by bringing together the various actors concerned.

Such active collaboration occurred at a further two events: the International Symposium on Urban Studies in September in 2013 and the Central American Forum in Urban Studies from September in 2014. Both events brought together national and international speakers (from Central America and South America), students and teachers from various universities, as well as representatives of civil society organizations, state institutions and the general public. Over three days, experiences were shared through multiple events and activities: lectures, discussions panels, hands-on labs, group workshops, field visits, a cultural programme, book presentations, documentaries and the exhibition of the work developed by the students from both universities for the Candelaria district.

The challenge: The network of academics and professionals
These events were of crucial importance because they brought together various actors who would go on to form the basis of a national and international network of Architects and Urbanists. This network was further strengthened by the Urbanist_Xchange programme, whose seven internships helped forge new links through to South American countries like Argentina, Chile and Colombia.

The project's interdisciplinary approach made it possible to incorporate the different visions of all the project partners and participants to achieve a highly inclusive project and generate practical contributions for the population of Barrio Candelaria. The newly created network of architects and urban planners should help to bridge gaps between actors in the territory, promoting synergies that are relevant to both professional practice and the academy.

To ensure the continuation of these initiatives, the Central American Forum of Integrated Urban Development Studies will become an annual event to be organized by the Central American University with the support of the network of professionals. This work, although complex, is obviously urgent and necessary. The challenge starts now.

3.4.3 Transforming city: The challenge of developing the centre of Managua

by Roland Krebs

Managua – a city without a true urban centre or *urbanity* – is transforming rapidly. The government and municipality carry out numerous new urban projects, mostly in public spaces. The city is changing, mostly in its historic centre, but this leaves uncertain the future of approximately 64,000 inhabitants from about 11,000 households, most of them with unresolved property title issues, living in very low urban density and under poor conditions. This multi-sector phenomenon not only requires new and innovative planning tools, but also skilled urban planning professionals who are capable of understanding the complexity of sustainable urban transformation.

In this light, the Urban_Managua project started a process of discussion of and reflection upon the past (Managua's planning history, starting from 1954), the present (the actual status of informal settlements) and the future (how to deal with such informality) of the urban

The centre of Managua, newly renovated but without people

core of Managua. Our hypothesis was that the city should include the informal settlements and their inhabitants in a broader, integral development strategy that included cultural, social, economic and ecological dimensions. Efforts to create *urbanity*, *proximity*, cost-efficient *urban development* and at least a sense of *being a city*, are supported by existing urban projects in public spaces, but other interventions are also needed, such as social housing, rehabilitation of traditional quarters like La Candelaria, inclusionary public space, local economic development, cultural activities that foster social cohesion and good governance and management.

During the two years of the project, we developed, tested and investigated various urban models and typologies for inclusionary human development of the central informal areas, such as incremental housing models, cultural activities as catalyst for urban development and participatory planning techniques, among others. We invited numerous urban experts from Colombia, Argentina, Brazil and Guatemala to share experiences and solutions to problems from their cities and also sent seven Nicaraguan researchers to Chile, Argentina and Colombia to investigate specific research topics in the context of the situation in Managua.

The discourse started at just the right time, because the historic centre is becoming an observatory or living laboratory of urban transformation. The experience, *know-how* and *know-why* gained during Urban_Managua has helped to develop new strategies for urban development. This was without a doubt an excellent opportunity for the city, the academic sector and urban professionals alike.

El Barrio La Candelaria, our main research focus

El Barrio La Candelaria is located in Managua's historic centre

Accelerated urban growth

The Municipality of Managua is the leading city, regionally and nationally, in Nicaragua, and is part of the so-called *Metropolitan Area of Managua*, consisting of nine municipalities with a population of approximately one million inhabitants, equivalent to 29% of the national population. However, the structure of the metropolitan area is characterized by its remarkably accelerated pace of spatial urban growth, with dramatically negative economic and social consequences. Among these negative effects are the institutional and administrative challenges of managing urban mobility and the use of territory. The city is growing at its fringes rather than within its existing urban fabric. It has a population density of 38.51 people per hectare, which is a relatively low figure compared to other Central and South American capital cities. The regional average is 70 inhabitants per hectare, but in the city centre, the *Centro Histórico*, this figure is even lower, with only about 30 inhabitants or fewer per hectare. It is estimated that 40% of all settlements in the city centre of Managua are informal.

Managua's leading urban planner Leonardo Icaza analyzes the La Candelaria sector and it's problems

Managua as a highly vulnerable city

In December 1972 the city centre was devastated by an earthquake with a magnitude of 6.2 on the Richter scale, which left approximately 20,000 people dead and most of the centre destroyed. As a result of the earthquake, whose epicentre in Lake Managua was only about 28 km from the capital city, the area of Laguna Tiscapa deepened. Most of the residential and office buildings in downtown Managua collapsed and were cleared by the then Somoza government. The central area was nationalized (in other words *expropriated*) which meant construction in the downtown area was discontinued. The reconstruction of Old Managua was made impossible. These measures resulted in the decentralization and fragmentation of the city's spatial development, encouraging the sprawl of informal residential structures.

A further phenomenon is the growth of the Mercado Oriental, which was just one single city block in size before the earthquake. Today the market is uncontrolled, a site of urban anarchy stretching about 200 hectares. Urban growth, mostly residential, has taken place around the destroyed area, on the outskirts of the city. As a result of the centre's extinction, its central urban functions were dispersed and disrupted. Due to a lack of control over construction projects, the condition of the built environment is very poor. Should an earthquake, storm surge, flood or such occur, severe damage will ensue.

The urban fabric of the Old Managua and the new centralities

Many people, especially researchers and visitors, might ask: *Is Managua an urban place?* It at least *used to be*. Until the earthquake in 1972, the central square, the Plaza de Revolución and the adjoining Central Park were the most meaningful and important places in a then densely residential urban fabric. The design outline of the old Managua is a rigid orthogonal, a classic Spanish system, with the main square as the most iconic and important place in the city. Today we would not call it *urban*. Due to its low population density, the area looks empty except for the occasional tourist inspecting the national monuments. Nowadays, roundabouts and shopping malls shape new centralities in the city. These are Managua's real everyday meeting places. Roundabouts are, however, rapid transit spaces and therefore provoke social exclusion. Malls are places of commerce, where people must buy and consume. But although these places are not truly public spaces, people use them as meeting places nonetheless.

Shopping as a new centrality in Managua. The Plaza Inter, the only shopping centre close to the historic city centre

88　　3 The Central American Context

Roundabouts as urban centralities in Managua

Shaping public space with political messages

Unexploited opportunities and investments
After more than forty years of decay and deterioration, the municipality of Managua and the Sandinista Government have, in the last ten years, taken serious steps to renew the historical city centre. Several initiatives in the centre, mostly in public spaces, are being developed: a) the articulation of 'Avenida Bolívar' as an urban boulevard, b) the rehabilitation of urban parks such as 'Luis Fernando Velázquez', c) the construction of the waterfront and boardwalk and d) the renewal of two parks, the *Puerto Allende* and the *Paseo Xolotlán*, with a very nice city model of the Old Managua. However, these investments have occurred in a highly arbitrary manner, following neither an overarching master plan nor an investment plan, and seeming to pop up at random as foreign investment or donations become available.

The challenges of making city
In Managua and other Latin American cities, the most important challenges for urban development are rapid population growth and its management in the context of urban planning. In the context of Managua, the main question is how to manage the city's spatial growth along with the formation of informal settlements. The city has planning instruments in place such as the Land Use Plan, but these legal instruments are not adequate to combat severe poverty and urban informality.

It is very clear that the existing urban planning tool-kit, which was invented around the beginning of the last century, no longer serves to regulate and guide accelerated urban growth. The city is too *dynamic* and *complex* to be dominated by a mono-dimensional regulation plan, for example a *zoning plan*. What is now required is a programme of integral short-, mid- and long-term activities that allow a dialogue between *the people* who are affected and the ones who plan, meaning *the administration*. The main issue is that projects need to be based on a clear vision for transforming the city. This vision must be multi-dimensional in order to tackle other pending problems of urban development, including

The development of experimental housing typologies. Source: Urban_Managua, 2014

Proposals for dense residential developments in the city centre of Managua. Source: Urban_Managua, 2014

poverty, inequality, mobility and the growth of the urban footprint with all its environmental and social consequences.

The role of the Urban_Managua Project in discourse
With the aim of reflecting upon and contextualizing these urban development challenges, we organized two urban forums: the International Symposium in 2013 and the Urban Forum in 2014. The main goal was to establish a network of actors concerned with urbanism, planning and architecture in Latin American countries, to exchange experiences and good practices regarding the treatment of informal settlements in other countries and compare it to the situation in Nicaragua. In turn, this would help establish creative local strategies to combat urban poverty, informality and the risk of disaster. The specific objectives of the symposia were to:

- Strengthen relationships and cooperation between academics and professionals in the field of planning and urban studies.
- Create a network of actors concerned with urban design, planning and architecture in the countries of Central and South America, to promote future knowledge exchange and creativity to combat urban poverty, informality and natural disasters.
- Determine the characteristics and conditions of informal settlements in Central and South America to compare with those in Nicaragua, especially Managua.
- Update knowledge on experiences and best practices in the upgrading of informal settlements in the countries of Central and South America, which would form the basis for generating proposals for the treatment of informal settlements in Managua.
- Establish a platform for the dissemination of research results from Urban_Managua or other such initiatives, giving exposure to student's urban proposals.

The international participants of the workshop at the International Symposium 2013: Academics, planning professionals, and members of the urban planning office in Managua

- Create a forum for local researchers and improve the quality of research practice.
- Create an annual forum for architects and urbanists dealing with urban studies.

The Charta of Managua: A manifesto for the integrated development of informal settlements
At the Central American Forum on Integrated Urban Studies organized by Urban_Managua from 24th to 26th September 2014, we held an intensive urban workshop with approximately 60 students, urban development professionals and architects from the city administration. This activity was accompanied by an excursion to downtown Managua and the site of a comprehensive urban development project undertaken in the former informal settlement of *La Chureca*. This excursion helped participants contextualize potential projects for redevelopment in the central area of the city. We discussed this successful project, its comprehensive and multi-disciplinary urban strategy and analyzed the lessons learnt. We concluded that urban strategies need to include all urban actors in the design process and that an interdisciplinary development focus is required when intervening.

In this context we created the *Charter of Managua*, a manifesto of principles and commitments for the integral development of the slums in the historic centre of Managua. The focus of the charter is the preservation of the historic centre as a whole by including the informal settlements and their inhabitants, particularly in the traditional neighbourhoods of La Candelaria, Santo Domingo, San Antonio and San Sebastian. The charter promotes a comprehensive and integrated approach to the development of urban projects, with a thoughtful and autonomous organizational structure and private sector participation. At the same time, the social inclusion of the population in the development and implementation of projects is an indisputable precondition for redevelopment programmes in historical city

The participants of the 2014 Urban Workshop

centres, for example through the elaboration of the new Master Plan for the Central Area (PMAC).

In the medium and long term, the administration has to start to plan and manage the city in a pro-active manner in order to avoid further urban sprawl. The creation of a holistic vision of an *urban* Managua and the activation of centralities like the one at the historical centre is only possible with well-educated planning professionals and an energetic academic sector that are capable of reflecting upon and contextualizing the built and social environment. The project Urban_Managua came at the right time and initiated an important and overdue discussion about sustainable urban development. We should continue this dialogue and so energize the spirit of an *urban Managua*.

3.4.4 Enumeration of results

Results based on academic capacity-building

- The International Urban Design Laboratory was prepared, implemented and monitored, and feedback on the results of the laboratory was provided through the exhibition and physical delivery of the projects to the inhabitants of Barrio Candelaria.

- Accompanying interdisciplinary research was conducted throughout the project in open public spaces in Spontaneous Human Settlements (SHS). Two research studies were developed in the community: 1) *Spontaneous Human Settlements. Candelaria Case*. Application of bi-variate analysis and factor analysis of demographic variables and indices of happiness of the inhabitants. (2) *La Candelaria. Annotations of a Social Space*, a qualitative study, focussed on the study of spaces and the construction of meanings from the standpoint of users.
- Architectural urban and popular habitat methodologies were strengthened, as were the capacities of the faculty and students via participation in these courses during the two years of the project.
- A model for staging international events that promote the inclusion of a larger number of lecturers, diverse topics and discussions, and participatory methodologies, as well as broad dissemination of the results was produced.
- The project's blog and Facebook page contains information about Urban_Managua activities and SHS planning and research at national and regional levels.

Results based on the development of a dialogue between professionals and academics

- The International Symposium on SHS Urban Studies was prepared, organized and monitored. It was kicked off with a debate on urban planning and development in Nicaragua followed by a presentation of best-practice projects in Latin America.
- Contacts were coordinated to establish an interdisciplinary network between Nicaraguan academics, architects, planning practitioners and stakeholders with urban developers and planners of Latin America, who will give continuity to their own initiatives after the project comes to an end.
- The Urbanist_Xchange scholarship programme was established, coordinated and disseminated for urban planners and practitioners who visited best-practice projects in South America.
- The systematic integration of innovative methodologies began with the presence of local and/or international professionals in the new curriculum of the discipline of architecture based on the curricular review proposed by the UCA authorities.
- The Central American Forum on Urban Studies was prepared, implemented and monitored at the end of the project.

Results based on the development of urban research and participatory development

- Awareness of Nicaragua's need for improved urban planning and urban studies instruments and practices was encouraged.

- Community workshops, cultural activities, and artistic endeavours supported by the project were prepared, implemented and monitored.
- Local capacities were strengthened through discussions and ownership of the project based on the results of the International Urban Design Laboratory.

4 THE CONTEXT OF THE PALESTINIAN TERRITORIES

4.1 Capacity Building for Rural Development in Occupied Palestinian Territory

Project Coordinator: Samar Al Nazer
Coordinating Institution: Birzeit University (BZU), Department of Architectural Engineering
Partner Institution: Graz University of Technology (TU Graz), Institute of Urbanism
Associate Partners: University of Natural Resources and Life Sciences, Vienna (BOKU), Institute of Landscape Planning, Vienna University of Technology (TU Wien), Department of Spatial Planning
Partner Country: Palestinian Territories
Project Duration: 1 September 2012 – 31 August 2014

4.1.1 The project – RURAL DEV

Rural communities are increasingly threatened by economic change and the rise of neoliberal remedies. Economic change and the emerging suburbs reduce available agricultural lands and lead to an attendant loss of rural identity and sense of place. Palestinian rural communities are no different, witnessing an increasing disparity in socio-economic development between rural and urban areas. This leads to migration from villages to cities, rising economic and political dependency on cities by marginalized areas and their inhabitants, the superimposition of neoliberal realities and the decline of rural settlements. The political obstacles of Palestine and the ongoing neoliberal system of the state are major reasons of the deterioration in rural areas. In this context, future planning and developmental measures – such as protection of the indigenous landscape, enhancement of local communities' quality of life and management of the environment, agriculture and natural resources – are of particular importance. Hence, there is an urgent need to train local spatial planners and researchers to lead the planning, construction and implementation of such measures.

Our project "Capacity Building for Rural Development in Occupied Palestinian Territory" developed an academic training programme in rural planning and community development between the Architectural Engineering Department at Birzeit University (BZU) and the Institute of Urbanism at Graz University of Technology (TU Graz). It also established a spatial planning research cluster that includes academics from BZU, TU Graz, Vienna University of Technology (TU Wien) and the University of Natural Resources and Life Sciences, Vienna (BOKU), who worked together to organize an international conference entitled "Rural Areas: Exploring Challenges and Opportunities for their Conservation and Development".

The project aimed to enhance rural communities' quality of life, acknowledge and respect a diversity of needs and perspectives through the provision of educational opportunities and interdisciplinary research, as well as foster knowledge transfer between Birzeit University and the local community organizations in Occupied Palestinian Territory and encouraging intercultural exchange between Palestine and Austria. Academic training was also supported by contributions from other Austrian academic institutions, in particular BOKU and TU Wien, through their expertise on natural resources, environmental and spatial planning issues.

The project encompasses higher education, research activities and knowledge transfer under its major theme of spatial planning and rural community development. Collaboration has been instrumental in the transfer of knowledge between higher education partners in the area of spatial planning and its application within the new context of Occupied Palestinian Territory. Higher education measures involved developing a Spatial Planning Programme curriculum, establishing the spatial planning lab at Birzeit University and organizing international workshops on spatial planning and rural community development at Birzeit University and TU Graz. Joint research between participating universities has also occurred via co-supervision of bachelor's theses and other projects.

Knowledge transfer has been achieved through workshops and conferences. Two international students' workshops were organized which focused on rural development case studies. An international conference on development and planning in rural areas was held at Birzeit University in April 2014. In these venues, international researchers met and exchanged ideas with their local academic counterparts as well as those from local organizations in Palestine. Students also benefitted from participating in such forums.

The project's main aim was the enhancement of spatial planning studies in general, especially rural planning and community development, in the Architectural Engineering Department at Birzeit University through development of partnerships with enterprises and on the basis of local and international practices and experience. The specific objectives were to:

- Evaluate the current status and practices of spatial planning studies in the Architectural Engineering Department programme, in order to assess their effectiveness for addressing current and future planning problems and challenges in general and rural planning and community development challenges more specifically.
- Develop a curriculum to foster change in spatial planning studies in the Architectural Engineering Department on the basis of international experience and identified deficiencies within the sector, especially deficiencies in rural planning and community development.
- Exchange knowledge and know-how resulting from the experience gained at the Institute of Urbanism at Graz University of Technology in spatial planning studies in general and in rural planning and community development studies more specifically. Development of partnerships with spatial planning and development enterprises.
- Enhance skills capacity, raise awareness, develop partnership with enterprises and improve communication among different societal groups, women in particular, and other stakeholders involved (directly or indirectly) in spatial planning issues and enterpris-

es such as the municipalities, the village councils, the Ministry of Local Governance (MoLG), Municipal Development and Lending Fund (MDLF) the Ministry of Planning and Development (MoPAD), research centres, NGOs, etc.

4.1.2 The project's importance

by Grigor Doytchinov

Towards the strengthening of an established network
A cooperation project presupposes established contacts, the mutual confidence of the partners involved and last but not least a professional interest on both sides. In this sense, a look back to the background and prehistory of the partnership is required in order to explain the project's motivations.

The Institute of Urbanism of the Graz University of Technology engages in a wide range of international activities and has given consultation and assistance in Palestine since the 1990s, supported by relevant Austrian institutions. The project "Concept for Preservation and Adaptation of the Historic Centre of Nablus", initiated by the Municipality of Nablus and supported by the Austrian Development Agency, marked the beginning of our work on topics related to Palestine. The project was conducted in cooperation with local experts. As well as partners from the town, the work was supported by information from teachers and researchers from local universities and institutions. This information exchange extended the pool of knowledge about the Palestinian occupied territories in general and of the professional problems under consideration more specifically. It generated new scientific questions and opened new fields of research.

Academic interaction between partners did not finish with the successful completion of the Nablus project. Since that time, five colleagues from Palestine have successfully presented their dissertations at Graz University of Technology and begun teaching at Palestinian universities including Birzeit. If the number of PhD students is impressive, their activity and engagement in Palestine has been more so, something that can be taken as evidence of the success and sustainability of the partnership. In this sense, that original initiative can be seen as the seed for a functioning and fruitful network. The partnership has, from the very beginning, been one of mutual respect and interaction rather than a unidirectional, sender/receiver relationship. The preceding activities hence served as the foundations upon which we built the project cooperation currently under discussion.

Towards the professional definition and resolution of problems
Development of rural areas in Palestine is an acute economic and social problem. Landscape preservation is not, however, a specifically "Palestinian" issue. This globally relevant subject is also of topical interest in central Europe. It is of special interest for the state of Styria and therefore for the Graz University of Technology.

Whatever the aims and objectives of the visits of the Austrian experts to Palestine, they have always been fascinated by the rural landscape of Palestine, acknowledging the extremely high artistic and historical value of the rural areas in the occupied territories. The topography is determined by gentle hill formations with steep slopes. The towns and villages on the crests of the hills and on the mountain ridges form the high points of the natural elevations and create a distinctive silhouette, pinpointed by minarets or, on occasion, church towers. Only on closer inspection does a visitor notice that the hills are completely terraced and planted with small olive trees. The stone terraces characterize the specifically horizontal stratification of the topography, a centuries old tradition of landscape cultivation preserved to the present day. Together with the remarkable number of ensembles and individual objects of religious value, the interaction of natural forms, towns, villages and cultural landscapes generates that specific picture thought of as "biblical". Palestine's traditional rural areas present a system of interconnected cultural elements, illustrating significant historical periods. They are an outstanding example of a traditional way of life and are connected to ideas and objects of universal significance.

These areas currently suffer considerable development pressure. As a result of rapid population growth, towns and villages are expanding unchecked. The need to extend areas of designated building land and its associated infrastructure is destroying this inherited idyll and progressively changing its historical appearance. The terraced olive groves are yielding to the pressure of the extensive settlement development. The disposal of rubble and waste is a particular problem too. A lack of expertise and regional development tools further fuel these nascent environmental problems. Planning activities, sporadic and small-scale, are based on a combination of sometimes contradictory regulations from differing periods of rule - the British Mandate period, the former Jordanian administration and the Israeli occupation regulations. Sustainable regional planning is made problematic by the geopolitical situation and the fragmented zoning of the country after the Oslo Peace Accord. The country's fragmentation makes it impossible for any decisions on large scale spatial concepts to be made. The Israeli settlements, some of which have been established illegally and are being sealed off, also limit the opportunities for an orderly development of the area and for any control regarding changes to the landscape. Above all, the landscape is blighted by security installations. All these aspects pose are a serious danger to Palestine's valuable rural areas and, if nothing else, a source of social and political tension.

The call for a sustainable policy for the development of rural areas and the cultivation of the cultural landscape becomes ever more relevant; this was the impulse for the project.

Towards the meeting of the Palestinian partners' expectations
That the project topic be defined by the Palestinian partners, who initiated the project and have set its programme, was of the utmost importance. Equally, it was important that the content of the project be defined by local academic experts. In order to achieve successful and sustainable outcomes, we took a broad view of the topic from the very start. This included the enhancement of spatial planning know-how in general and focused specifically on rural planning and community development. The very clear deductive approach of the Palestinian partners greatly assisted the Austrian partners' understanding of the issues and hence their involvement in the project.

The Palestinian partners took a particular interest in an academic training programme in rural planning, developing and discussing the new curricula in intensive workshops with the Austrian partners. An important requirement for project success was that we do justice to the richness and diversity of the topic. Consequently the partners decided during the project preparation to include as associated partners two relevant Austrian universities – the Vienna University of Natural Resources and Life Sciences (BOKU) and the Vienna University of Technology (TU Wien).

- For our Palestinian colleagues, it was very important to train the implementation of didactic know-how by organizing student workshops, as it is practiced at Austrian universities.
- Knowledge has been transferred between the institutions through collaborative curricula development and intensive student programmes.
- The international conference was intended not only as the project's finale but as a confrontation of standpoints and opinions.

The three project blocks were supported by the Austrian partners and were seen as a basis for further activities like the establishment of a spatial planning research cluster and of partnerships with local and international academic institutions and planning offices and not at least with rural communities in Palestine.

Towards the meeting of the expectations of the Austrian partner
The relevant professional interests and the international experience of the Institute of Urbanism of the Graz University of Technology were without doubt the decisive requirement for starting the project. The institute had existing professional and personal contacts with BOKU's Institute of Landscape Planning and TU Wien's Department of Spatial Planning, Infrastructure and Environmental Planning. The interdisciplinary nature of the project necessitated these institutions' involvement. In this sense the project offered a chance to deepen networks and knowledge transfer activities within Austria.

Professional interest in information and innovation was an important motivation for the project partnership and the coming together of this network of universities. Every modification to the professional topic and object of research provokes new problems and questions. To reply permanently to new professional questions is a principle part of the development of the scientific discipline of urbanism. The "new" is in the case of the project the professional change of mind when dealing with outer European topics, the check of the steering functions of the urban planning and the limits of its acceptance from cultures, different from the European ones. The advantage for the Institute of Urbanism is seen in the extension of its information pool and of the contents of its courses at the home university as well as an impetus for a critical reflection on the own practice. It is a way of holding one's own in the international professional stage as well as of the own image and authority. The Institute of Urbanism is finally feeling obliged to support the intercultural exchange between Palestine and Austria.

4.1.3 Cross-cultural exchange and teamwork

by Samar Al Nazer and Dima Yaser

Here we detail the lessons learnt during the joint Appear project between the Architectural Department of Birzeit University, Palestine and the Department of Urbanism of TU Graz, Austria. This partnership exposed partners to each others' experiences and cultures. The lessons learnt cover aspects of culture and rural development, as well as the specific comparative problems and challenges faced regarding rural areas and their development in Palestine and Austria. The exchange of academic experience was very beneficial and insightful for both students and lecturers from both partner institutions.

This project included several activities, amongst which were a variety of workshops, student exchanges and an international conference. The two partner institutions experienced each others' cultures through student and staff visits and learned a lot about the challenges and problems they face in their communities, especially in rural areas.

Five workshops were held in the two countries, two of which focused on the development of the new bachelor's programme in spatial planning and design at Birzeit University. These two workshops sought to review and improve the proposed curriculum. Our Austrian partners from TU Graz, TU Wien and BOKU shared their own experiences in this regard and provided us with feedback that enriched the new programme. They suggested an emphasis on concepts of village renewal, landscape protection and conservation regulations. Additional suggestions included the integration within the course curriculum of excursions to rural and other areas, in order to provide the students with first-hand experience of the areas they study. The first workshop was held at Birzeit University's Department of Architecture in September 2012 and the second was held at TU Graz in Austria in late February and early March 2013. This academic workshop was very insightful and the exchange of ideas between different faculty members and different academic systems were very beneficial to the new study programme and to the faculty members themselves.

Two other student workshops compared specific challenges for rural areas in Palestine and Austria. The first workshop was hosted by the Department of Architecture at Birzeit University in September 2013, where students from TU Graz worked with students from Birzeit University on issues related to the village of Jifna. Students formed teams which sought to understand and propose solutions to Jifna's physical, social and political challenges. The second students' workshop was hosted by TU Graz in July 2014, and paralleled the first, in that students of Birzeit University participated, and groups studied and discussed physical and social issues relating to the Styrian town of Hartberg, proposing solutions for the challenges in that area. As a result, students were able to expand their understanding of rural lifestyles, spatial planning and tourism in rural areas. The workshops involved excursions to rural areas, in which both students and staff members were exposed to rural cultures, activities and landscapes. The workshops also allowed the students to work in teams in order to better deal with different planning regulations.

The last workshop targeted community outreach and was held at Birzeit University in August 2014. The local councils of rural areas were invited to a workshop that aimed to blend academic and professional policy experience, to highlight the linkage between urban/rural planning and strategic planning, and to raise awareness of the importance of rural planning for the development of rural areas. The workshop covered physical planning within rural and urban communities, developmental plans and strategic planning. The participants visited Al-Bereh city hall and the staff there presented Al-Bereh's physical plan (in process) and the city strategic plan. Workshop participants, who came from village councils and municipalities, were able to identify crucial issues in planning processes, and recommended further cooperation between stakeholders such as the Ministry of Local Affairs, academics and professionals, and the holding of further workshops.

Finally, an international conference related to rural development entitled "Rural Areas: Exploring Challenges and Opportunities for their Conservation and Development" was held at Berzeit University in April 2014. Conference participants came from different countries, which allowed for a lively exchange of experiences and discussion of a variety of subjects. In this way, participants gained knowledge of other countries, including in the areas of cultural heritage, sense of place, rural tourism, resource management and socio-economic issues, land use conflict in rural areas, agricultural land preservation and landscape maintenance and capacity building for rural development.

Through cross-cultural exchange and teamwork, the conference allowed us to collaborate for the common good and to share experiments and experience on both a faculty and a student level. Much was learnt on both sides, including awareness-raising of responsibilities towards rural areas and natural resources among the official bodies and institutions that took as well as among the local community. There were also contributions from local institutions that highlighted their work in these areas, such as WOJOOD center for sustainable development in rural areas, networking and development. Other contributions from the international participants presented their own experiences in village renewal, rural conservation and sustainability and the preservation of natural resources.

4.1.4 Enumeration of results

Evaluate the current status and practices:
- A one day needs assessment session with Alumni and employers was held to identify the current situation of spatial planning education.

Enhance knowledge of rural development and planning:
- Two curriculum development workshops were held at BZU and TU Graz.
- Core and elective course outlines and syllabus were prepared
- Spatial planning lab was updated
- BZU acceptance of the Spatial Planning B.Sc. programme (University Board, Academic Affairs Unit)
- Accreditation from the Palestinian Ministry of Education and Higher Education (MoE-HE) is in process

Exchange of knowledge and know-how in the field rural development and planning in the South:
- Three graduation projects and two dissertations were co-supervised by professors from BZU and TU Graz each year.
- International students' workshop was hosted at BZU for 7 days.
- International students 'workshop was hosted at TU Graz for 7 days.
- International conference on rural planning and community development was held at BZU (27th-29th April 2014).

Enhance skills capacity and raise awareness of planners and municipality engineers:
- Architectural Engineering Alumni supporting group was founded.
- Two workshops and two lectures by Birzeit Alumni working in the field of rural development and planning were conducted.
- Documentary on rural landscape was produced.
- Several meetings to identify training needs for village council engineers.
- A 30 hour (5day) training program for 14 municipalities was conducted.

Austrian and Palestinian students visit the town of Rawabi

4.1 Capacity Building for Rural Development in Occupied Palestinian Territory

Photo exhibition by Martin Grabner: Jifna village was the research area of the first student workshop

Round table at the conference: Rural Areas. Exploring Challenges and Opportunities for their Conservation and Development, April 2014

Conference poster

Workshop with students at Birzeit University

Kick-off meeting with project coordinator Samar Al Nazar (first row, first left)

Rawabi, the first town in the Palestinian Territories that was designed on the drawing board

4.1 Capacity Building for Rural Development in Occupied Palestinian Territory   105

Workshop in Ramallah and excursion to surrounding rural areas

Workshop with students at Birzeit University

4.2 Conflict, Participation and Development in Palestine

Project Coordinator: Samia Al-Botmeh
Coordinating Institution: Birzeit University, Centre for Development Studies (CDS)
Partner Institution: University of Vienna, Department of Development Studies (DDS)
Partner Country: Palestinian Territories
Project Duration: 1 August 2011 - 31 July 2014
Project Website: http://cds-ie.univie.ac.at/en/home.html

4.2.1 The project - CPDP

The project has successfully established an academic partnership between the Centre for Development Studies (CDS) at Birzeit University in Palestine and the Department of Development Studies (DDS) at the University of Vienna. The two main components that have formed the basis of this partnership are:

- capacity building in the area of development studies and research, and
- the enlargement of knowledge on development issues, theories, and practices.

Firstly, capacity building has been achieved in development studies, methodologies and research methods relating to development issues through the setting up of courses in the Institute of Women Studies program, the training of a new cadre of field workers for the CDS by experienced field workers and the development of a handbook on research methods. This handbook is based on the reflections and discussions of CDS field workers, and builds on their experiences of both bridging the gap between research theory and practice and implementing an exchange program between the CDS and DDS. Secondly, the enlargement of knowledge on development issues in the "Global South" generally, and Palestine specifically, has been achieved via the creation of a research cluster on Conflict and Development (CD) at the DDS.

Both these components of this cooperation have been systematically combined in two ways: through an exchange programme between Birzeit academics, CDS field workers and DDS faculty members and students in Birzeit and Vienna and through the introduction of the above mentioned research methods handbook into the syllabuses of the development studies programmes at the CDS and the DDS.

This project has proved highly successful in building capacity at both universities. This has involved enhancing research capacity, student engagement in articulating theoretical approaches to development issues, as well as enhancing the capacity of field workers to conduct fieldwork. The project has also helped to progress debate and discussion between scholars in the north and the south. In addition, an innovative contribution to knowledge has been produced in the form of a qualitative and quantitative research handbook that focuses on fieldwork in conflict areas.

The partnership between an institution in the Global North (University of Vienna in this case) and another from the South (Birzeit University) has proven mutually beneficial and constructive. The support provided by the APPEAR team has also been invaluable to the success of the project.

In terms of possible future prospects for further cooperation between Birzeit University and the University of Vienna, the two partners discussed the extension of the project to encompass Palestinian communities in neighbouring countries (Jordan and Lebanon). This entails training fieldworkers and engaging in debate about the implementation of qualitative and quantitative research. Other points of possible future cooperation that were discussed include collaboration in capacity building, including training in qualitative and quantitative research conceptualization rather than just implementation, which was the focus of the current project.

4.2.2 Emancipatory knowledge production under occupation

by Helmut Krieger

During the three years duration of our project *Conflict, Participation, and Development in Palestine*, we had to meet a variety of challenges that, at root, derived from the complex realities of a country still confronted with ongoing mechanisms of control by occupying Israeli forces. All aspects of life are affected by this occupation including, of course, the scientific landscape. If knowledge production and knowledge transfer are essential tasks in any scientific project that consists of partner institutions from the Global South and North, then these issues were of particular importance in our project. What does knowledge production mean under occupation? In such restricted circumstances, how is knowledge to be produced that does not merely reproduce existing asymmetries of power? How can critical knowledge emerge in a project that is defined *per se* by its time limitation? How can a Eurocentric knowledge production be avoided? What are the necessary preconditions for reaching a common understanding not only of the way our knowledge production must be organized, but also of basic political, economic and societal problems which in turn strongly influence scientific work?

In order to adequately meet the challenges associated with these questions, we had to establish an approach that systematically integrated a decentring of hegemonic (Western) knowledge. Hence, we had to find a way to deconstruct existing models of development (in Palestine) and reconstruct a critical understanding of the situation on the ground, as well as of global conditions of knowledge production. This dialectical process of deconstruction and reconstruction has proven to be a necessary epistemological approach in order to establish a common understanding of what knowledge is needed, without reproducing power asymmetries. Given the existing conditions in Palestine, and discourses on the Israeli-Palestinian conflict in general, this was a challenging task.

Development in Palestine as multiple crisis
Even a cursory glance at the situation in Palestine shows the multiple crisis the country is

facing. Although more than twenty years have passed since the Declaration of Principles was signed in Oslo in 1993, it is obvious that the current project of state formation in the West Bank and the siege on the Gaza Strip have led nowhere, to neither peace nor justice. As opposed to developments in the Gaza Strip, it seems that the "West Bank first" strategy, adopted by both western powers and Israel, links together two basic elements: the implementation of a development agenda that is strongly biased towards neoliberalism and continued support for the current political and economic elites in Ramallah. At the same time, occupation practices continue through various means, such as the confiscation of land in order to establish and extend existing settlements. This process of neoliberal state formation under an occupation regime in the West Bank is not just about the restructuring of 'state' apparatuses, their ideological legitimacy and economic underpinnings, but also about a process of societal restructuring.

The Palestinian National Authority (PNA) in the West Bank serves as an institutional body responsible for enforcing a neoliberal economic agenda that at the same time seeks to centralize its repressive apparatus, under the guidance of international donors. This has led to the construction of a client 'state' without solving the main issues of the Israeli-Palestinian conflict. The crucial factor for the (political) survival of this West Bank elite is the aid industry that supports it financially. This aid keeps the occupied Palestinian territories (oPt) from total breakdown and allows Israel to continue its security regime. With more than 17 billion US-dollars disbursed since 1993, aid to Palestine, in the form of official development assistance, is among the highest in the world per capita. In sum, under the fundamental conditions of ongoing occupation, the creation of a highly dependent authority has been and will be a contested one. With that, a multiple crisis in Palestine that also affects the academic landscape worsens.

Given these main conditions, the issue our project needed to address was whether it was able to contribute to a critical understanding of development in Palestine.

Components of our project

Designed as an academic partnership between the Centre for Development Studies (CDS) at Birzeit University and the Department of Development Studies (DDS) at the University of Vienna, our project was based on two main components: capacity building in the area of development studies and empirical social research and, secondly, a critical re-reading of knowledge on development issues, theories, and practices. Hence, the following four components were linked systematically:

- Establishment of a MA programme in development and conflict at the CDS and the setting up of courses as part of the Institute of Women Studies MA in gender and development,
- Development of participatory research methods among CDS field workers,
- Establishment and institutionalization of an exchange programme between Birzeit University and DDS' scholars and students, and
- Institutionalization of a thematic (conflict and development) research cluster at the DDS.

Our project was based on the demand, identified by the CDS, for a more participatory and critical approach to development education and research in Palestine. Hence, the MA programme and research methods training were designed to institutionalize development education and research at Birzeit University, while the conflict and development (CD) research cluster at the DDS in Vienna provided the opportunity to analyze societal developments in both the Arab world in general and Palestine in particular. The activities required to establish a MA programme, to set up courses, to build up participatory research methods among CDS field workers and to establish a research cluster, were only possible in as much as we were able to create a space where extensive discussions on development theories and practices (in Palestine) could take place. Crucial to this process was the willingness to critically reflect on and to redefine one's own (geopolitical, class, etc.) position and its related standpoints. The facility for self-evaluation and self-reflexivity as well as the ability to cooperate and act as one in the face of new tasks thus became essential prerequisites in a process of creating a common base of knowledge. Hence, it became possible to discuss the main aspects of our project without over-emphasizing ideological, political, or epistemological differences.

First-hand experience and decentred knowledge
One of the basic preconditions for achieving this crucial process of self-reflexivity was the exchange and mutual learning that took place between Birzeit University and DDS scholars and students. Over the past three years, a number of researchers, academics and field workers from Birzeit University have engaged in exchanges with DDS. Their visits to the DDS were exceptionally productive, as they systematically combined historically informed analyses of the Israeli-Palestinian conflict with reports of current developments in Palestine. In doing so, they not only deepened our critical knowledge of the overall situation in the occupied Palestinian territories, but created an increased interest in dealing with those issues more systematically within DDS' research cluster. By providing fresh insights and reshaping established orthodoxies, they created a space for discussion and reflection which was further extended via visiting research fellowships at the CDS. From 2012 to 2014, DDS nominated a number of students, all of them members of the research cluster, to engage in research at the CDS during visits that each lasted a number of weeks. During their stay they had the opportunity to gain first-hand experience of preparing research proposals and applying research methods. Furthermore, they could gain invaluable insights into the academic system and general current political and scientific discourses on the situation in Palestine. In summary, it can be concluded that the exchange programme created the liminal space in which a decentred knowledge, in the proper sense of the phrase, could emerge. Given the overall situation in Palestine, it is obvious that knowledge production regarding issues of development depends significantly on the ability to gain a critical distance from hegemonic approaches. Rethinking development in Palestine thus requires a paradigm shift, away from mainstream development concepts deeply associated with theories of modernization theories and towards theories of critical development which themselves constitute a field of unresolved tensions. As we learned to move within this area of tension, we were able to create a critical knowledge that was and is needed at both Birzeit University and the University of Vienna.

4.2.3 Ethics in conducting fieldwork in conflict areas – Occupied Palestinian Territory

by Samia Al-Botmeh, Ayman Abdul Majeed and Abaher EL-Sakka

A main project task was the production of a qualitative and quantitative research handbook, whose particular focus was to be the carrying out of fieldwork in conflict regions, and in this case Palestine. The following is a reformulation of some of the recommendations of the resultant manual by Mr. Ayman Abdel Majeed and Dr.Abaher El-Sakka of Birzeit University.

- The idea for developing a quantitative and qualitative research handbook emerged from the more than fifteen years of accumulated fieldwork experience of the survey unit at the Centre for Development Studies (CDS), Birzeit University. The increase in the number of surveys conducted in the occupied Palestinian territories (oPt) since the mid-nineties – in which the CDS played a pioneering role – is a clear indicator of the need for such a manual. This is particularly true, given the fact that the focus of the surveys that have been run over the past 20 years was on issues relating to the repercussions of the Oslo Accords which define the relationship between the Palestinians and Israelis along the lines of peace partners. In other words, the focus of the past surveys was relatively narrow and at times, distant from reality. Therefore, important issues were left out, including those that are the outcome of framing the relationship between the Palestinians as a colonized people and the Israelis as colonisers. This research manual has aimed to address these shortcomings and engaged in discussion of issues not limited within the narrow definitions of the Oslo Accords.
- The handbook critically presents various models in order to get to grips with fieldwork mechanisms by engaging in an extensive reading of reality which focuses on the frailty of the society and its exposure to external central factors, and especially the "occupation/colonization" effect. Accordingly, the manual puts forth a key proposition: "field work must pursue interactive approaches that are based on partnership with the surveyed Palestinian society in order to establish a partnership that is capable of understanding and analyzing the colonial reality, that allows those surveyed the principle opportunity to express and show their experiences of suffering, shows the impact of the external effects and their internal interactions, as well as presenting field research tools based on active and flexible participation."

Fieldwork ethics when working with people living under occupation
When conducting fieldwork in areas exposed to colonialism, the following can prove useful:

- *Clear research objective:* Why am I in Palestine? Is there any person from the local community who knows and supports me? Am I here to prove a theory about an occupied community? Or does occupation have nothing to do with people's lives?
- *Language issues:* Do you ask questions that lead to political answers?

- *Awareness Issues:* Are you aware of the risks that people face and that could result from participating in research? What is the level of your awareness of the confidentiality of information? Making people's names public or other failures of confidentiality could cause imprisonment or loss of life. The confidentiality of information presented in the research includes non-disclosure of the identities of people participating with you.

Participation should be voluntary with no incentives. Be aware that sometimes certain kinds of topics can be hurtful to the lives of people under colonialism. Hence try to avoid questions that may cause any moral, psychological, physical or ethical damage. Research should be independent with no hidden political agenda pushing you towards goals that are beyond the scope of the research. You should seek the good of the local community being researched, whether politically or morally. Do not go into local communities without a clear message but enter with a clear message that proves good intentions. Respect the culture of the local community. Do not offer material or moral bribes for the purpose of gaining access to information with an unclear purpose.

Tips for enhancing partnership with communities in field research:
First: Challenges caused due to violations of the occupying power
Challenge 1: Inability to access certain communities within the Palestinian Territories, such as Palestinian villages in the seam zones, firing zones, border zones or lands near to borders such as the Jordan Valley and Jerusalem. Some organizations exclude these locations automatically from their research due to their being difficult to access and the high cost of conducting fieldwork there. Research centres, however, should strive to develop strategies to overcome these difficulties.
   Proposed interventions:
- Training a local team that improves local capacities to collect local data from the different communities.
- Dialogue with local communities through opening communication channels with various groups and also organizing meetings with the surrounding communities to help facilitate tasks.
- Exercising flexibility in addressing communities in order to achieve research objectives.

Challenge 2: Checkpoints and curfews
   Proposed intervention:
- It is essential not to tie the research to specific periods of time or to the personal interests and the financial interests of institutions, but rather to deal with issues with a high level of flexibility. Always maintain the personal safety of the research team and respondents when entering the targeted locations.

Communication with local communities exposed to the daily risk of occupation violations significantly contributes to the expression of unity with these communities, enhances resoluteness and keeps morals high.

Second: Lack of trust within the community
- Local communities don't trust research. Research is viewed sometimes as a tool for collecting information for certain political parties or organizations. This is due to the internal political conflict and lack of security and stability in the Palestinian Territories.
- Hence it is important for researchers to build relationships with the community through local community-based channels (bottom-up) rather than imposing a relationship through an organization (top-down).
- It is also important to organize initial awareness meetings with the local community regarding the issue in question and its significance to their lives.

Third: Challenges while communicating with respondents
Sometimes, researchers will encounter potential respondents who request payment for their participation in the research. Data emerging from such a process is often misleading. A number of institutions working in the area of data collection do provide such payments, which is a highly unethical form of relationship between the data gatherers and respondents.
Therefore, this source of data should be discarded.
- There is no trust or credibility in this kind of a relationship between the respondent and the researcher or organization. A sense of partnership should be in place before starting the research.
- The objective of the research should be explicitly clarified to respondents via an official letter from the organization or a presentation from the researcher.
- It is forbidden for researchers to give promises, even if the result would otherwise be the loss of the participation of a certain respondent.
- The researcher should be aware of the conditions put in place by local communities to ensure their safety and security. It is important not to cause any immediate or future harm for them based on their participation in the research.
- Researchers can enhance trust by carrying identifying documents to show to community members during their fieldwork. Such documents include ID card, research identification card and business cards.

Direct examples: Security and taxation conditions imposed by the Israeli occupation on East Jerusalemite community cause confusion for people who live there regarding how to respond to research interviews or questions, especially if there are specific questions on their financial or income status. Another example is that carriers of Jerusalemite identity cards who live outside Jerusalem but maintain their Jerusalem address might be hesitant to respond to research questions because of the complexity of their situation.

4.2.4 Enumeration of results

- Training of 75 field researchers in the West Bank and Gaza Strip in qualitative and quantitative field research.
- Drafting of 10 research papers by field workers on various socio-political issues related to life under occupation in the West Bank and Gaza Strip.

- Drafting and printing the qualitative and quantitative research handbook focusing on the conducting of fieldwork in conflict areas, particularly those under occupation.
- Conducting exchanges between academics and students from the University of Vienna and Birzeit University. These exchanges involved joint visits by academics from the Department of Development Studies at the University of Vienna and academics from the Centre for Development Studies and the Institute of Women Studies at Birzeit University. Field workers from the West Bank and Gaza Strip also participated in these exchanges. The exchanges involved discussion of work aspects, lectures, presentations and learning experiences. At the same time, students from the University of Vienna visited the Centre for Development Studies for periods of between three and eight weeks over the course of the past three years. The students participated in the research programs of the Centre, as well as in drafting research proposals and contributing to seminars.
- Setting up a research cluster at the University of Vienna. The main activities of the research cluster were focused on strengthening research into issues of development in conflict areas. This involved four public lectures, four workshops, and a lot of informal debates on the process of development within conflict regions, particularly in the occupied Palestinian territory. In addition to working with students and academics, the research cluster engaged in the organization of the international graduate student conference 'Rethinking Palestine' that was held at the University of Vienna from 13th to 15th of December 2013. After receiving a surprising number of applications from all over the world (over eighty), we decided to structure the workshop sessions in such a way that important issues regarding not only the occupied Palestinian territories, but also the Palestinian diaspora as well as Palestinians inside Israel could be covered. Hence, the following panels were held at the workshop:

- Cultures of Resistance
- Neoliberalism, Whiteness, and Solidarity
- Gendered Orientalism, Protest, and the Thirdspace
- Political Islam in Palestine
- Sumud and Return

Selected papers from the conference workshop will be published soon.
- Conducting a joint final seminar at Birzeit University. The final seminar for the project was held on October 13, 2014 under the title "Development as power - learning from the field". The seminar's programme focused on the understanding of development as power within conflict-stricken Palestinian territories and the manner in which fieldwork is conducted under such conditions. The workshop was conducted simultaneously between the West Bank and Gaza Strip - using a video conference link between the two territories. The seminar was attended by the 75 field workers as well as members of the general public, students and academics. Colleagues from the DDS, Helmut Krieger and Ramin Taghian, also took part in the deliberations of the seminar. Field workers

were granted a certificate to testify to their participation and completion of training in quantitative and qualitative fieldwork. The certificate carried the logos of both Birzeit University and APPEAR.

- Developing two courses to be taught as part of the existing MA program in development and gender at the Institute of Women Studies. The first course has been finalized under the name "Foundations of Development and Alternatives in the South". The second course is titled "Trajectory of Economic Development in the Occupied Palestinian Territory". The work also focused on developing a diploma in development studies. The diploma is directed at the local community and makes prime use of the manual that was developed as part of this project. This has been done in close cooperation with the DDS.

Audience at final seminar

Ayman Abdul Majeed

Fieldworkers attending training at the Birzeit University

Fieldworkers workshop in January 2012

Graduation ceremony for fieldworkers

Prof. Rema Hammami is giving a lecture at the University of Vienna

Project coordinator Samia Al-Botmeh (left) with a member of the Austrian based research cluster at the APPEAR gender workshop in November 2013

Final project seminar

Fieldworker Tahrir Asfour

Training of fieldworkers in Jenin

5 THE NEPALESE CONTEXT

5.1 Development of an Academic Programme on Energy Systems Planning and Analysis in Nepal

Project Coordinator: Tri Ratna Bajracharya
Coordinating Institution: Tribhuvan University, Centre for Energy Studies, Institute of Engineering
Partner Institution: Vienna University of Technology (TU Wien), Institute for Energy Systems and Thermodynamics
Partner Country: Nepal
Project Duration: 17 July 2011 – 16 July 2014

5.1.1 The project – ENERGY

The Human Development Index ranks Nepal in 157th place. Access to reliable and affordable energy services is fundamental to reducing poverty and improving health, increasing productivity, enhancing competitiveness and promoting economic growth. Though Nepal possesses an enormous hydropower potential of 83,000 MW, to date just one percent of it has been harnessed and the country remains perilously dependent on imported fossil fuels. The country continuously faces dire energy crises, whether 18-hour-a-day power-cuts or the frequent supply crises affecting gasoline, diesel and LPG. The need exists for effective mechanisms to help develop qualified human resources and guide policy-makers and stakeholders planning and implementing sustainable energy systems in Nepal.

Considering this problem of poor energy access and ineffective energy systems planning and management, the Centre for Energy Studies (CES) at the Institute of Engineering (IOE) of Tribhuvan University in Nepal teamed up with the Institute for Energy Systems and Thermodynamics (IET) at Vienna University of Technology. The objectives of this partnership were to build Nepal's capacity for energy systems planning and sustainable energy policy development and to create awareness of universal access to electricity. This South-North cooperation project was funded by the Austrian Development Cooperation under the APPEAR programme. The project was based on the innovative approach of combining an academic programme with research and development activities in the developing country.

The main goal of the project was to further Nepal's development through the effective utilization of better human resources in the field of energy systems planning and management. Specific project objectives were:

- To establish the Energy Systems Planning and Analysis Unit (ESPAU) at the Centre for Energy Studies (CES), Institute of Engineering, Tribhuvan University.
- To involve ESPAU in the creation of doctoral and post-doctoral research groups at CES which would develop energy systems models, perform policy analysis and make planning recommendations to the government, policy-makers and related stakeholders.
- To develop and implement the curriculum of a M.Sc. programme in Engineering in Energy Systems Planning and Management.
- To strengthen South-North cooperation between Nepalese and Austrian partners for sustainable development in Nepal.

5.1.2 Energy as a crucial element for sustainable development

by Tri Ratna Bajracharya

Energy is a crucial element for a country's sustainable development. Energy resources are regarded as key strategic natural resources, with the potential to be a catalyst for a country's general economic growth and development. Unless a country's energy sector is geared up for efficient and indigenous sustainable resources, along with their sustainable harnessing, its economy cannot move forward on its path to higher growth. Every economy requires secure access to modern sources of energy. But while many developed countries are focussed on domestic energy security or decarburizing their energy fuel mix, many developing countries like Nepal are still seeking to secure enough energy just to meet basic human needs.

Total energy consumption in Nepal was about 292 Peta Joule (PJ) in 1995/96. It increased by a total of 29% in the period from 1995/96 to 2011/12, an annual growth rate of 1.6%. The use of fossil fuels has increased at a growth rate of 5.8%, due mostly to a rapid rise in LPG and coal consumption. This indicates that the trend of energy consumption is towards increasing dependence on imported fossil fuels, raising issues of energy supply security. Electricity, mostly from hydropower, has increased at an average growth rate of 8.0% indicating the increasing role for hydropower in fulfilling the growing demand for modern commercial energy. GHG emissions from energy use has increased by 76%, from 4.1 million tons CO_2e in 1995/1996 to 7.3 million tons CO_2e in 2011/2012 (3.6% annual growth rate). The per capita GHG emission has increased from 0.20 ton CO_2e/capita in 1995/1996 to 0.27 ton CO_2e/capita in 2011/2012. This indicates the energy consumption pattern is shifting towards carbon intensive fuels, raising issues related to global and local environmental sustainability.

Though Nepal possesses an enormous hydropower potential of 83,000 MW, to date just one percent of it has been harnessed and the country remains perilously dependent on imported fossil fuels. The country continuously faces dire energy crises, whether 18-hour-a-day power-cuts or the frequent supply crises affecting gasoline, diesel and LPG. The Human Development Index ranks Nepal in 157th place. Access to reliable and affordable energy services is fundamental to reducing poverty and improving health, increasing productivity, enhancing competitiveness and promoting economic growth. In terms of access to modern energy, the per capita electricity consumption is only 93 kWh, which is very low in comparison to averages for Asian countries and those in the developed world. This also points towards a potential future increase in electricity demand due to economic and population growth. In its long term economic development approach paper, the Nepalese government has already set as its goal the transitioning of Nepal from least developed to developing country by 2022.

On the electricity supply side, there were no power cuts a decade ago when installed capacity (mostly from hydropower) met peak demand. As time has gone on, however, and new hydropower capacity has remained uninstalled due to political instability, the country has been forced to adopt scheduled loadshedding (intentionally engineered electrical power shutdowns). In the country's commercial and industrial sector, there has been an increasing trend of installing captive gen-sets (generators) to overcome the effect of ongoing loadshedding, as is evident from the sudden increase in diesel demand from 2008 onwards. This has had a huge impact on the trade deficit of the country, as reflected by fast growth in the expenditure of foreign currency surpassing the total amount earned from merchandize exports.

A clear need therefore exists for effective mechanisms to help develop qualified human resources and guide policy-makers and stakeholders planning and implementing sustainable energy systems in Nepal.

In the aftermath of the peace process, the investment picture has improved and there is now increasing investment in the hydropower sector. As of 2013, 708 MW of hydropower plants are in operation and an additional 732 MW are under construction. Altogether, 1,892 MW of hydropower are planned for construction under the Nepal Electricity Authority (NEA), a government body. A power purchase agreement has been made with independent power producers for an additional 928 MW of hydropower by 2013. The NEA projects that peak load demand for electricity will be 3,679 MW by 2027/28 under present electricity intensity levels, but this figure could be much higher if we consider the government's goal of transitioning Nepal to developing country from least developed one. Recently, the government signed a power trade agreement with the Government of India, paving the way for increasing investment in hydropower, not only for domestic consumption but also for export. To address a research gap in the hydropower sector, the APPEAR programme has sponsored two PhD students to conduct demand-side and supply-side analyses of the sustainable use of hydropower in the country.

To address this problem of poor energy access and ineffective energy systems planning and management, the Centre for Energy Studies (CES) at the Institute of Engineering (IOE) of Tribhuvan University, Nepal, teamed up with the Institute for Energy Systems and Thermodynamics (IET) at Vienna University of Technology. The objectives of this partnership were to build Nepal's capacity for energy systems planning and sustainable energy policy development and to create awareness for the universal access to electricity. This South-North cooperation project was funded by the Austrian Development Cooperation under the APPEAR programme. The project was based on the innovative approach of combining an academic programme with research and development activities in the developing country.

The project was able to set up the Energy Systems Planning and Analysis Unit (ESPAU) at the Centre for Energy Studies within the first year of the project. The unit has since been actively involved in the organization of numerous training and awareness raising events, which has aided its visibility and recognition among public and private sector bodies in Nepal as an energy sector think tank. The unit has provided services to the Nepalese Ministry of Environment's Alternative Energy Promotion Centre for a "Study on Revision of Subsidy Policy on Renewable Energy Technology". The recommendations made by the study have since been accepted by the Government of Nepal and put into practice. ESPAU has also provided consulting services to the Carbon and Climate Unit (CCU) of the National Renewable and Rural Energy Program (NRREP) for a Study on the Role of Renewable Energy Technologies in Climate Change Mitigation and Adaptation Options in Nepal. The unit is also involved in the development of the Water Resources and Energy Sector Vision 2050 for the Water and Energy Commission Secretariat, Government of Nepal. Amongst other central strategic documents, it has been actively involved in the formulation of "National Energy Strategy 2012", "Low Carbon Development Path 2013" and "Biomass Energy Strategy 2013". The unit also assists faculties and students in publishing research work related to energy systems planning and analysis in national and international peer reviewed journals and at national and international conferences.

ESPAU successfully developed and implemented the curriculum of the MSc Engineering in Energy Systems Planning and Management (MSESPM) programme. The curriculum was approved by the Subject Committee, Faculty Board and Academic Council of Tribhuvan University. The project also supported selective scholarships for deserving students from the MSc programme's first intake and funded small-scale research works based on energy system planning and management for the programme's first and second intakes. Student enrolment has since increased due to demand from the student body. After the end of the project, the programme was incorporated into the regular list of master's programmes offered by the Institute of Engineering. In its third year it established itself as the top choice among 18 masters programmes offered, with more than 5 applicants for every available place. As a result of the establishment of this valuable master's programme, students receive a specialized, high-level of education regarding energy systems planning and management, making them more qualified for higher levels of employment. Visits and teaching stays from the Austrian partners provided the students with additional input, with the international view on special aspects of hydropower-related topics especially invaluable. In addition, the project also supported the Institute of Engineering's in-house capacity building by supporting four students to pursue their PhD degrees at Vienna University of Technology, Austria and Tribhuvan University, Nepal.

Cooperation between the Austrian and Nepalese partners has been instrumental to the success of the project. As both partners had known each other for a long time before the project was established, cooperation was intensive. Visits led to a rich exchange of experiences and teaching approaches on both sides. The visits from the Austrian partner to Nepal allowed a broader perspective on the needs of this country and the Austrian members were able to share academic knowledge and teaching materials with their Nepalese counterparts. The Austrian partners, meanwhile, profited by gaining experience in teaching abroad and through the chance to see circumstances in a developing country first-hand. The site visits were of especially high interest for the Austrian members and gave them a more detailed impression of the challenges involved in establishing a Hydropower Plant in such remote places. Meeting with Nepalese officials gave the Austrian members background information for the guidance of the two Nepali PhD candidates in Austria. The results of the project are expected to be helpful in establishing an effective mechanism that can help to develop qualified human resources who will be effectively involved in guiding policy-makers and stakeholders in sustainable energy systems planning and implementation in Nepal.

5.1.3 How to see technical problems from a different point of view

by Eduard Doujak

The following contribution aims to give an insight into the project from the Austrian partners' point of view. It starts with the beginnings of the relationship between the Nepali and Austrian partners and progresses chronologically, giving special consideration to what we have learned from each other and how our knowledge, in particular that of the Austrian members, has been enhanced. From our point of view it is not only interesting to reflect on whether the project went well and all goals were achieved but also to reflect on the individual development of the project members. Therefore this contribution will also comment on what we have learned from each other and from visiting a previously unfamiliar country. The starting point for this long-term relationship was the conference participation of Dr. Tri Ratna Bajracharya at the Viennahydro in 2004, where he presented his PhD work at an International Conference on Hydropower Plants. Since that first meeting, contact has been maintained and resulted in the successful proposal for this project. Thanks to the support of the Austrian government, via the APPEAR programme, we got the chance to further develop a long-term relationship and to increase sustainable energy capacity in Nepal.

None of the Austrian project team had previously been to Nepal, and therefore the first journey in October 2011 at the start of the project was of high interest. All Austrian project members undertook the first trip full of expectations. Our first major impression was of the warm welcome afforded to us by the Nepalese team members. Other than the architectural differences compared to a European city like Vienna, we experienced our first culture clash with the highly social way of life. Crowded streets, filled with masses of vehicles and motorcycles led one to think that transport was almost totally private. It seemed that the public transport was all underground. Only small electric vehicles and buses were noticeably part of a mass transportation system. It soon became clear that fossil fuels were a highly important resource, which had to be imported as Nepal itself has no such resources.

After the kick-off meeting and discussions with members of the newly established Energy Systems Planning and Analysis Unit (ESPAU), we (the Austrian partners) were astonished to learn that most of the imported fuel was not used for transportation, but for electricity generation via individual diesel generator sets due to power shut-downs in the electrical grid. This was definitely a big difference to the European style of living and understanding of electricity supply. From that moment on, right at the beginning of the project, the importance of energy planning and analysis was clear and was to be advanced at every opportunity.

Studying the country's electricity demand and supply sides, it quickly became clear that the situation was unsustainable. Therefore it was thought necessary to include these facts in the development of the master's course by installing modules on various renewable energy sources, along with consideration of their attendant technologies and respective difficulties in energy conversion. These courses aim to equip students with knowledge of supply side possibilities. For the demand side, some special lectures were included to teach different estimation methods. Following much discussion, a comprehensive and sustainable curriculum for the master's course in Energy System Planning and Analysis was established.

A major lesson we learned at this stage was the need to include all stakeholders right from the beginning. During Austrian partner meetings at the Austrian Agency for International Cooperation in Education and Research (OeAD), we heard that where such stakeholder inclusion is lacking, projects can fail to be accepted. Luckily our project did not have this problem. This can be attributed to the role of the coordinator, responsible for project management as a whole.

After recruiting the first batch of master's students, classroom teaching began and this led to the Austrian project team's next visit. Among other courses, the focus was given to hydropower engineering and development due to the initial research unit findings that the hydraulic potential of Nepal is enormous. Many of the problems with power cuts could be solved if existing hydropower resources could be suitably developed. Therefore, classes on hydropower engineering and development as well as maintenance and refurbishment of hydropower plants were led by the Austrian partners. This was intended to further educate Nepali students on this topic, and hence to have more educated persons in this field in the future.

Capacity building was, and continues to be, a central aim of the project. From our home institution, we knew that while classroom teaching can provide theoretical knowledge transfer, an excursion to an existing hydropower plant or a power plant under construction can deliver a deeper insight into practical matters. Therefore the Centre of Energy Studies at the Tribhuvan University organized a one day excursion to the hydropower stations Kulekhani I&II (in operation) and Kulekhani III (under construction) to see the practical conditions on site. Members of the Austrian partner team joined this student excursion and we learned that a combination of theoretical background and practical site visits is extremely important both for Nepali and Austrian students. This approach is seen as the best approach for teaching younger scientists worldwide.

In addition to the student excursion we also had time to visit other hydropower stations under construction or refurbishment. The project team had the chance to get to understand the difficulties involved in constructing a hydropower plant in rural locations. Experiences were exchanged, which fed into the further development of the project. Table 1. lists the power stations visited throughout the project.

Site name	Type	Capacity	Development stage
Upper Tamakoshi	Run-Off River	456 MW	Under construction
Kaligandaki	Run-Off River	144 MW	In Operation
Middle Marsyangdi	Run-Off River	70 MW	In Operation
Kulekhani I and II	Storage-Type	60 MW + 32 MW	In progress
Trishuli	Run-Off River	60 MW	In Operation
Maikhola	Run-Off River	22 MW	Under construction
Kulekhani III	Storage-Type	14 MW	Under construction
Andhikhola	Run-Off River	9.4 MW	Upgrading from 5.1 to 9.4 MW

Hydropower Plants visited during project meetings

Some of our experiences should be described here in more detail due to their remarkable difference to European expectations. For example, visiting Upper Tamakoshi showed that huge investments had had to be made just to install the infrastructure needed to make access to the hydropower station's location possible. Although transporting goods and materials to the site is costly and difficult, when fully operational, Upper Tamakoshi will be Nepal's biggest hydropower station and so be a major help in meeting the demand for electricity. Despite this, however, there will still be a lack of electricity in the electrical grid. When looking at the project consortium and development companies, it was noticeable that foreign companies are responsible for the development, construction and building of this hydropower plant. While the finances for the project are covered by the government and Nepalese companies, it is striking that there is a lack of skilled and well-educated people to support a project like this. Further, all sub-suppliers are also from outside Nepal, which lacks the manufacturing base to deliver goods and materials for such a big power station. Seeing this big hydropower station first-hand, we also learnt that developing the enormous potential of hydropower in Nepal requires a lot of well-educated people – something that made the project's establishment of the MSc programme all the more important.

Andhikhola was also a very interesting project. This old hydropower station is due to be upgraded and for an additional machine unit to be installed. This would not be such a big task if the powerhouse cavern were easily accessible. In this case, though, the powerhouse cavern can be reached only by a 250m long vertical shaft and all materials must be lowered by gantry crane. Hence, the size of individual machine parts is limited by the diameter of the vertical shaft and the gantry crane's payload.

Just these two examples show the difficulties of developing a hydropower station in rural places in Nepal. Austrian project members know very well the construction problems and challenges within Europe, but these challenges pale in comparison to the troubles and restrictions in Nepal.

The Nepali project members also visited hydropower stations in Austria to see the typical machine setup and operational boundaries here. This led to some excellent knowledge-transfer on technological and economical matters. An especially important aspect of this visit for our Nepali guest was the chance to see High Head Storage plants, which will become necessary in Nepal in the future. Austria is a world leader in this kind of technology and therefore it was very important for the Nepalese project partners to witness this technology in action. Nepali members were very impressed with the huge size of our storage power plants and got a good idea about the technology needed to increase electricity supply in Nepal.

Knowledge-transfer was achieved not only by site visits, important though they undoubtedly are. We also tried to organize an experience exchange with Austrian manufacturers of small hydro equipment as well as suppliers of turbines for large hydro applications. As the Institute of Energy Systems and Thermodynamics organizes an International Conference on Hydropower Plants every two years, in 2012 and 2014 we had a good opportunity to share insights, experiences and research results with the international participants of this conference. Sharing visions, ideas and possibilities led to a more complete understanding of the energy situation in Nepal and opened the eyes of European suppliers to future market possibilities. Learning was hence not limited just to project members, but also extended to some 350 conference delegates.

One of the biggest challenges presented by the project was also to have two Nepali PhD students here in Vienna. Through this intercultural exchange of knowledge, ways of life and mindsets, both sides learned a lot about each other. Indeed, I believe one of the biggest advantages and opportunities to be gained from development projects is the chance to understand the needs and mindset of the southern partner. Respect and individual dignity sometimes count more than money. Therefore we are happy to have these students here and I hope they have learned a little bit about our way of thinking.

To summarize the main lessons learnt in this project:

- If you are part of a development project you have to ask about and reflect upon your position prior to meeting your southern project partners. It is of the utmost importance to remain aware of your partners' dignity. And be there! Do not try to manage such projects without leaving your office. Be there, visit the country and witness first-hand how people live and think.
- Educate yourself about the situation in the southern country. Try to speak as much as possible to many different kinds of people as well as high officials.
- One of the most important things to be aware of when setting up courses, such as the master's in energy planning and analysis, is to make sure to include all necessary people and officials. The better informed and included such people feel, the better the chances for success.
- In terms of preparing material for the classes, it was very helpful to first teach there and so get an impression of general levels of skills and education. This is of immense importance as you cannot rely on skill levels being the same as in countries like Austria. International rankings might perhaps help but will never surpass personal experience.
- We learned that Nepal has huge amounts of hydropower resources. In the future, a major challenge will be to harness this great potential and supply it to the people

who currently lack electricity. The biggest challenge we will never solve, however, for this is a political one. As long as the country lacks a stable government that embraces hydropower with vision and energy, the country's hydropower potential shall remain just that. The development of Hydropower Plants can only go so far without further improvement of the electrical grid. This is a major regret for this project – to witness the potential resources and also the willingness of private investment, but also the deficiencies of the electrical grid due to legal property rights. As long as this matter remains unresolved, Nepal's development cannot truly start.

- Austria is one of the biggest suppliers of components for Hydropower Plants. Due to the International conference organized by the Institute of Energy Systems and Thermodynamics we had the possibility to share information. Next to the visits to Nepal, this was one of the biggest opportunities for learning and dissemination within this project. Project members and delegates alike learned a lot at this event, which acted as a multiplier by sharing information with manufacturing companies and consultants.
- Personally, every Austrian project member learned to see technological problems from a different point of view. It was wonderful to carry out this project and to help our southern partner in terms of capacity building and the development of their country.

By the project's end, we had all learned a lot and we are all very glad that the Austrian Development Cooperation supported this project financially.

5.1.4 Enumeration of results

Establishment of the Energy Systems Planning and Analysis Unit (ESPAU) at Centre for Energy Studies, Institute of Engineering, Tribhuvan University:

- ESPAU installed within first project year.
- Established as an energy sector think-tank in Nepal.
- Conducted several energy policy related research exercises for government agencies and development partners.
- Involved during formulation and revision of several government policies including Subsidy Policy on Renewable Energy Technology, National Energy Strategy 2012, Biomass Energy Strategy 2013, Water Resources and Energy Sector Vision 2050, and Low Carbon Development Path 2014.

Development and implementation of the curriculum of the M.Sc. in Engineering in Energy Systems Planning and Management (MSESPM):

- Curriculum for master's programme MSESPM was developed in collaboration with Northern partner and implemented from November 2012. It is in the process of a second revision with active feedback from related stakeholders.
- First two intakes of students successfully taken through the programme within the APPEAR project period.

- Third intake has been successfully registered under the IOE's regular programme of master's courses.
- MSESPM has been able to establish itself as top choice among 18 master's programmes offered by IOE, indicating the sustainability of the programme after the APPEAR project funding.

South-North Cooperation:

- Northern partner shared knowledge and teaching material in delivering international level course.
- Visits from Northern partner to Nepal further increased experience of teaching abroad and gave a broad view about the real needs of this country. Technical expertise was directed towards addressing those needs.
- Visits from Southern partner to Austria helped in the capacity building of Nepali expertise and provided an opportunity to interact with international development partners.
- Established a platform for further South-North collaboration in development activities.

First evening of kick-off visit of Austrian partners in October 2011

Spinning prayer wheels

Main building of the IOE campus at Tribhuvan University in Kathmandu

Students of the first batch at discussion

5.1 Development of an Academic Programme on Energy Systems Planning and Analysis in Nepal

Excursion with students of the first batch to the Khulekhani Hydropower plant

Access road from power house cavern to inlet structure side at Upper Tamakoshi Hydropower Plant. Elevation difference is about 600m

Drilling of the vertical shaft between inlet structure and power house cavern. Drilling length is about 600m

Official visit of the project team and our leaders of the construction site

The only access to the power house cavern of Andhikhole Hydropower Plant is this 250m deep vertical shaft

Eduard Doujak, Prof. Bharat Raj Pahari, former dean of the Institute of Engineering, Julia Lichtkoppler, APPEAR programme officer, and Prof. Tri Ratna Bajracharya, current dean and project coordinator

Prof. Tri Ratna Bajracharya at High Head Hydropower Plant Silz in Austria in June 2014

Students of the second batch

Final Project Completion Meeting in October 2014 in Kathmandu. Members of the project team

6 THE CONTEXT OF MOZAMBIQUE

6.1 Strengthening Universities' Capacities for Improved Access, Use and Application of ICTs for Social Development and Economic Growth in Mozambique

Project Coordinator: Thomas Grechenig
Coordinating Institution: Vienna University of Technology (TUW), Information Technology Services (ZID)
Partner Institution: Universidade Eduardo Mondlane (UEM), Department of Mathematics and Informatics (DMI)
Partner Country: Mozambique
Project Duration: 1 July 2012 – 30 June 2014
Project Website: www.ict4dmz.org

6.1.1 The project – ICT4D

The Vienna University of Technology (TUW), the Universidade Eduardo Mondlane (UEM) and the non-profit organization ICT4D.at set up a sustainable research partnership between the two universities. The project supported the implementation of new IT infrastructure and the improvement of teaching, learning, research and gender equality at the Department for Mathematics and Informatics (DMI) at the UEM. Furthermore, the project supported the development of a local intellectual property (IP) transfer office at UEM to foster innovation and the exploitation of research findings.

The project goals were the attainment of a higher quality of education at the department of Mathematics and Informatics at UEM and a strengthening of its research capacities, in order to produce research outputs in the areas of rural development and poverty reduction that are relevant to Mozambique's strategic economic sectors. Improvement of information technology programmes and technological infrastructure, along with the formation of a sustainable research partnership between UEM and TUW, are the project's main developmental achievements. These achievements mean that the practical results of the project can be made sustainable for the processes of teaching and research and will contribute to the Mozambican private and civil sectors, as well as the economy as a whole.

Mozambique has a demand for skilled IT graduates to meet the needs of its growing economy. The demand for graduates from the DMI at UEM exceeds output, both for the economy and the university, which relies on graduates to fill faculty positions. In order to meet the quantitative and qualitative demands of the market in Mozambique, as well as its own internal staff requirements, the DMI is in need of updated IT equipment, a redesign of its IT related programmes, capacity building of both faculty and staff, and improved resource management.

Currently, 30 students are admitted to the IT master program at UEM annually. However, this number does not seem to reflect the rising interest in the ICT field and the increasing demand for skilled professionals in the economy. There are, though, entry barriers to the master's programmes, including high levels of tuition fees, a lack of infrastructure, a shortage of places for students in the programmes, and a lack of trained professors.

With better trained staff and possibilities for student involvement with projects, innovative changes in areas of resource management and administration can be realized and internal processes and services can be improved. With improved infrastructure and a higher quality of education, more innovative projects can be realized.

After completion of a new project-funded IT laboratory, the DMI is now able not only to connect its existing IT labs to the Internet, but can also efficiently manage the access and usage of this infrastructure. The infrastructure is set up in a way that new projects can easily build on this environment, as the infrastructure allows a high number of additional servers to be hosted virtually, which will enable upcoming projects to focus less on infrastructural issues and more on the training of staff members.

Furthermore, as a result of the IT lab and workshops, a virtual server has been set up which enables the usage of the e-learning software 'Moodle' within the department. This is the first step towards a successful application of e-learning tools at DMI. Additionally, three courses have been created, based on the usage of this IT lab and the equipment that was introduced at the women and IT workshop.

An important part of the project was the implementation of two software engineering projects by students at UEM. Preparations started in September 2013, with several workshops on developing concepts and requirement analysis. The software had to simultaneously meet the demands of the broader population while also offering a practical guide to students on how to further develop a project idea to create a software concept. The two developed concepts were later implemented under the supervision of two Informatics master's students from the Vienna University of Technology from February to May 2014. During three weeks in Maputo, the two Austrian students Philipp Schnatter and Paul Spiesberger presented state-of-the-art software development methods and tools like GIT, design patterns, scrum and many more. Using these new methods, two groups of students from the UEM implemented the following applications:

- Complaint Center: This application provides an interface between customers that have bought a product and want to file a complaint, and companies tasked with taking care of this complaint as a platform for customer support. Company ratings, based on their previous responses to complaints, can help future customers to decide where to buy a product. The basic requirements were developed by Florian Sturm and Anders Bolin from ICT4D.at and the live version of this platform will be implemented together with this institution.

- Find UEM: The second student group has been working on an Android app for students to find points of interest (POIs) like lecture rooms, Wi-Fi hotspots or public power plugs on the UEM campus. The locations of the user and other POIs are marked on a Google map similar to a navigation system. The focus for this project is partly the application of geographic information systems and partly a user-friendly implementation of the Android user interface guidelines.

The topic 'gender in ICT' was emphasized, following discussions with female students at DMI, via the development of a workshop at a local school in Maputo. We demonstrated the possibilities of technology to secondary school students using two programmable LEGO Mindstorm sets and succeeded in awakening their interest. As young people in Mozambique have to decide very early if they want to later go to university, the only way to increase female participation in higher education is to increase awareness in schools. This workshop was a test run and will be further evaluated at the DMI for the next steps.

Finally, a big success for the project and the sustainability of the whole activity was the grant awarded to a lecturer from UEM to enable her to complete her PhD studies at the TUW in Austria. She is, and will be, involved in all upcoming activities and acts as a steady link between the two universities.

6.1.2 The project's importance

by Emílio Mosse and Andrei Shindiapin

Education has always been a beacon for the development of nations and people. The ICT4D project is part of a concerted effort by our department to improve educational conditions through national and international partnerships. The Department of Mathematics and Informatics (DMI), within the Faculty of Sciences has been responsible for teaching IT at the University Eduardo Mondlane since 1987. In 2002, the DMI started to offer further courses such as Mathematics and Statistics, and in 2007 an additional specialization in Geographical Information Sciences was introduced.

Graduates from DMI are in high demand with employers, both because of the growth of the Mozambican economy and a high level of innovation within the department and UEM. Currently, the DMI has about 100 staff members, some of whom are part-time lecturers. Additionally, there are 22 technical staff members responsible for the provision of general services.

The establishment of the ICT4D project relied heavily upon contacts established by Mrs. Joanna Knueppel who had been working in Mozambique for some time, as well as the initiative of Paul Pöltner, the project manager. Initial correspondence resulted in extending contacts to Emilio Mosse and Andrei Shindiapin, both of the Department of Mathematics and Informatics (DMI), Faculty of Science, University Eduardo Mondlane.

A series of meetings between Maputo and Vienna ensued, with the aim of finding a common understanding of the project. These encounters were supplemented by contact via email, SMS and Skype. Initially, the project team weighed the idea of a project in the area of Geographic Information Sciences (GIS), a specialization taught in DMI. The project partners eventually decided, however, that the project's focus should not only encompass GIS but rather cover to the full spectrum of the department's competences.

Eventually, the project's ambitious goal was determined: to strengthen DMI's ICT infrastructure with the support of TUW. The objective was in line with the aims of DMI, the Faculty and UEM, particularly regarding budgetary constraints on the purchase of laboratory equipment, and aligned in general with the need to improve the training of students in order to support their integration in the workforce.

In parallel with the meetings between Maputo and Vienna, there were also discussions at a departmental level within DMI regarding the composition of the project elements. The team comprised three DMI staff members. We were glad to welcome several female experts to the project in various roles, since there are few female DMI staff members. The involvement of one female project member from the university in Maputo helped to attract female students to take courses similar to the one taught at DMI.

The project arrived at crucial time for UEM, with changes occurring across the higher education sector imposing an imperative to rethink the aims of the UEM and the demands for skills and knowledge that graduates from UEM face when they enter the labour market. At the same time, there is a conditional requirement for student learning and training processes to be further aligned with specific societal problems.

The project had four broad objectives, namely:

- *To improve university infrastructure by meeting the basic conditions for a high quality study programme and research activities.* Such infrastructure includes a computer lab with GIS equipment that supports the UEM IT programmes.
- *To further develop educational programmes by improving the quality of teaching, learning, research and gender equality.* The project partners worked together to improve curriculum development, teaching practices and resource management at UEM by financing educational exchange between core members of the team and supporting the dissemination of knowledge throughout the department at UEM. Activities will be designed and implemented to encourage the participation of female students in IT at UEM throughout the course of the project. Comparatively, Mozambique has a low percentage of women with higher educational degrees, although from known studies this is not such an issue in IT-related programmes.
- *To establish a sustainable partnership between UEM & TUW to collaborate on projects and research relevant to the needs of the university and strategic economic sectors in Mozambique, that will assist with rural development and poverty reduction via the use of ICTs.* The project aimed to establish a partnership for sustainable collaboration on research and projects in software engineering, change intellectual property management practices and develop software to meet the needs of UEM and the demands of NGOs and businesses in Mozambique.
- *To enhance the local intellectual property transfer office at UEM to guarantee the application of research findings to both society and the economy, assisting with sustainable social development and economic growth in the long term.* ICT4D supports UEM in building a sustainable research program that facilitates exchange between the uni-

versity, society and the economy, in order to facilitate a sustainable means of financing university research activities.

These highly ambitious objectives naturally raised concerns for their achievability within the project's short two year duration. A particularly contentious area was the urgently needed enhancement and the extension of the Geographic Information Science curriculum and the revision of the Informatics curriculum. We were aware that changes of this scale would require high-level approval within the university, and that their implementation would take a long time. These and other issues were discussed and debated during project meetings until the correct focus and scope of the project was agreed upon.

These discussions led to the installation of an IT laboratory to act as a hub for other activities. This lab facilitates research into specific societal problems and also serves as a motivational centre in the search for talent within DMI with the potential to assist in developing solutions to some of the above mentioned problems. Questions about the preparation and frequency of submission of reports were also discussed at project meetings.

The project organized several workshops on various topics:
- Coordination meetings analyzed and answered questions regarding the development and status of the project.
- A communication and file sharing platform "Alfresco" was established, where relevant project documents were made accessible to all project partners for further discussion.
- Workshops in the application of e-learning and m-learning (mobile learning) in education were held. These workshops addressed new methods of cooperative work involving the e-learning software 'Moodle'.
- A workshop on "Equipment Management" created a space for participants to discuss emerging issues, challenges and possible solutions associated with print management in the Faculty of Science. Following this workshop a guidance document was produced that will serve as a roadmap for future improvements, helping us to allocate existing resources more efficiently and significantly reduce costs.
- Students' project work: During this workshop, students were advised on how to plan projects to best meet the needs of the population. During this workshop, two groups of students developed two systems:
  - *Find UEM: a smartphone application that allows users to locate places in UEM.*
  - *Complaint Center: a complaint management interface application that links consumers and manufacturers.*

The project generated knowledge on all sides. Austrian and Mozambican members engaged in mutual learning and the exchange of experiences. One particularly visible result of the partnership between EMU and TUW was that a PhD student started her studies in Vienna under APPEAR funding. This student can be seen as a sustainable link for the continuation of the collaboration. The project organized capacity-building training for administrative staff from the entire faculty. This training focused on administration and management of material resources, as well as the capitalization of a computing laboratory.

To conclude, we can certainly state that the project has led to the consolidation of a sustainable cooperation between TUW and DMI. Based on this success, the way has been cleared for other departments at UEM to establish partnerships with Austrian partners. The installation of a laboratory, now in its final stages of implementation, should be considered one of the project's great achievements. Additionally, lessons have been learned from the successful resolution of emergent problems at both a management and a technical level (for example, a recurring point in the workshops was the need to have a fully dedicated infrastructure manager, not only for DMI but for the entire faculty).

6.1.3 Between high expectations and daily routine

by Thomas Grechenig, Paul Pöltner and Philipp Schnatter

One of the ICT4D project goals was to plan, implement and support two software projects by students of the Universidade Eduardo Mondlane (UEM) in Maputo, Mozambique. The project was to provide an additional and non-mandatory course on top of the UEM's regularly scheduled lectures, for motivated students to deepen their knowledge of software development by realizing an exciting and relevant project together with their colleagues. Having been closely involved with this part of ICT4D by both assisting DI MMag. Paul Pöltner with project management and by supporting the 'Complaint Center' group as one of two students from Vienna, I (Philipp Schnatter) would like to tell a story about the problems we faced and the solutions we developed, our expectations as they compared to the reality we confronted and the 'workarounds' we came up with to cope with the unforeseen and unexpected.

In order to involve the students as much as possible, in September 2013 planning started at the UEM under the supervision of DI Florian Sturm. Professor Emílio Mosse had preselected two groups of five to seven students based on two main criteria: good grades (the additional workload should not endanger the positive completion of regular lectures) and that the students be in their third or fourth semester of the bachelor's programme. Both measures ensured that students would be equipped with the basic experience and knowledge required for this project.

Florian completed several workshops with the students during his three weeks in Maputo to develop concepts for the two applications. Ideas came directly from the students, who after an initial brainstorming session settled for two projects: 'Safe Maputo', an application for smartphones using maps and crowd-sourced data to show safe areas in Maputo and 'Complaint Center', an application that provides a platform for consumers to express their complaints about a product and for companies to handle that customer feedback. In the ensuing workshops, Florian and the students worked on the project specification and documentation. Use case diagrams, lists of system components, UML diagrams and user interface mockups were created and each student given one or two specific roles within the group: coordinator, sub-coordinator, software architect, GIS expert, documentation expert, quality assurance and testing expert and programmer.

After the project had been successfully kicked off by Florian, Paul Spiesberger and I joined the student projects in October 2013. As students of the Informatics master's programme at the Vienna University of Technology (TUW), we had the opportunity to combine our master's theses with the coordination of the student groups, including a three week trip to Maputo for intensive workshops to start the implementation phase. Paul and I established regular Skype meetings with the students every second week to further refine the documentation. The students were extraordinarily motivated in regard to programming but a little less so about writing documentation. Documentation being an absolute necessity for modern software development, however, we had to convince them of the upmost importance of documents like 'Project Definition', 'User Stories' or 'Software Architecture'. Of course, the students gained greatly from this (perhaps sometimes tedious) paperwork when we started writing code in February.

But before that our project suffered a setback that delayed our time-table by several weeks. Professor Mosse was informed by high representatives of the Interior Ministry that the 'Safe Maputo' application was under no circumstances to be realized in this form. While I do not want to comment on this directive, I do understand there were possible issues regarding legal aspects and liabilities. In any case, the result was that we had to find another topic instead of 'Safe Maputo' and almost restart from scratch. So, together with the students, we decided upon a 'Find UEM' application and revised all prior documents. 'Find UEM' is an Android app for students to find points of interest (POIs) like lecture rooms, WIFI hotspots or public power plugs at the UEM campus.

In Maputo, Paul and I organized a kick-off meeting to become acquainted with our colleagues from the UEM. Each participant was invited to tell the others about himself (sadly, the only female student had left our group due to scheduling issues in November), his hobbies, likes and dislikes. Despite the extremely tight schedule, we considered this meeting just as important as the following workshops. We talked to the students about their experience as programmers and about the tools and technology we were planning to use. After this initial evaluation of the students' level of knowledge, Paul and I developed topics for our upcoming lectures. As a result, we held presentations on GIT software and source code management (SCM), human computer interaction (user interfaces), Play Framework as a fast web application development framework, the software development framework Scrum, development for Android, software design patterns and database design over the course of the first week. Every lecture started with such a presentation and after a discussion and a break, we practised hands-on implementations of the presented theory.

Thanks to the work of Professor Emílio Mosse and his colleagues at the UEM, all students had a very good understanding of programming, so we were able to focus on more advanced and project-specific topics not usually covered in classical programming courses. We deliberately set aside a lot of time (one week out of the total two and a half weeks) for these seminars, because we wanted to show students new methods, tools and frameworks. The aim was to communicate alternative approaches to known software engineering problems that would expand the abilities of the students, arouse their interest and provide best-practice examples from state-of-the-art of modern software development as practiced by industry. The learning curve for using GIT during the programming phase was steep, but on every subsequent day Paul had fewer 'merge conflicts' to solve and ultimately the students were able to operate the software autonomously. Another success came almost instantly. We were positively surprised when, during a workshop break, we noticed that some students were independently using GIT rather than Dropbox as a versioning system for their own side projects!

Our three weeks in Maputo were scheduled to take place in February, during the break between the winter and summer semesters. Our time-frame was very tight, however, since of the 22 days we stayed in Maputo, only 12 days were normal workdays. When we arrived on the Thursday, we were informed that our planned meeting with the students on the next day had had to be cancelled, because the president of Mozambique had at short notice declared a public holiday. Hence, subtracting two days for arrival and departure, one public holiday, the last day as a cushion for unforeseen events and six days accounting for three weekends, we had a mere 12 days to work with the students.

Then, of course, the students had regular lectures, seminars and exams during our stay. Professor Mosse excused them from his own lectures, but they were not allowed (and neither did we ask them to) to miss other lectures. To emphasize again: the students came to our workshops in their free time. They spent time working on the project instead of studying, working, doing sports or social activities. We could not and did not coerce our colleagues to appear, to participate, or to work at home. So instead of compulsion, which would have required instruments to which we had no access, we tried hard to make the lectures interesting, motivating and amusing! Nonetheless, our project was quite demanding. Students had the opportunity to attend an average of about 12 hours per week of workshops. Additionally, we also asked them to do some homework, because the few hours we had at the university were not enough to make noticeable progress within a software development project.

Outside of students' already busy university workloads, the scheduling of the workshops during our 12 working days was quite a challenge for various reasons. We quickly realized that making appointments by email did not work, as many students did not have access to the internet at home and could only access their emails at the university. As a solution, we spent more time with our students agreeing the schedule for the upcoming week. Planning a whole week ahead ensured that students had more time to react to any changes.

Another aspect that had a big impact on time-management was our almost impossible struggle to start the workshop meetings on time. Students would arrive 45 minutes late, shortening the already restricted possible time we can spend together. Through discussion with the students, we learned that they were regularly delayed by traffic jams. Most of them had to take the bus, and students coming from outside of Maputo needed more than one hour to get to the university. Knowing that the source of the problem could not be resolved, we adapted our schedule accordingly. From the second week on, the first hour of our meetings was dedicated to questions, a recap of previous lessons and discussions. That way we were able to use the available time in a meaningful manner, while waiting for the others to arrive.

As I already mentioned in the introduction, our groups consisted of students in their third and fourth semesters. Naturally, they had to attend various lectures and seminars. On many occasions, half of them would have lectures in the morning and be free in the afternoon, while the other half's schedules were exactly the opposite. Hence, Paul and I conducted some workshops twice: once in the morning and then again in the afternoon. This was the best solution to ensure that students did not miss an important workshop and fall behind their colleagues.

Considering all these circumstances, challenges, and the fact that we could not give grades or ECTS points, we were amazed at the enthusiasm and motivation displayed by the students. They really wanted to improve their software engineering knowledge and learn new things for their university studies and later careers. Thanks to the students' motivation, we were able to lead a total of 34 hours of workshops during our stay in Mozambique.

The infrastructure at the UEM confronted us with surprising challenges. The Department of Mathematics and Informatics features free WIFI within the building. While the WIFI network *per se* was stable, Internet access was only rarely possible. For our work with the students, access to the internet was essential. While programming, we required access to our GIT repository, documentation websites of the used frameworks and tools and a search engine as a first address to consult when bugs or errors occur. Kindly, the students helped Paul and me to buy SIM cards for our smartphones and showed us how to load them with prepaid data volume. From that point on, Paul and I used our phones as mobile WIFI hotspots where students were able to connect during workshops. The 3G coverage in Maputo proved to be excellent and so the students were able to work efficiently with stable internet support.

Accommodation for our workshops was not an issue at all. Thanks to the efforts of Professor Mosse, we had more than enough room. Paul and I even had access to a small office where we could prepare. To allow for the fact that we had two groups with very different software projects, we often split up and used two adjoining lecture rooms, each equipped with a projector, which would have otherwise been empty. These ideal conditions enabled us to focus on our projects. Another positive aspect was that almost all students brought their own laptop or shared one with a colleague.

After the workshops in Maputo, Paul and I continued to support the further progress of the application development via Skype and email. At one point I was shocked to find that the students had themselves changed a part of the software, only later informing me, but all my worries about missing the deadline were unnecessary, because the change did not cause any delays.

With the project complete, I am thankful for the productive and delightful hours we were able to spend with our colleagues from Maputo, the rich experiences we gained in that beautiful country and the countless lessons we learned during our role as student tutors. The applications are in beta-stage and ready to be officially presented at our project conclusion event. I am impressed by the effort and skills of our colleagues and am positive that the applications will very soon go live to the public. Big thanks to Alfredo, Camilo, Chilengo, Delmiro, Elton, Gautchi, Inacio, Job, Jordao, Mauro and Paulo! I am looking forward to keeping in touch and observing the future of our applications.

6.1.4 Enumeration of results

Results of objective A - *To improve university infrastructure through provision of basic conditions for a high quality study program and research activities:*

- Implementation of IT/GIS lab

Results of objective B – *To develop educational programmes by improving the quality of teaching, learning, research and gender equality:*

- Report on requirements and impact analysis
- Improvement and expansion of "Licenciatura" (corresponds to Bachelor) geo-based information systems program
- Improved and revised curricula of IT aspects of all graduate programs in DMI
- 20 faculty staff members with enhanced teaching skills, research methods
- 1 publication on university capacity building
- Dissemination of knowledge of capacity building in Maputo
- Raised awareness of gender in ICT

Results of objective C - *To establish a sustainable partnership between UEM & TUW to collaborate on projects and research relevant to the needs of the university and strategic economic sectors in Mozambique, that will assist with rural development and poverty reduction via the use of ICTs.*

- Developed joint local demand-driven research strategy for ICT4D
- Realization of 2 six-month research projects
- Realization of 10 student projects
- Publication of 4 papers
- Joint Research Partnership agreement beyond project

Results of objective D - *To enhance the local intellectual property transfer office at UEM to guarantee the application of research findings to the society and economy, leading to sustainable social development and economic growth after the project period:*

- Enhanced IP transfer office
- 20 staff members trained on IP

Márcia Juvane, lecturer at UEM, received an APPEAR grant to complete her PhD studies at the TUW in Austria

Starting two software engineering projects

Software engineering projects with students

Workshop on „Women and IT" at a secondary school in Maputo

The new building of the Faculty of Science

6.1 Strengthening Universities' Capacities for Improved Access, Use and Application of ICTs

Team meeting with the project coordinator Prof. Thomas Grechenig (fourth from left) at the Eduardo Mondlane University in December 2013

Research scenario seminar for students

Institutional and technical support for the student project in Mozambique

7 THE EAST AFRICAN CONTEXT

7.1 Master's Programme in Medical Anthropology and International Health

Project Coordinator: Ruth Kutalek
Coordinating Institution: Medical University of Vienna, Department of General Practice and Family Medicine, Unit Ethnomedicine and International Health
Partner Institution: Gulu University, Faculty of Medicine
Partner Country: Uganda
Project Duration: 1 October 2012 – 30 September 2015

7.1.1 The project - MA-MEDANIH

The main goal of this project is to train social scientists and health scientists at master's level in Medical Anthropology, with a focus on Global Health. We wished to create a new generation of postgraduate practitioners who have a broad interdisciplinary background and are able to do applied and participatory research work in communities in Uganda and elsewhere in Africa.

Medical Anthropology is a growing multidisciplinary field. It focuses on health, illness and disease from a social-cultural and socio-economic perspective. Drawing its theory largely from the social sciences, humanities and philosophy, it is firmly rooted in applied research in the medical field. Concepts of Medical Anthropology are therefore important not only for medical doctors working in primary care, promoting community health or as cross-cultural psychiatrists, but also for policy makers, public health practitioners, epidemiologists and social scientists. Persons who hold a Master of Medical Anthropology engage in both qualitative and quantitative research and they bridge the gap between biomedical disciplines and the community by contributing their perspectives on health, illness and culture.

The course in Medical Anthropology's strength lies in its enhancement of qualitative research capacity, which will provide policy makers with relevant baseline information to plan for development projects. Graduates will be able to conduct high-quality qualitative research on various issues related to healthcare and be able to represent and advocate for the communities they study and with which they work. In addition they will acquire competencies in the theory and applied work of Medical Anthropology and Global Health which will enable them to interact with other scholars worldwide.

Students of the master's course are admitted as members of the Faculty of Medicine at the Department of Mental Health at Gulu University. They hail from various fields, so that an interdisciplinary approach is guaranteed in the classroom. Currently we have nine students who hold degrees in arts, guidance and counselling, education, social work and community development as well as population and development studies. All receive a scholarship through the project. The national and international lecturers are from Uganda, Kenya, Austria, Germany, the Netherlands, and the United States of America, with disciplinary backgrounds in medical anthropology, transcultural psychiatry, general medicine and epidemiology. These international connections will enable further cooperation between countries from the North and Uganda and hence enhance research capacity and education.

This course is innovative in its theme, its needs-based approach, its new strategy in higher education and its excellent teaching and tutoring quality. The first master's course in Medical Anthropology in Africa, it is a pioneering course that addresses cross-cultural perspectives in healthcare which are much needed across Africa and in Uganda specifically. The modules are designed to draw from the context of local communities in Uganda. For instance, the situation of armed conflict and its aftermath are analysed in modules focusing on studying health and disease. From a cross-cultural perspective, human rights issues in biomedicine, infectious diseases, non-communicable disease, mental health and social politics in health care are considered.

Through many years of financing of PhD students from Austrian and international funds, we were in the fortunate position to be able to draw from a broad base of research and teaching expertise in Medical Anthropology in Uganda. However, a lack of highly qualified human resources remains an issue in many academic settings in Africa.

This course enables students to attend a master's course in a relevant field in their own country. Outstanding students will be given the chance to progress to an international PhD, with the precondition that they undertake teaching and research in the framework of the course upon their return. In this way, the strengthening of sustainable institutional capacities is guaranteed.

Furthermore, we were able to attach two Ugandan PhD candidates to our project, who have been independently financed via an APPEAR PhD grant since 2013. Both are registered in the Social Science Programme at the University of Vienna and are currently conducting medical anthropology fieldwork. At the time of writing, early 2015, a third Ugandan candidate is completing his PhD studies. We are thus slowly building highly qualified human resources, making Uganda a hotspot for postgraduate education in medical anthropology in Africa.

7.1.2 The Southern perspective

by Grace Akello

In this short essay I will briefly discuss the history of the Master of Medical Anthropology programme, the process of programme development, implementation and other success stories. While so doing, I will highlight the importance of the Austrian Partnership Programme for Higher Education, Research and Development (APPEAR) and how the grant from this programme facilitated the initiation and implementation of the master's programme.

History of the programme

I conducted my doctoral fieldwork in northern Uganda over a one-year period in 2004 and 2005. In addition, I was offered three opportunities by the Amsterdam School for Social Sciences to do a follow-up study with my respondents in 2006 and 2007. Due to the nature of my topic, "wartime children's experiences and quests for therapy", during my fieldwork I worked closely with professional healthcare providers in Gulu Regional Referral Hospital, and sometimes Lacor hospital. Most doctors in these two hospitals are also honorary lecturers at Gulu University. This is how I was introduced, indirectly, to the University system, culminating in my appointment as a Lecturer in November 2007 in the Department of Mental Health within the Faculty of Medicine. During this time, I was still writing my thesis, but the University was patient with me during my frequent absences in The Netherlands, until my return final in October 2008, after submitting my doctoral thesis to Leiden University Medical Centre.

Upon resumption of my duties, I realized that Gulu University's Faculty of Medicine would benefit enormously from not only teaching medical students, but also some master's courses. I followed this idea with a proposal, in which I argued to members of the Department of Mental Health, and later board members at the Faculty of Medicine, the importance of introducing a Master of Medical Anthropology in Gulu University. Although all members at both department and faculty level were receptive, they raised many questions. For instance, who would teach the master's students, supervise their research, and which facilities (lecture rooms, textbooks, computer laboratories) would they use? And if they wanted to do ethnography, how would they be supported financially? At this management level, it was decided that although the idea was good, and indeed a by-then six-year old faculty should have some master's courses, there were insufficient facilities to support a Master's Programme.

The idea for what would become a pioneering programme of its calibre in East and Central Africa was hence put aside in November 2008. At that point in time, the Faculty of Medicine had only two lecture rooms, one small library and most courses were taught in hospitals. Ultimately, the then dean of the Faculty did not report the idea to the higher decision making bodies in the University, for instance the Senate, because at the faculty level there were too many difficult questions to answer. Fortunately, the Faculty of Medicine received guests from the Medical University of Vienna in December 2009 who were seeking collaborative opportunities, with the aim of advancing research capacity. Having introduced themselves as Medical Anthropologists, the dean retrieved a file copy of the concept presented to the faculty a year ago. This is how the process to introduce the Master of Medical Anthropology in Gulu University with financial support by Austrian Development Corporation within APPEAR was initiated.

Although I only learnt about this visit and the content of the discussion much later, to me this was a God-sent visit, a rare moment of serendipity. This is because my training in Medical Anthropology was, for me, not just an additional diploma, but had become a way of life, influencing my daily way of doing things, through critical thinking, empathy and introspection. If medical students and indeed other practitioners were taught these skills, I constantly told myself, they would be better professionals. This strong belief kept my hope alive, even when all circumstances around me seemed to suggest that it would not be possible to realize such a dream. It should be noted that it was fear of lack of capacity to support a master's programme within the faculty and within the university that prevented officials from the Academic Registrar's office from sharing ideas about curriculum development with interested academic staff. For it was argued, if we trained such academic staff to develop curricula, how would the university support such programmes given that it struggled to even accommodate existing programmes? I will come back to this issue and how financial support from APPEAR instilled confidence in the academic registrar's office about the possibility of successfully implementing the programme – and their technical support in developing the curriculum.

Master's programme development

Within the Ugandan academic system, when a university would like to introduce a new academic programme such as the Master of Medical Anthropology, there are specific policy guidelines to follow. For example, the highest decision making body, the National Council of Higher Education, has to approve a curriculum for the proposed programme. The process can take from one year to many years to complete. This is because the curriculum has to be approved by the different hierarchical structures within the University and also at the National Council of Higher Education. Questions from the different boards, for instance the Faculty Board, must be satisfactorily answered before they can forward it to the next decision-making committee. That is how our Master of Medical Anthropology Programme took about four years from concept stage to implementation.

In the previous section, I mentioned how a lack of facilities and staff had been as an insurmountable challenge, and that therefore, in 2008, there had been no attempt to discuss the idea with any higher decision making bodies. In my experience, I have seen that taking risks is part and parcel of any project adventure. To quote an old adage, if one aims for the stars, he or she might not catch them, but they might at least reach the sky. For example, it was through this risky presentation of a concept to introduce a master's course within the faculty in spite of a dire shortage of resources that guests from Vienna were later presented with a good idea for collaboration. Fortunately for us, in June 2012, we were awarded a grant by APPEAR to support the initiation of the Master of Medical Anthropology programme at Gulu University. Professor Ruth Kutalek would be the project director, based in Vienna and Dr. Grace Akello the programme coordinator, based at Gulu University.

It should be noted that it was only when collaboration with the Medical University of Vienna to initiate the master's programme was discussed with the University Senate, that the Academic Registrar's office became actively engaged with the programme. Although internal university dynamics and bureaucracy led to extreme delays in the process of receiving accreditation from the National Council of Higher Education (NCHE), in December 2013 our master's programme was accredited.

The delays we endured helped us learn to handle work-related pressures and stress, especially when the window for funding is limited. For instance, while the APPEAR grant had to be utilized before October 2014, other than making preparations to receive our master's students, no other activity could be done prior to receiving accreditation from the NCHE. This is where I had to sometimes take unprecedented steps. For instance, instead of waiting to hear from the NCHE via the Office of the Academic Registrar and (through the Dean, the Faculty of Medicine) about the status of our curriculum, I went directly to the NCHE on my own initiative. As a result, tensions occasionally developed between me and the Academic Registrar, who felt the reporting system was being ignored. How could it be possible that a relatively junior officer would update her boss about the current status of the Master of Medical Anthropology Programme?

But this issue was later resolved when I learnt to first contact the Academic Registrar, asking him whether I should bring any information from the NCHE, since I was already at the NCHE office to visit friends, and was told that there were some documents regarding how to improve the curriculum for the master's programme. This way of doing things was important, as one learns that in any hierarchical arrangement, perhaps one of the errors is to act on behalf of a higher authority. No matter how well meant or regardless of all good intentions, it is never good to interfere with this hierarchical establishment and their way of doing things. To further resolve this issue of a junior officer seemingly acting on behalf of an important office, the Director of the NCHE visited Gulu University to offer advice and make suggestions for how the NCHE could work directly with a programme developer.

It was during this trying time that guests from Vienna, including Professor Andreas Obrecht, visited Gulu. Although the aim was to receive concrete feedback about timing, about when the master's students would be admitted and lectures would commence, nobody who understood the structural hierarchies and obstacles would state the exact dates. This was a source of frustration to all stakeholders, who felt it almost demonstrated a lack of seriousness or commitment. This is how I learnt that the Academic Registrar would sometimes tell donors what they wanted to hear, even though he knew such deadlines were not possible. I later asked him why he did this, and he told me that under certain circumstances one has to learn what the other wants to hear and tell them exactly that. This, according to him, enabled him to sometimes diffuse pressures in his office. To this time, I am not sure if I agree with this approach. I still believe it is always better to discuss realities and possibilities openly. Doing so not only saves the time that would be wasted on false hopes and expectations, but also provides the listener a clear framework within which he or she can act and innovate.

The course curriculum is organized into thirteen modules including social and cultural anthropology, medical anthropology, anthropology of infectious diseases, cross cultural psychiatry, health and healthcare in Africa, research methods, epidemiology and biostatistics, biomedicine, human rights and culture, current debates in anthropology, child health and well-being, reproductive health and a cross cultural perspective. After approval of this curriculum, we followed the university regulations in admission and implementing the programme. There is now no looking back, and the academic programme has excellent prospects for the future, as is evident from the many inquiries we have received about the next intake and requirements for enrolment from students in Uganda and elsewhere.

At Gulu University, there are up to five full time staff who could ably teach any of the above modules. However, with the financial support from APPEAR, this programme was technically supported by various international universities, including Universiteit van Amsterdam, Universiteit Leiden, the Medical University of Vienna, Free University in Berlin, Kansas University, University of Ottawa, and the Catholic University of East Africa.

Implementation of the programme and international cooperation
With financial support from APPEAR, it was possible to access both infrastructural facilities and seek technical support from the universities above. For instance, after Gulu University allocated a building to host the Master of Medical Anthropology programme within the Department of Mental Health, funds from APPEAR were used to purchase furniture, textbooks, netbooks, internet facilities, desktop computers and support students through awarding scholarships which cover up to 50% of the total tuition fees. APPEAR funds also supported the salaries of four staff over a period of two years. Furthermore, international visiting lecturers and professors were supported through the meeting of travel and accommodation costs.

Perhaps as a result of good management and acknowledgement of the project's progress, the Master of Medical Anthropology programme has attracted attention from many visitors to Gulu. For example, a multi-country consortium from the UK visited the programme in December 2014. One of the objectives was to seek opportunities for collaboration and to propose a base at the institution which hosts this programme. Furthermore, professors from other universities have expressed interest in offering technical support free of charge. In another proposed consortium, it is planned that a technical team from Germany will visit Gulu to teach about trust, security and preparedness for disease epidemics, perhaps in the form of a one-week seminar. Although the Master of Medical Anthropology students will be the main beneficiaries, colleagues and students from other departments will be invited to participate.

7.1.3 The Northern perspective

by Ruth Kutalek

Grace has already said it all! She has explained the various challenges we had to face during the project, and has stressed the success we have already seen.

On two occasions we were very near to terminating the whole project. The first occasion was when I had to insist that Gulu University first provide the space for conducting the course before we proceeded with the project. They did so very slowly and reluctantly but in the end they provided us with a wonderful 1930s building in the middle of a green meadow. The second occasion was the postponement of the accreditation process, which threatened the start of the master's course and the project as such. These two substantial delays not only caused severe concern (and headaches) among our team but also created a stir in the APPEAR organization. I had sleepless nights. During the worst times, my superior severely doubted that the project would yield any positive results. I had the same doubts, but for some reason I went on – we went on. I thought to myself that this place has just come out of a decade long civil war and that we needed to be a bit more patient. In these hours I called the project "my exercise in sobriety". Retrospectively I can confidently say that if we managed to succeed under these circumstances, we can manage anything.

Today, we have nine students who have completed all the modules and are ready to go into the field for their master's thesis research. Nine might not sound a lot, but compared to other planned and implemented postgraduate courses at Gulu University and other Ugandan universities, we are doing very well. Our students are committed and eager to learn. They will be the first generation of master's students educated in medical anthropology in Africa.

Allow me to stress why building capacity in medical anthropology in Uganda and its neighbouring region is so important, using the current Ebola epidemic in West Africa as an example. Immediately after my most recent project visit to Gulu in August 2014, I was invited by the World Health Organisation to support them in the Ebola response in Liberia. The WHO recognize that including medical anthropologists in their social mobilization and mental health teams is vital in dealing with the community response to the disease. They were actually the first organization to employ anthropologists in an Ebola response. Doctors without Borders (MSF) followed and today many major organizations involved in the Ebola response, such as UNICEF, the US Centers for Disease Control and Prevention, Oxfam, the International Rescue Committee (IRC) and others, have medical anthropologists in their teams.

Most anthropologists working for these organizations come from countries from the Global North, very few are Africans. Compared to the thousands of medical anthropologists in the US and Europe, there is a lack of African medical anthropologists in Africa. Remedying this is the aim of our course. Before this current outbreak, the worst Ebola epidemic was in Uganda in 2000, mostly affecting the northern area around Gulu. Due to this epidemic and other smaller ones, Uganda has very broad expertise in dealing with viral haemorrhagic fevers. At the very beginning of the outbreak, it was able to send a team of 14 doctors and health workers to Liberia to support their colleagues in caring for patients, training health workers and maintaining infection control measures.

In future I envision that not only Ugandan doctors and health workers will be part of teams supporting medical emergencies in Africa, but also Ugandan medical anthropologists. But they will also work in other medical fields in the country – in mental health, non-communicable and chronic disease, health and human rights, migration and health, in sanitation and so on, and with national and international NGOs, in transnational health organizations and in the governments of their home countries.

7.1.4 Enumeration of results

- Development of a Master of Medical Anthropology curriculum
- Equipping of the course building (also called the "APPEAR building") with furniture, electricity, water, wireless internet, a library and computers
- Application for the accreditation of the curriculum by the NCHE
- Accreditation of the first African Master in Medical Anthropology curriculum
- Selection and recruitment of students and Appear project staff
- Selection and appointment of national and international teaching staff
- Hosting of national and international teaching staff in Gulu as moderators for different modules
- Very satisfying gender balance
- Very experienced team in project management
- High-quality teaching of all modules within a very limited timeframe
- Pioneers in conducting digital examinations for master's students
- Transparent methods for assessment of students' results
- Selection of research topics for students' master's theses

The project team (from left to right): Vice Chancellor Nyeko Pen-Mogi, project coordinator Ruth Kutalek, Armin Prinz, Grace Akello, Constantine Loum

On the way to Gulu in the North of Uganda

Landmines near Gulu town, heritage of the reign of terror of war lord Joseph Kony

7.1 Master's Programme in Medical Anthropology and International Health

Gulu town is surrounded by remote and extremely poor villages

The project sign

The adapted project building

One of the offices equipped by the project

Andreas J. Obrecht, head of the APPEAR programme, and the Ugandan lecturer Constantine Loum are visiting a rural health centre, that works closely together with the Faculty of Medicine at Gulu University

7.1 Master's Programme in Medical Anthropology and International Health

Our course with staff and international lecturer Sjaak van der Geest

Guests and management at the kick-off event of our course in August 2014: Grace Akello, David Kitara, Robert Kiduma

7.2 Strengthening Universities' Capacities for Mitigating Climate Change Induced Water Vulnerabilities in East Africa

Project Coordinator: Paul Nampala
Coordinating Institution: Regional Universities Forum for Capacity Building in Agriculture (RUFORUM)
Partner Institutions: University of Natural Resources and Life Sciences, Vienna (BOKU), Centre for Development Research (CDR), Egerton University, Department of Crops Horticulture and Soils, Makerere University, Department of Agricultural Extension/Education Associate Partners: Horizont3000, Participatory Ecological Land Use Management Uganda (PELUM)
Partner Countries: Uganda, Kenya
Project Duration: 1 April 2011 - 31 March 2014

7.2.1 The project – WATERCAP

The project "Strengthening Universities Capacities for Mitigating Climate Change Induced Water Vulnerabilities in East Africa", abbreviated as "WATERCAP", was conceived as a direct response to stakeholder demand for university-community engagement to address development challenges. Over the last decade, climate change induced water vulnerability and uncertainty have negatively affected agricultural performance in both Uganda and Kenya. While equatorial precipitation has increased, dry spells and droughts have become more frequent on marginal lands and in ecologically disadvantaged regions. Climate change induced water vulnerability and uncertainty jeopardizes food security and poses a great risk to a rural population that largely depends on rain-fed small-holder farming. The resultant effects are multi-dimensional, encompassing the technical, social, economic and political, and hence require multi-stakeholder engagement through partnerships to ensure efficient water use in small-holder agriculture. Public and private development actors have always criticized universities for not being responsive in the development domain, including in the area of water resources and climate change threats. Often the blame is found to lie in universities' irrelevant curricula. If universities are to be responsive, they must engage more with their communities and other development actors to learn collectively. Through such interaction, universities will be able to make their curricula and research more relevant, improve teaching and learning approaches and enhance the problem-solving competences of their graduates.

WATERCAP was therefore designed to establish partnerships between universities (Makerere University in Uganda, Egerton University in Kenya and the University of Natural Resources and Life Sciences (otherwise known as BOKU) in Vienna, Austria), development actors and the community that focused on efficient water use, with the aim of helping to mitigate climate change induced water vulnerability and uncertainty in small-holder agriculture in Uganda and Kenya. The universities and their partners also aimed to strengthen their capacities in addressing this issue. Four broad activities were successfully implemented over a period of three years, which sought to achieve key results in five thematic result areas, as indicated in the following table.

Planned Project activities and Results

	Major Activity implemented	Key Result Area
1	Assessment of internal and external constraints and opportunities for effective partnerships between universities, development agencies and community for mitigation of climate change induced water vulnerability and uncertainties in rural areas.	Internal and external constraints and opportunities for partnerships between universities and development agents assessed.
2	Initiate and manage partnerships between universities, development agencies, policy makers at various levels and farmer groups for mutual learning on efficient water use in smallholder agriculture through water innovation platforms.	Innovation platforms for interaction between universities and development agents developed and facilitated.
3	Reviewing and updating curricula, improving training approaches, and procedures for demand-driven based on lessons learnt.	Lessons learnt for improvement of training and research in universities to be more relevant to development derived and utilized.
4	Development of strategies for sustainable partnerships between universities and the development actors for addressing climate change induced water vulnerability and uncertainties in smallholder farming.	Framework and strategy for incubation, outreach and up-scaling of innovations derived both from University and from development actors. Framework and strategy for scaling-up and sustaining partnerships between universities and the development actors developed.

The project has made a significant contribution, with key outputs including improvements in the relevance of curricula and research, innovation platforms, mutual learning among partners in both academia and non-academic spheres, knowledge and technology verification and exchange between farmers and local communities, universities and other actors in the agricultural value chain. These achievements were only possible through engagements that have, among other results, promoted institutional adjustments and changes in mindsets and practices among the universities and their partners in a process of mutual learning. Overall, the project has achieved its target of increased innovation capacity through partnerships for outreach, research and training. There is evidence of strengthened collaborative capacities among researchers, lecturers and future graduates as innovation partners with non-academic actors in rural development.

7.2.2 Enhancing the relevance of partnerships between higher education institutions and development partners

by Michael Paul Nampala, Washington Odongo Ochola, Emmanuel Okalany, Kenneth Senkosi and Adipala Ekwamu

Summary

Public and private development actors have always criticized universities for not being responsive in the development domain. The expectation is that universities should exercise agility in generating knowledge solutions and innovations to solve global development challenges including emerging issues such as climate change threats. Recent discourse in the higher education sector regarding its contribution to improving rural livelihoods through participatory agricultural research has focused on how to blend various forms and intensities of stakeholder participation with quality agricultural science (training and research), moving beyond the simple "farmer-first" ideology of the 1980s and early 1990s to more intense engagements that aim to empower multiple actors along commodity value chains. Strategies such as the Farmer-Field Schools and Innovation Platforms, which have the potential to address commodity value chain constraints while promoting joint-learning between researchers and value chain actors using interdisciplinary and multidisciplinary approaches, have gained prominence.

In this project five innovation platforms were established, two in central Uganda and three in western Kenya, to facilitate the implementation of a project that focused on strengthening the capacities of universities and their partners to adequately address climate change induced water vulnerability and uncertainty in smallholder agriculture in Eastern Africa. The project was a unique engagement of academic and development actors that aimed to increase innovation capacity through partnerships for enhancing research, training and outreach. After three years of implementing a range of activities anchored by the principle that all stakeholders should be participants in the innovation platforms, the project has made a significant contribution to development by addressing the need for universities and development actors to engage in impact-oriented research that links university outputs to markets and the formulation of practices, social and business innovations for adoption in smallholder agriculture systems.

Introduction

Awareness of the contribution of Higher Education Institutions to national and global sustainable economic development has increased over the last two decades. Concerted efforts to understand the underlying challenges for higher education and to engage universities to realize development goals have increased over the last decade, especially in Sub-Saharan Africa where the Human Development Index is low. A study by Bloom et al. (2006) for the World Bank reported Sub-Saharan Africa as having the lowest enrolment as of 2004, with the lowest enrolment growth rate of 5% per annum. About four years later Montanini (2013) reported a rate of 7% per annum, a mere 2% increase. Analysis of global investments in higher education show similarly low figures for Sub-Saharan Africa, a directive attributable to a previous World Bank recommendation based on the findings that lower returns compared to primary and secondary education in its previous studies (Montanini, 2013). However, recent trends of returns in Higher Education have changed, with recent studies showing that Sub-Saharan Africa has the highest current and future returns to investments in Higher Education. Montenegro and Patrinos (2013), in a World Bank study for the period 2000 to 2011, reported Sub-Saharan Africa as having the highest overall returns to schooling of 12.8%. The region also had the highest returns to tertiary education of 21.6%, which was larger than the global average of 16.8%. The increasing trends are due to an increasing demand for skilled labour to tackle increasing development challenges in Sub-Saharan Africa. This has placed more demand for relevant technologies to mitigate or adapt to increasing development challenges, which in turn has made the role of universities as producers of human capital more recognized in economic development. This demand necessitates more and sustained funding to Higher Education Institutions from national governments and international donor policies targeted at increasing the contribution of universities to national and global economic development. It also implies an increased contribution to development as part of social accountability. The challenge, however, has been the lack of contextualized approaches for involving universities in addressing challenges to sustainable economic development such as climate change, gender disparities, HIV/AIDs and food insecurity. Various models have been implemented on best practices for engaging universities to contribute to national development through relevant, quality training and research. Available evidence indicates that most effective approaches necessitate the involvement of a range of trans- and multidisciplinary stakeholders (Neef and Neubert, 2011). Based upon the premise of trans- and multidisciplinary teamwork, the RUFORUM network, in partnership with Makerere University in Uganda, Egerton University in Kenya and the University of Natural Resources and Life Sciences (otherwise known as BOKU) in Vienna, Austria, came together to implement a project titled "Strengthening Universities' Capacities to Mitigate Climate Change Induced WaterVulnerabilities in East Africa" (WATERCAP) to train students and develop appropriate technologies with non-university actors for mitigating climate change induced water vulnerabilities.

Fostering networking for capacity building among universities
The WATERCAP project successfully brought together three universities - Makerere University, Egerton University and University of Natural Resources and Life Sciences (BOKU), Vienna. Networking between the three universities was initiated in the proposal development process, when the staff of the three universities came together to discuss development challenges in their respective countries and institutions, and to share their experiences in developing technologies that sustainably mitigate climate change induced water vulnerability. Partnership among universities, especially in the South, has until now been far from the norm, and this has often led to duplication of effort. As recommended by USAID (2014), institutional Higher Education transformation requires partnerships between fellow institutions since they understand the dynamics of challenges and opportunities that exist in the

sector. The WATERCAP project initiated and managed a partnership for mutual learning on efficient water use in smallholder agriculture through water innovation platforms between a diverse group of stakeholders consisting of universities, development agencies, policy makers at various levels and farmer groups. The social dynamics observed in the communities engaged the research team to develop relevant technologies and processes to mitigate climate induced water stresses in smallholder agriculture. The five innovation platforms provided the opportunity to contextualize research and focus on multiple commodities while taking into account the technological, business and social complexities that reflect the reality of smallholder agriculture. Consensus was guided by the partners' previous experience and complementing staff disciplines from the partner institutions. The involvement of a diverse group of experts, including social scientists, civil and water engineers, climate change experts, agronomists and animal scientists, afforded an opportunity to study many different dimensionalities of the smallholder farmer complex in relation to climate change induced water vulnerabilities. This was particularly useful in situations where the innovation platform community was less receptive to the established technologies despite high levels of participation in selection and establishment. The engineering team saw this as a hurdle yet the social scientists saw it as a research opportunity. The challenge also promoted peer-learning by leading to the recruitment of students into a multicultural and multidisciplinary research team.

The universities were engaged in developing the research agenda for the project and agreed by consensus that a students' "master class" be constituted where African and European undergraduate, master's and PhD students undertake research together with a team of supervisors. Co-supervision of students further strengthened the collaboration among the partner institutions. Kenyan and Ugandan supervisors interacted continuously both with each other and the northern partner, BOKU. In terms of capacity building, the project saw master's students graduate in good time and generated knowledge products (publications) within the project period, a rare achievement in other projects. The engagement continued beyond student supervision, to the sharing of teaching and research experience across universities. The agenda-setting process for research conducted in the innovation platforms was participatory and guided primarily by challenges identified by the researchers and development actors.

The level and rate of institutionalization of the project varied among the three institutions, something observed to be attributable to the experience of the implementation team members and the position they held in their respective departments or universities. Institutions where the project team occupied senior positions such as Head of Department or Dean of Faculty were faster to adopt the project. This shows that in transforming universities, it is important to engage champions, a lesson which chimes with recommendations from studies reported in USAID (2014) that the use of champions who are highly familiar with the organization and policy structures in African universities enhances the sustainability of capacity building initiatives.

Universities, development actors, the private sector and communities learning together to enhance innovation capacity

For universities to contribute to economic development, they must understand the economic environment in which they operate, especially the challenges differing actors face and the university's role in addressing these challenges. Universities should therefore strategically position themselves to make a contribution to the development of the community they serve. This is quite challenging for university staff, who usually balance heavy workloads. Yet staff cannot ignore the call for their participation in development. The WATERCAP project deployed the innovation platforms approach to bring together universities and non-university actors to jointly develop climate change adaptive water technologies while building their own institutional capacities.

Five innovation platforms (IPs) were established and used as mechanisms for facilitating interactive learning between universities and development actors. The IPs demonstrated the promise of sustainability and hence attracted partners that were not initially part of the WATERCAP project. The IPs remain relevant field excursion sites for undergraduate and postgraduate training and research, following the reaching of an understanding with local communities and non-governmental organizations operating in these areas.

At a national level in Kenya, a platform for engaging a consortium of universities, the Inter University Forum for Climate Change (IUFCC), was established with support from the Office of the Prime Minister. Five universities have signed a memorandum of understanding to work together to address climate change and related issues in the country. The platform will keep universities engaged in the incubation, outreach and up-scaling of technological, social and business innovations within the broader area of climate change adaptation and mitigation in the region.

The project's training of young scholars contributed to capacity-building in the area of human resources. A total of 11 undergraduate, 12 master's and 2 PhD students were supported to conduct research at the innovation platforms. As a direct result of the hands-on training they received, all the students supported by the project have either found employment, started personal businesses or are advancing their careers by doing master's or PhD programmes. This is uncommon for three year projects but the trans- and multidisciplinary nature of the project enabled this massive capacity-building.

The project contributed to social development through the realization of a proactive community of practice engaged in research and training. The project's multidisciplinary team of university researchers and development actors worked closely throughout the project and will certainly stay in touch beyond the project's lifespan.

13 courses in 8 programmes have been modified as part of curriculum reforms at Egerton University and Makerere University. This is the start of what will be a continuous process of regularly adapting university teaching to the dynamic demands of the labour market for research and graduates.

Two short courses on climate change, water and agriculture were also designed to benefit practitioners dealing with various aspects of climate change adaptation.

Finally, several spill-over effects from the project should be noted at Egerton University, where two masters programmes focusing on agri-enterprise development were developed and launched and the Industry Liaison Office at Egerton University and other outreach mechanisms (internship and Field Attachment Programmes) to facilitate formal linkage of the university with non-university actors were reinstated.

Conclusion

The aim of the WATERCAP project was to create a partnership between university and non-university actors to build capacity and generate technologies for mitigating climate change induced water vulnerabilities in Uganda and Kenya. The project's achievements and lessons detailed above show the efficacy of such engagements in enhancing universities' contributions to economic development. The IPs and the IUFFC, students trained, community of practice established and the short courses are ignition instruments which strengthen these partnerships.

As observed by Brown et al. (2007), in the wake of climate change, appropriate water techniques and innovations must be urgently found to curb the vulnerability of farmers who depend on agriculture for their livelihoods. The WATERCAP project has made an effort to work towards mitigating this threat through science, integrated knowledge and practice as well as policy interactions. Traditionally, universities have a substantial portfolio of research projects, in many cases involving interaction with farmers, communities and other end-user categories (stakeholders). Unfortunately, the results of such research often remain bunkered within academia, rarely converted into user-friendly, contextualized information for wider dissemination. Changing this situation will require a change in approaches to university outreach programmes, which are currently conducted as *ad hoc* activities with very limited (if any) institutionalization of such activities. The WATERCAP project has demonstrated that innovation platforms can promote greater participative (rather than merely consultative) engagements with stakeholders. The Regional Universities Forum for Capacity Building in Agriculture (RUFORUM) uses the Community Action Research Programme (CARP) approach to promote the institutionalization of research projects, and their associated outreach as well as innovation components. It is important that universities do not merely remain training institutions, but transform themselves to facilitate the creation of fully-fledged structures that provide an enabling environment and/or institutionalized mechanisms for the effective generation of research and innovations with clear up-scaling pathways for the wider adoption of good-practices and tested solutions.

References

Brown, O./Hammill, A./Mcleman, R. (2007): Climate change as the new threat: Implications for Africa. International Affairs, 83 (6): 1145 – 1154.

Montanini, M. (2013): Supporting tertiary education, enhancing economic development. Strategies for effective higher education funding in Sub-Saharan Africa.Working No. 49. Instituto per GliStudi di Politica Internazionale. Pp38.

Montenegro, C. E./Patrinos, H. A. (2013): Returns to Schooling around the World. Washington D.C.: The World Bank

Neef, A./Neubert, D. (2011): Stakeholder participation in agricultural research projects: a conceptual framework for reflection and decision-making. Agriculture and Human Values, (28): 179–194.

USAID (2014): African Higher Education: Opportunities for Transformative Change for Sustainable Development. Pp.139

7.2.3 Does knowledge really emerge when knowledge is needed?

by Florian Peloschek

Each day I try to understand myself within the context in which I work and so I search for knowledge that helps me better cope with complexity. I work in the field of research on sustainable farming, food security and secure livelihoods. My main interests are inter- and transdiciplinary research approaches and establishing multi-stakeholder engagement through partnerships to sustain research interventions.

In my academic work, meeting challenges through education and capacity building is key. I believe it it useful to deal with a 'systemic challenge', not a piecemeal of scientifically prepared solutions will help. In our ressearch context we are restricted with environmental borders, economic structures, policy process, societal preferences and - oursleves.

Never throughout history have we known more about our planet and its boundaries. Peak oil, climate change, globalisation, adequate supply of drinking water, deforestation, conservation of biodiversity, population growth, fight against poverty…there are many issues where knowledge is available, and constantly developed. Therefore to cope with them should be easy. So, do we really need 'new' or 'more' knowledge to cope with the challenges?

Sustainable farming, food security and secure livelihoods are among the key tasks. In an attempt to build sustainable community resilience, an Austrian-Ugandan-Kenyan academic partnership designed and implemented the project "Strengthening Universities Capacities for Mitigating Climate Change Induced Water Vulnerabilities in East Africa (WATERCAP)". The challenge of water vulnerabilities among communities in eastern Africa is enormous. Competences that allow universities and research organization to facilitate rural livelihood improvements among poor farmers and communities are required. Multi-stakeholder engagement through partnerships to ensure efficient water use in smallholder agriculture helps to secure livelihoods and is a pillar of the project logic (WATERCAP project proposal 2011). From this multi-stakeholder engagement, knowledge emerged.

Among other issues, WATERCAP looked at aspects of participation and management in communities as important factors for sustaining the interventions brought into them. To work closely together, innovation platforms (IPs) in Uganda and in Kenia were formed across major agricultural domains (horticulture, stable food crops, livestock, water harvesting and irrigation). A key question for the project was how viable agricultural development could be achieved while also addressing crosscutting issues such as sustainable farming is a key focus. The goal of the IPs was to use the lessons learnt to achieve a more versatile and realistic delivery of professional content by universities. In Uganda, the organisational structures within the IP have been assessed vital to ensure the project's sustainability, as the infrastructure provided by WATERCAP can be considered technically appropriate for its purpose and stakeholders can maintain it. In Kenya, offering farmers within the IP training sessions and technical advice from other stakeholders does not imply that they finally perceive good interaction.

In the IPs, university experts had the chance to facilitate some rural livelihood improvements focusing on water security and were able to gain competences in outreach, research and training. As academic actors appear in IPs as partners of communities and practitioners rather than lecturers, interventions are more likely to be sustainable within the communities and thus help build sustainable community resilience. An open knowledge and learning system has been identified which integrates a diversity of actors and institutions. Personally speaking, learning to learn from other stakeholders helped me to deal with complex and dynamic challenges.

There are difficulties in making concepts reality, especially if these concepts are new for the implementers, as IPs were for us. Composition and initiation, multi-stakeholder engagement, incentives and the timeframe of the IP, among other factors, added complexity to our previous assumptions and beliefs about the way we did our work. In the end, though, such complexities made the project a more rewarding learning experience. The partnerships developed and fostered by the project provide new avenues and networks for future academic contributions. The IP processes highlight the need for institutional support and willingness to engage in transdisciplinary interventions.

Transdisciplinary research helps to focus on actual global problems and addresses structural, cultural and cognitive barriers. It is not about formalization. It is not about following mainstream discourse. Transdisciplinary learning supports us in becoming aware of our own assumptions and expectations in our research work. The participatory approach of IPs encourages us to try out other teaching and learning methods and to explore new methods of creative and collaborative knowledge generation to meet new challenges. Personally, choosing a new path in my research and exploring innovative ways of knowledge transfer and collaboration helps to cope with complexity.

We need fresh knowledge, but we also need innovative competences to apply it. Although so much technical knowledge already exists, the IPs were nonetheless incubators for new discoveries among most of the project's participants: knowledge about societal preferences, knowledge about traditional societies, knowledge about social structures and so on. In this regard, our capacities to be competent partners for development have been enriched. Capacities for mitigating climate change induced water vulnerabilities in the academic institutions have been markedly strengthened. Strong attempts have been made to develop human capacities beyond the academic partnership and to become facilitators of newly established partnerships with civil society agents and organizations.

WATERCAP was designed to create new competences that would allow universities to facilitate rural livelihood improvements among poor farmers and communities. The intense involvement of WATERCAP researchers is crucial to the continuance of research as an interactive process. Different facets of WATERCAP build the foundations for this. In the long run, the footprints of this project will serve as a pathway for development-oriented multi-stakeholder research.

7.2.4 Enumeration of results

- Five Innovation Platforms (IPs) established and used as mechanisms for facilitating interactive learning between universities and development actors. The IPs have demonstrated the promise of sustainability and have attracted partners that were not initially part of the WATERCAP Project. The IPs still remain the relevant field excursion sites for post graduate training and research.
- One platform for engaging a consortium of Universities in Kenya, the Inter University Forum for Climate Change (IUFCC) has been established. 5 Universities have signed a memorandum of understanding to work together to address issues of water vulnerabilities in relation to climate change. The platform will keep Universities engaged with incubation, outreach and up scaling of technological, social and business innovation.
- Capacity in terms of human resource developed as part of training young scholars. A total of 11 undergraduate, 12 Masters and 2 PhD students were supported to conduct research at the Innovation Platforms. All the students supported have either found ready employment, started personal businesses or are advancing their careers by doing masters or PhD programmes because of the hands-on training they received.
- A pro-active community of practice engaged in research and training as a contribution to social development. The multi-disciplinary team of university researchers and development actors involved in the project have continued to work closely throughout project implementation and will certainly remain in contact beyond the project's lifespan.
- Several spill-over effects including two university programmes focusing on agri-enterprise development, a Masters programme launched at Egerton University. Other spill-over effects include institutional changes such as reinstatement of the Industry Liaison Office at Egerton University and other outreach mechanisms (internship and Field Attachment Programmes) to facilitate formal linkage of the University with non-university actors.
- 13 courses in 8 programmes have been modified as part of curriculum reforms at Egerton University and Makerere University.
- Two short courses on climate change, water and agriculture were designed to benefit practitioners dealing with various aspects of climate change adaptation.
- Several knowledge products have been generated and disseminated widely. These include 15 manuscripts on various scientific aspects of the project, 2 research papers and 7 policy briefs, two of which were presented at the RUFORUM Biennial Conference.

Animals watering from a concrete trough constructed by WATERCAP

Farmer in Rakai irrigating a cabbage crop

Farmer with tomatoes cultivated using rain water harvesting, Lare, Kenya

7.2 Mitigating Climate Change Induced Water Vulnerabilities

Farmers presenting their accounts in Rakai, Uganda

President Uhuru Kenyatta (right) attends exhibition that featured WATERCAP with Prof. Rhoda Birech

Spokesperson of the women group in Rakai, Uganda

Spring protection box at Elementaita, Kenya

Student fixing pipes in Rhongai

7.2 Mitigating Climate Change Induced Water Vulnerabilities 171

Villagers and team members in Rakai

Women group in Rakai

7.3 Promoting Gender Responsive Budgeting and Gender Mainstreaming

Project Coordinator: Elisabeth Klatzer
Coordinating Institution: Vienna University of Economics and Business (WU), Institute for Institutional and Heterodox Economics
Partner Institutions: Makerere University, Kyambogo University
Partner Country: Uganda
Project Duration: 1 April 2011 - 15 September 2014

7.3.1 The project - GENDER

This academic partnership focused on "Gender Responsive Budgeting" and "Gender Mainstreaming", long-standing research foci of two of the partners, Makerere University and Vienna University of Economics and Business (WU) and areas of high importance for the future development of Kyambogo University.

The project collaboration consisted of two main components, namely:

- *Research and Research Dissemination: Gender Responsive Budgeting* (GRB) as a strategy to engender the national development framework and development cooperation, in particular New Aid Modalities (NAM), with the aim of enhancing poverty reduction strategies and contributing to gender equality.
- *Strengthen Gender Responsive Management Capacities* at Kyambogo University, with the aim of strengthening gender equality in the university management by promoting organizational development on *Gender Mainstreaming* (GM) at the university.

The project combined activities in the field of research and research dissemination and in the field of building gender sensitive management capacities at Kyambogo University.
Thus, the overall objectives of the partnership were:

- To contribute to gender equality and poverty reduction in Uganda.
- To strengthen gender responsive management capacities at institutions of higher learning.
- To develop and strengthen links and research collaboration between participating universities in Uganda and Austria.
- To strengthen the implementation of gender responsive budgeting and gender mainstreaming through applied interdisciplinary research and teaching as well as stakeholder involvement.
- To strengthen civil society organizations (CSOs) through research collaboration and dissemination of research results.
- To strengthen South-South cooperation between the universities in Uganda as well as South-North cooperation.

Gender Responsive Budgeting (GRB)
Cooperation on this component evolved around a research focus at Makerere University and the Institute of Institutional and Heterodox Economics, WU, to develop strategies and instruments to assess and promote national and regional/local budgets and budget processes from gender perspectives. The specific objectives of the GRB cooperation component were:

- To analyse strategic documents like the Ugandan National Development Plan (NDP) and other national and international development strategy documents with regard to gender equality goals and objectives and possible gender gaps.
- To analyse the budgetary processes at a national level and in selected local communities from a gender perspective.
- To identify how the New Aid Modalities (NAM) can be popularized and communicated to empower civil society, especially women's organizations, and to identify entry points to integrate gender equality and GRB approaches at the level of NAM processes.
- To evaluate public service delivery from a GRB perspective (using the example of three sector budgets, education, health and agriculture) and systems of accountability of different stakeholders, especially to assess levels of downward accountability, transparency and participation in selected local governments.

A series of research reports, policy briefs and dissemination activities ensured the relevance of the work in the context of ongoing policy processes, especially the new national development planning cycle and ongoing debates about strengthening Gender Responsive Budgeting implementation. All researchers involved could build networks with national and local public institutions, the gender donor community, CSOs and other stakeholders, opening new venues for contributing to policy processes.

Strengthening management capacities at Kyambogo University: Gender Mainstreaming (GM)
Cooperation here focused on supporting organizational development and university management reform towards integrating gender mainstreaming in management at Kyambogo University with a view to promoting gender equality and women's empowerment in Kyambogo University (KyU). For KyU, the GM experiences of the other project partners were valuable points of reference and support in building its own capacities. GM has been an integral part of university management at Makerere University since 2002, while WU has long experience in GM implementation at an institutional level and in applied research at the Institute of Institutional and Heterodox Economics.

Mainstreaming gender activities in the context of KyU's organizational development involved the areas of university management, teaching, learning, research and knowledge transfer partnerships and networking. Specific objectives and results of the GM project component were:

- To identify gender gaps at KyU as a basis for further developing and institutionalizing gender policies.

- To mainstream gender in the context of organizational development by promoting and advocating for the enactment and effective implementation of gender responsive policies.
- To work towards the establishment of a Gender Mainstreaming Unit promoting gender equality and women's empowerment within the university.
- To promote sensitivity and capacity development among university staff and students regarding gender equality issues.
- To promote teachers as multipliers for advancing gender equality in the country through gender-sensitive teaching methods and sensitization.
- To advocate for the gender responsiveness of university access, especially for women from disadvantaged backgrounds and those in science disciplines and to contribute to the enhancement of quality education and the shaping of responsible citizens.
- To support GM in teaching and learning through the engendering of the university curricula and university academic programme.
- To engender knowledge transfer partnerships and networking.

The project substantially contributed to gender equality and gender sensitivity at KyU, promoting gender responsive management capacities among top management. With KyU's formal adoption of their Gender Policy, the basis for sustainability has been built. After the end of the project, the focus will be on this Gender Policy's implementation.

7.3.2 To hear and to be heard: Reflecting on power relations and knowledge production from a postcolonial perspective

by Susanne Dietl, Luise Gubitzer and Elisabeth Klatzer

We, three white, Austrian female researchers, would like to share our thoughts about our experiences of the project on Gender Mainstreaming and Gender Responsive Budgeting with Ugandan researchers. There were researchers from three universities involved, the University of Kyambogo (KyU), Makerere University and the Vienna University of Economics and Business Administration (WU). The objective of the Austrian Partnership Programme in Higher Education and Research for Development (APPEAR) "is to strengthen institutional capacities in higher education, research and management in the key regions of the Austrian Development Cooperation (ADC) through academic partnerships with Austrian academic institutions … as a contribution to sustainable reduction of poverty" (APPEAR).

Within this objective lies the notion of cooperation and collaboration between different researchers for sustainable partnerships. In our project this involved four researchers from Uganda and three from Austria. We will here reflect, using concepts from a post-colonial perspective, upon the many challenges and difficulties we faced as project members from Austria during the project cycle with our partners and colleagues from Uganda. Following the post-colonial approach's postulate to look at the individual position, we first reflect as the Austrian team and then each individually from the perspectives of the different roles we held in the project.

Post-colonial theory

The post-colonial perspective tries to analyse whether and how various patterns of relation and effects of colonial dominance persist in today's theories and discourses. This also includes the effects of the knowledge production of the "other". Post-colonial theories are predominantly concerned with examining the effects of colonialism on the level of representation, as well as the discursive construction of identities and concepts which legitimate certain practices. They argue for continuity and parallels to colonialism in today's reality, analysing the politics of knowledge and its modes of creation, control and distribution. In addition, post-colonial theories critically reflect on the representations of the colonizer and the colonized and also on ways of viewing and of being viewed. In this light we have chosen our title "To Hear and To Be Heard", as we believe that many of the difficulties we faced in our project related to issues of communication. Spivak asks whether the subaltern can speak and answers "no". This, in simple terms, is due to tension between cultures, social realities and languages. This means that the colonizer, the Global North, must unlearn its language and its knowledge in order to learn and to hear the subaltern speaking (see Spivak 1994).

In his book "Orientalism", Edward Said (1978) explored how the Orient and the Occident are constructed through colonial discourse and identified an ontological difference which leads to the homogenizing and the stereotyping of the orient, of both the region as a whole and its people. He concentrated his research on the question of how Europeans represent(ed) "others". According to him, orientalism constructs humans in the orient as others, as different from "us". Hence we speak of us, the West, and them, the rest. We argue that this can also be translated in today's world, where the Global North often constructs the Global South as merely "the other", as their "counter-image". This alone might not be very harmful, but this construction of the other comes along with certain categories and stereotypes that are often perceived as being inferior to the western world and its culture. Further, the term orientalism homogenizes a whole variety of different continents, countries, people, languages, customs, thoughts and so on.

As partners from Austria, we want to critically reflect upon our roles within this project, among them our being white, being project coordinators and being the channelers of project money to southern researchers. When discussing and thinking about our role in the project, we were aware that we risked falling into the same "colonial trap" that we ourselves critique, but such a risk is necessary in order to write about intimate matters such as our communication patterns or power relations. We have identified postcolonial concepts that we think helpful to this analysis. Hence, the next few pages are organized according to the following concepts: homogenizing and stereotyping from the research assistant's perspective, communication, knowledge and its creation from the perspective of the institutionalized academic researcher and also power and dependency from the project manager's perspective.

Homogenizing and stereotyping

This short theoretical background should help to ask whether the individuals in this project were themselves guilty of stereotypes and homogenization. Having studied post-colonial theory for some years and also agreeing with the need to reflect on oneself, and neither to homogenize nor to stereotype different cultures, people, societies or places, I (Susanne Dietl) found myself dealing with thoughts and being exposed to thoughts of the so-called "others" that I thought belonged to (my/our) past.

There were a few incidents where I noticed that I started to think: "oh this is so African." At first I noticed a positive bias towards "Africa". I talked about or justified delays in communication or delivery of agreed products with phrases like "African time" and the "African way".

However, upon reading the first contributions from Uganda for this project and embarking in an exchange with our partners on how to improve it, I realized that there are large differences with regard to the level of ambition. Repeatedly reading papers which for example didn't have a clear line of the argument or had with incomplete citations and references or tables without titles and data without sources was a frustrating experience. I found myself confronted with a picture of the "African" as someone not willing to write a paper according to scientific standards, and very soon a picture of the "African" started to materialize that I did not like and I started to have assumptions, prejudices and hypotheses that I did not want to have. This made for uneasy feelings and discomfort – I did not want to think in this way. This shows that images that have been created over many decades and centuries about the alleged "others" are still there and if certain persons or situations fit into those old assumptions and prejudices, they again manifest themselves.

Further, I noticed that we started to talk about our colleagues as "them". The pronoun "them" also always needs its counterpart, "us", and all of a sudden we were in the trap of "us" and "them", especially in the sense of us trying to communicate about the papers. I would argue that this was especially true when things were not going the way we had expected rather than when the collaboration was working. Somehow, in spite of many efforts, as project members of Austrian and Uganda we never really managed to create a sustainable spirit of "us", namely in the sense of an understanding of all project members as a research group working jointly towards joint products. As a project we made progress and delivered, especially in the last months of the project a series of papers and policy briefs were produced, but a certain degree of separation among the Austrian and Ugandan research group work remained until the finalization of the project.

Knowledge and its creation: The process of scientific work
One analytical category of post-colonial theory is the exercising of power by means of universalisms. In this project the universalism I (Luise Gubitzer) used is that of researching and writing according to western scientific standards which formed the basis for the process of scientific work.

I first encountered the Ugandan researchers according to their curricula vitae. The CVs showed that all hold PhDs, have published extensively in scientific journals from the Global North, have presented papers at international conferences, have experience in international (scientific) development cooperation and projects, and have an excellent command of the English language. Thus I was very much surprised when I received and read their first papers, which constituted basic papers for our fields of research in Uganda, but found they did not meet the scientific standards which I had expected. This brought me into a complicated and uncomfortable position. All of a sudden I was confronted with the question of who was responsible for setting the standards for our joint scientific work, as this topic had not been discussed at the project initiation meeting. The question emerged of whether I was allowed to ask for these standards or if I would have to unlearn my knowledge and assumptions in order not to impose western scientific standards onto our project partners and not to become another colonizer who in the eyes of the Ugandan partners held the power over knowledge. Even though we tried to discuss this point at a joint project meeting by establishing commonly agreed standards for our research work, it continued to be a sensitive issue throughout the whole project.

Another central post-colonial question is that of the rhetoric of partnership (Ziai 2010: 409), where current development discourse emphasizes collaboration as equals. This is also true for the APPEAR programme, as mentioned above. Besides the notion of equality and partnership, there were underlying issues of dependency. In analysing the communication patterns throughout the project duration, two issues emerge as repeatedly raised concerns, namely "too little money" to carry out project activities from Ugandan partners and "lack of delivery according to agreed standards and timelines" from Austrian partners. This involved underlying issues of mutual dependency: The Ugandan team was dependent on the money from the North and the Austrian team was dependent on the local knowledge and field research in the form of papers and information from the Southern partners and on their willingness to cooperate, e.g. by keeping to agreed deadlines. In the project we tried to dismantle this imbalance and power inequality but we did not succeed. The question remains: why?

Another experience of imbalance throughout the project involved rationality and irrationality which Ziai (2010) defines as further categories of post-colonial theory. I would argue that nowadays the development "industry" makes it possible to rationally use development projects to make and get money, preferably from the northern donors. My idealistic aim had been to contribute to the well-being and empowerment of women in Uganda from a feminist economic perspective. This proved to be irrational in the context of the project. Hence, there were two very differing approaches in the project, a divide which remained until the end as talk about money never stopped.

Power and dependency in project management
With the project management in my (Elisabeth Klatzer's) hands, a certain imbalance of power was inherent in the project's organization which could be interpreted as a dichotomy between the holder of the power (money) and the receiver of money (power) from a post-colonial perspective. It had been our intention to organize project cooperation on the basis of equality, but by the end of the project, I had come to realize that imbalances of power had not decreased, but had actually increased during the project. To me this was not a unilateral shift, however, but rather a complex web of different forms of dependency and the exercise of power. I initially considered my role as a project manager to be that of facilitating smooth project implementation and collaboration, as well as communicating with and reporting to APPEAR and communicating APPEAR procedures and regulations to partners.

On reflection, I realize that a major shift occurred rather early on in the project work, during the writing of the first research papers. In our view, these papers were intended to be background papers to stimulate further research work and thus essential to subsequent project work. It was agreed that Makerere University partners would write a first draft. The drafts were sent with major delays. The first 1-page graph for one of these papers was received after 1.5 years. Such delays, quite apart from questions of research standards discussed above, had a significant impact on my perception of myself as a project manager. I understood my role to be one of assuring smooth project work, including ensuring that agreements, including deadlines, were kept. Non-delivery over many months, which continued in different forms over the whole project cycle, pushed me into the role of acting with "erhobenem Zeigefinger" (a wagging finger), as I had to frequently ask about the outstanding drafts and send reminders to the Ugandan researchers. I now realize that one effective form of pushing me into powerlessness was simply not responding to messages. I had a strong feeling of not being heard, whatever form of communication I tried. Countless times, my messages were simply ignored. During a late night chat over some drinks after one project meeting, a member of the southern team joked that my email messages would be sent to the trash bin right away. I still do not know whether this was a joke.

My understanding of and criteria for successful project advancement, namely to fulfil mutual agreements and responsibilities vis à vis the APPEAR programme, were seemingly not shared in the same way by our partners. Similar feelings of powerlessness arose when information about the non-participation of the Ugandan researchers at agreed project meetings was twice communicated at the very last minute, with attendant monetary cancellation costs. I felt neither listened to nor taken seriously.

At the same time, it may be the case that I did not properly appreciate the meanings of the messages from our southern partners. Initially I thought we had a common interest in good project work and joint advancement, and assumed we had a basis of mutual trust. But even now, at the end of the project, I can not see what interests were shared by all project members. It seems I missed a lot. Even now, though, going back through all our communications, it is not clear what. The messages sent repeatedly by our Ugandan partners stated that the money was insufficient to do this or to do that. My response was to repeatedly explain budgetary issues and make them transparent. That might have been the wrong answer. It might well be that I did not properly hear what our partners said, or what they meant by what they said. Even now I do not really know what or how I could have communicated to lead us to a path of better understanding and listening to the different needs of each other.

Conclusion

This reflection reveals important underlying aspects of project work when researchers from different backgrounds work together in the creation of scientific knowledge. These aspects were not, and perhaps could not, be explicitly addressed in the form of this APPEAR project. However, when designing a project format where researchers from all over the world work together, issues of power, dependency, universalism, homogenizations, stereotypes and different underlying interests arise. If not addressed explicitly, these can emerge as major hurdles.

Hence, we believe that for successful collaboration, it is important to be aware of such issues and to work explicitly to "overcome" them. Addressing these issues by taking the time to get to know one another and appreciate researchers' differing backgrounds, as well as engaging in continual mutual confidence-building, might help avoid falling into the trap of the dichotomy of "us" and "them". This needs more time beyond the time for actual research work. The design of such a research cooperation programme could explicitly allow for more time and support researchers from the Global North and the Global South to explicitly address these issues. This might help researchers to better listen to and hear each other.

References

Austrian Partnership Programme in Higher Education and Research for Development (appear): Website. Accessed in July 2014 at http://www.appear.at/appear_infos/gene-ral_information/

Said, E. W. (1978): Orientalism. New York: Pantheon.

Spivak, G. C. (1994 [1988]): "Can the Subaltern Speak?" In: P. Williams/L. Chrisman (ed.): Colonial Discourse and Post-Colonial Theory, Hemel Hempstead: Harester Wheatsheaf, p. 66-111.

Aram, Z. (2010): Postkoloniale Perspektiven auf „Entwicklung". In: PERIPHERIE Nr. 120, 30. Year 2010, Verlag Westfälisches Dampfboot, Münster, p. 399-426.

7.3.3 The prospects of and constraints upon gender budgeting and mainstreaming in Uganda

by Consolata Kabonesa, Henry Manyire and Tabitha Mulyampiti

Introduction

Uganda's efforts at gender mainstreaming over the last two and half decades have achieved mixed results. On the positive side, since 1988 Uganda has had a national machinery for the advancement of women and gender equality, in the form the Ministry of Women Affairs, which later became the current Ministry of Gender, Labour and Social Development. The Ministry is responsible for the overall formulation and coordination of policies on women and is a catalyst for making government bodies sensitive to issues of gender. Uganda also has several constitutional and policy provisions that protect and promote gender equality. The 1995 Constitution has several provisions that guarantee equality of the sexes, promote affirmative action for marginalized groups and prohibit laws, cultures, customs or traditions which violate the dignity, welfare or interest of women and/or which undermine their status (Republic of Uganda 1995). The Land Act, 1998, and the National Land Policy, 2009 protect the land rights of women and other vulnerable groups, particularly children and persons with disabilities (Republic of Uganda 1998; 2009).

At a policy level, Uganda has a National Gender Policy, whose guiding principles include gender equality, affirmative action, addressing unequal household and family relations, and promotion of GAD (gender and development) and WID (women in development) approaches (Republic of Uganda 2007). Uganda's policy frameworks for governance and development have also been gender conscious. The major policy frameworks have been the Poverty Eradication Action Plan (PEAP) which was implemented between 1998 and 2008 (Republic of Uganda 2004) and the National Development Plan which succeeded the Poverty Eradication Action Plan and is being implemented between 2010/11 and 2014/15 (Republic of Uganda 2010). These political, constitutional and policy provisions have brought gender into the domain of public space and debate, and have witnessed affirmative action for women in admission into public universities and in national and local governance structures. The provisions have further seen an increasing number of women serving in public administration as Judges and Magistrates, Cabinet Ministers, Permanent Secretaries, Commissioners, Professors, Deans and Heads of academic units.

In addition, government has made attempts to institutionalize gender equity budgeting (GEB) at the national and local government levels. However, gender budgeting (GB) was introduced by the Forum for Women in Democracy (FOWODE) together with the Parliamentary Caucus and other NGOs in 1997 mainly through creating awareness about GB, conducting research on and imparting skills for GB. Beginning with the financial year 2004/05, the Ministry of Finance Planning and Economic Development (MFPED) has been circulating the gender budgeting guidelines and a budget call circular as instruments of action to all government ministries and agencies to budget with an eye to gender. The MFPED has spearheaded GEB training in government units, GEB training of trainers, developing guidelines for GEB and training materials. Such initiatives aim at addressing gender inequalities by ensuring that the national budget responds to the needs of both men and women, as well as other vulnerable groups.

These government efforts to promote gender equality have also been supported by various donor agencies, most notably the Danish Agency for International Development (DANIDA), the UK's ODA and later DFID, SIDA and UN agencies such as UNICEF, UNIFEM/UN Women, FAO and UNFPA. Donor agencies have supported the Ministries of Gender, Labour and Social Development, Education, Local Government, Health and Finance and Local Governments in mainstreaming gender, especially in instituting gender budgeting, gender auditing, training staff and developing gender related policies, programmes and projects. Donor agencies have further supported the development of the academic and managerial capacities of Makerere University's School of Women and Gender Studies and the Gender Mainstreaming Division, respectively.

However, despite all these initiatives, a broader qualitative transformation of gender relations within formal and informal institutions is yet to be achieved. The same is true of transformation in the lives of the majority of girls and women, especially at household and community levels. There is still discrimination against women in Uganda through traditional rules and practices that explicitly exclude women or give preference to men, which is a key constraint on women's empowerment and socio-economic progress. At the community and household levels, women are still restricted from participating in important decisions such as resource use, family planning and access to services such as health and education. Women are also still marginalized in the ownership and control of land, in education, business ownership, skills development, access to financial resources, employment and inheritance rights. The culture of early marriages amongst girls increases the rate of early pregnancies and is partly responsible for the country's high maternal mortality rates and high fertility rates. And at all levels, a culture of ignorance regarding various forms of violence against women is still prevalent. There is also hardly any systematic implementation of GEB at any level. Women are also still restricted from participating in important decisions such as local government budget process and budget conferences.

Challenges to achieving broader qualitative transformation of gender relations within formal and informal institutions
Although as the Ugandan government has demonstrated good will towards promoting gender equality, translating the political, constitutional and policy provisions into actual, realistic and practical activities by the different stakeholders has proven challenging. The challenge arises from the inability of government, civil society organizations and many scholars to define and operationalize the problem of gender inequalities, its ideological roots, propagation, internalization and justification. Most gender documentation and awareness in Uganda only focus on the unequal outcomes of the current gender status quo, meaning the practical limitations to women's participation in development, (including inordinate roles, responsibilities and workloads, little control of and access to resources and existing attitudes and superior-male/subordinate-female power relations that curtail females' participation and possibilities). By ignoring the ideological roots and institutional propagation of gender inequalities, scholars, government and civil society organizations tend to "treat symptoms" rather than underlying causes. Thus, most interventions have been cosmetic and aimed at "political correctness". They have hence failed to achieve a transformation of the existing gender status quo.

For example, gender budgeting and its justification is little understood within central and local government, hence its implementation has been very low. This is epitomized in the statement from an MFPED officer "I need a whole lecture to convince me. Are the needs very different; is there a female hoe and male hoe? This is good … let's allocate more money for you (women) and you will actually work like obuloogoyi (donkeys). If we are farmers we all need crops/seeds and animals. You people you are taking things too far". Hence implementation has been very low. The MoH, MAAIF and MoES have gender officers and MoES has a gender unit and a gender policy, but their budgets continue to be gender blind. The Districts of Kabarole and Mpigi have gender officers who are limited not only in their financial resources but also in gender skills in their efforts to ensure that government pronouncements on gender budgeting are followed.

This study further revealed that there were gaps in donor funding for gender equality enhancement. For instance, the shift from project- to programme-focused aid through the general budget support (GBS) mechanisms raises concerns of how donors can support gender equity. It is noted that increasing the GBS portion of development assistance often means reduced major funding for gender projects. For GBS funds are not necessarily gender-equitable in design and implementation. Ensuring that GBS fosters gender equity concerns rather than threatens them has entailed the need to engage with strong bureaucratic systems and processes. In addition, the need to commit resources to increase capacity for women organizations is still a daunting task for both donors and the government.

On the part of donors, a trend of scarce gender targets among donor countries shows that much of the agriculture aid, for example, did not target gender at all. Only aid given by a few donors including Belgium and Canada targeted gender as a principal objective. Additionally, some donor countries such as Australia, Austria, Belgium, Canada, Germany, Japan, Netherlands and Norway extend aid based on significant objectives. With such little aid based on principal and significant gender objectives, it is not surprising that despite over 80% of women in Uganda being involved in agriculture, they continue to benefit little from agriculture projects. In sum, our findings suggest that the rhetoric of gender mainstreaming outstrips efforts to develop projects aimed at the empowerment of women and gender equality and that the concept may be being used to legitimize a decline in explicit focus on the empowerment of women.

The above mentioned challenges notwithstanding, the prospects for achieving the broader qualitative transformation of gender relations within formal and informal institutions and subsequently empowering women and girls are high. Dissemination workshops held with the health, education and agriculture sectors and with local government officials revealed that officials are willing to implement gender budgeting and mainstreaming if they are conceptually clear about what gender is and are equipped with the practical tools for doing so. Some sectors and local governments even asked for additional workshops to enable them better to understand gender budgeting and mainstreaming. From a gender budgeting perspective, this study noted that there were gaps in the availability of gender disaggregated data, skilled personnel to implement GB and training in all districts. In addition, the study found limited knowledge about the budget process both at the practice and conceptual levels, influencing the budgeting process at the beginning of the budget as opposed to ex-post budget analysis and a focus on women's basic needs rather than strategic needs. Priority areas and outputs remained aggregated and lacked gender specific targets and gender responsive evaluation indicators.

Conclusions

Uganda has the right structures and policies to promote gender equality and women's empowerment but actual implementation is still weak. So, too, is the actual practice of gender budgeting. For example, the process of determining budget priority areas remains unclear even at a national level. Sources of funds to promote gender equality remain largely private. In the long run, the activities of the women's movement should evolve to ensure that national budgets are gender sensitive by placing focus on gender awareness and gender mainstreaming in the budget process at national and local levels. There needs to be re-prioritization of expenditure and re-orientation of programmes within sectors to achieve gender equality and human development and monitoring of government revenue and expenditure to ensure that the inequality gap between females and males decreases. The women's movement should further highlight and ensure the putting into practice of three possible entry points for gender equality in relation to GBS: gender-sensitive indicators could be used in the design of the fixed and variable tranches while executing GBS; gender-sensitive indicators can be introduced in the annual Performance Assessment Frameworks (PAF); and Joint Assessment Reviews (JAR) in GBS and Sector Budget Support (SBS) could be "engendered".

7.3.4 Enumeration of results

The project has produced the following results and outputs:

Gender Responsive Budgeting Component:
The work in the frame of the GRB component contributed greatly to an informed reflection on GRB, national planning processes, development cooperation and new aid modalities. The research results have provided a basis for engagement with public officials, CSOs and other stakeholders, creating networks and opening new possibilities for influencing relevant policy processes. Dissemination activities via the research products listed below have ensured wide awareness of the issues raised, and contributed to ongoing policy debates. Thus, the project work substantially contributed to gender equality and the raising of gender sensitivity in Uganda's planning and budgeting processes, especially in the three focus policy areas of health, agriculture and education.

Policy briefs:
- GRB in the Agriculture Sector: A Tool for Gender Equality and Empowerment of Women
- Changes and Transformation through GRB in the Education Sector
- GRB in the Health Sector: A Pathway to Gender Equality and Well Being
- A Gender Analysis of the National Development Plan and its Implementation Process: The Case of the Agriculture Sector
- A Gender Analysis of the National Development Plan and its Implementation Process: The Case of the Health Sector
- A Gender Analysis of the National Development Plan and its Implementation Process: The Case of the Education Sector
- Engendering the New Aid Modalities in Health in Uganda: Opportunity for the Women's Movement
- Engendering the New Aid Modalities in the Agricultural Sector in Uganda: Opportunity for the Women's Movement
- Engendering the New Aid Modalities in the Education in Uganda: Opportunity for the Women's Movement
-

Research reports and articles:
- A Gender Analysis of the Uganda National Development Plan and Its Implementation Process
- Article: Changes and Transformation through Implementation of Gender Responsive Budgeting in Uganda: The Example of the Education Sector

- Working Paper: Downward Accountability for Gender Equality and Women's Empowerment in Uganda
- Working Paper: Scoping Study on Gender Responsive Budgeting in Uganda
- Gender Responsive Budgeting in Uganda: Scoping Study
- The Wish-List: Gender and the Budget Process in Uganda
- Changes and Transformation through Implementation of Gender Responsive Budgeting in Uganda: The Example of the Education Sector
- GRB in the Health Sector: A Pathway to Gender Equality and Well Being
- A Key for Transformation towards Gender Equality in Uganda: Scaling-up Work on GRB and Planning
- Engendering the New Aid Modalities in Uganda

Furthermore, a wealth of material documenting the work, especially participatory research, dissemination and meetings with different stakeholders is available.

Gender Mainstreaming Component:

At KyU University the project component was focused on organizational and university development and therefore firmly integrated in the university. The high level functioning of the overall project coordinator ensured fluent communication with university leadership.

The Gender Policy has been adopted, including the establishment of a Gender Mainstreaming Unit as a key institution to ensure sustainable implementation. Moreover, there has been a lot of knowledge transfer between appear project partners and considerable knowledge transfer and building of competences on gender analysis, GM and GRB has taken place.

The KyU Gender Policy formulation and approval strengthened the management capacities of all stakeholders involved in the formulation and approval process. The Gender Mainstreaming Programme of the office of the Vice Chancellor is slowly gaining visibility.

- Gender Policy prepared and adopted by the Kyambogo University Council
- Research report and article: Engendering Universities: Experiences and Practices in selected East African Universities
- Research report and article: Engendering Universities: Experiences of Formulating Gender Responsive Policies in Kyambogo University
- Research reports on Gender Mainstreaming experience at five universities
- Tools for conducting gender research and gender sensitive situation analysis have been developed, both at KyU and for affiliated institutions
- Consultation Report on the results of the KyU Gender Policy Formulation Consultation Process
- Paper on Experience at KyU presented at the Conference of the International Association for Feminist Economists (IAFFE)
- Situational Analysis of the gender terrain in KyU affiliated institutions has been carried out and the respective report is available

- Meetings and gender mainstreaming workshops conducted in 4 KyU affiliated institutions to engage in a process of building capacities and sensitize on gender issues in view of development of a gender policy for affiliated institutions
- Training material on GM/GRB at universities
- News reports on adoption of Gender Policy at KyU
- Working Paper: Gender Mainstreaming Experiences and Practices in 5 Universities
- Furthermore, numerous minutes and reports of meetings and workshops held throughout the project period are available

Uganda meets Austria. Project meeting at the Vienna University of Economics and Business: Susanne Dietl, Luise Gubitzer, Elisabeth Klatzer, Consolata Kabonesa, Elke Stinnig, Henry Manyire, Tabitha Mulyambiti, Harriet Kebirungi, Andreas J. Obrecht

Austria meets Uganda. Preparing for a project meeting in Kampala, Uganda: members of the project teams from Makerere University and Kyambogo University welcome the Austrian project team

Elke Stinnig, APPEAR, and Elisabeth Klatzer, project coordinator, meeting with the Village Budget Club in the Kabale District

Enhancing participation in budget processes: Meeting with civil society groups in the Kabarole District

At a meeting of villagers at parish level in the Kabarole District

7.3 Promoting Gender Responsive Budgeting and Gender Mainstreaming

Gender Responsive Budgeting in Practice

Engendering national plans: Researchers prepare for a meeting with the National Planning Authority

Ugandan community worker meets Austrian researcher

Welcome by the Village Budget Club in Kamwezi

... all take part in the welcoming ceremony

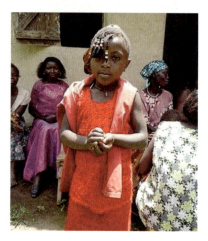

7.4 Promotion of Professional Social Work towards Social Development and Poverty Reduction in East Africa

Project Coordinator: Helmut Spitzer
Coordinating Institution: Carinthia University of Applied Sciences
Partner Institutions: Makerere University, Department of Social Work and Social Administration; University of Nairobi, Department of Sociology and Social Work; Institute of Social Work, Tanzania, National University of Rwanda, Social Sciences and Social Work Option
Partner Countries: Uganda, Kenya, Tanzania, Rwanda
Project Duration: 1 March 2011 - 28 February 2014

7.4.1 The project – PROSOWO

PROSOWO was a multi-dimensional project on the promotion of social work in the East African Community, with a focus on Kenya, Rwanda, Uganda and Tanzania. Social work in these countries is regarded as an upcoming profession which has the potential to play a key role in the development process, yet it faces a number of challenges which PROSOWO aimed to address. Firstly, social work training institutes suffer from a lack of institutional and academic capacities, including a strong research body. Secondly, social work training is mainly based on Western concepts and methods; hence, there is a big gap between theory, education and practice. Thirdly, social work is neither strongly recognized as a profession nor as a scientific discipline. As a consequence, social work educators and practitioners are hardly acknowledged as experts in the socio-political arena; on the contrary, most social workers find themselves dealing with the symptoms of social problems and have only very limited influence on the formulation of policies with regard to poverty reduction and development strategies.

PROSOWO started with the ambitious intention to address these intertwined challenges through a series of activities with the objective of strengthening social work at training, practice, institutional and policy levels. The project had already begun in 2010 under an APPEAR grant for preparatory funding. This grant enabled the team of African and Austrian researchers to conduct a workshop in Nairobi, Kenya, where the conceptual framework and the specific objectives of the project were formulated in a participatory manner.

The multi-dimensional character of the project is mirrored in its conceptual aim, namely to link research, education, practice, policy and capacity building. Consequently, the specific objectives of the PROSOWO project were:

- To strengthen the capacity of higher social work education institutions in the region through research, curriculum development and joint publications.
- To develop sustainable academic partnerships and networks in social work training and research in Africa and internationally.
- To conduct research on the role of social work in poverty reduction towards achieving the Millennium Development Goals.

- To develop more relevant social work curricula in alignment with national poverty reduction plans and social development strategies.
- To facilitate the process of drafting discussion papers on regulating the social work profession for discussions with relevant government authorities.
- To share outcomes of the project with the international social work academia and development stakeholders through publications, symposia and conferences.

In the first year of the project, the focus was on research. Comprehensive empirical field work was conducted in the four partner countries, covering 2,000 respondents (social work practitioners, educators, students, employers, policy decision makers and social work clients at grassroots level). Data were collected through of a set of questionnaires, qualitative interviews and focus group discussions.

As a next step, research findings were analysed and translated into already existing curricula at Bachelor level and/or into the formulation of new Master of Social Work programmes. This exercise turned out to be much more time-consuming than anticipated and is hence still ongoing in the partner countries. It is expected that future generations of social work students will benefit from the indigenous, evidence-based empirical knowledge generated through the project, which will increase their professional skills in handling poverty issues and related challenges in their respective localities and fields of practice.

From the beginning of the project it was envisaged that the project should also result in concrete academic outputs, particularly in terms of publications (both books and journal articles) and conference papers. In the course of the project, six books were published: four national research reports, one fieldwork manual (Uganda only) and a final publication on "Professional Social Work in East Africa", comprising both theoretical perspectives and empirical evidence on social work and its linkages to social development, the realization of the Millennium Development Goals and social equality, including gender equality. These publications will be disseminated to virtually all social work training institutions in the East African Community and serve as key references for social work training and education.

Apart from presenting project-related papers at international conferences in Austria, South Africa, Sweden, Uganda and Hong Kong, the PROSOWO team also launched two symposia (in Kenya and Austria) and one major international conference in Uganda. This conference coincided with World Social Work Day 2014 and attracted 450 delegates from East Africa and many other countries. The conference started with a march on the streets of Kampala to give social work a strong voice and to promote human rights and social justice. The conference gained broad national, regional and international recognition and is regarded as an important milestone in the process of professionalizing social work in East Africa and in the broader African context. At a political level, PROSOWO paved the way for the social work profession to gain more political recognition. A number of workshops and meetings were held in the partner countries to sensitize government authorities on social work and social development issues. It must be hoped that in future more social workers and social work scholars will be consulted with regard to the formulation of social policies, poverty reduction efforts and other instruments of social development.

In a parallel effort, measures were taken to initiate a dialogue on the formulation of a legislative framework to regulate the social work profession. In Uganda and Tanzania, initial steps were made towards the formulation of a Bill which, if all goes well, will lead to the establishment of a Social Work Council, responsible for the regulation of the social work profession.

At an institutional level, PROSOWO contributed to both individual as well as institutional capacity building. All team members have gained a lot in terms of research experience, academic expertise and project management skills. Some team members were promoted in their respective departments or are in the process of being promoted (e.g. from the status of Lecturer to Senior Lecturer). Additionally, three junior colleagues (one from Kenya, two from Uganda) were granted an individual scholarship for PhD studies in Austria.

The project has contributed to fostering a strong identity for the social work profession at the partner institutions. The PROSOWO research with its corresponding publications and events has gained institutional recognition and high visibility at the respective universities. This also applies to the Austrian partner institution.

Last but not least, PROSOWO also had a strong element of strengthening and sustaining South-South partnerships and networks. The team held a series of consortium meetings and regional workshops at different locations in the East African Community, including Burundi. In 2013, a partner institution from Burundi (Hope Africa University in Bujumbura) joined the project as "associated partner". Some elements of the project also liaised with the "Association of Schools of Social Work in Africa" (ASSWA) in order to facilitate an even more institutionally-backed and linked process.

7.4.2 Making cross-national academic partnerships work

by Janestic M. Twikirize

Drawing on the PROSOWO project, the article reflects on the process and nature of cross-national academic partnerships, highlighting the benefits as well as lessons learnt and underscoring the key elements considered to have contributed to the success of the partnership. The article is largely written from a cross-cultural, experiential perspective.

Introduction
International academic partnerships are as old as universities themselves, particularly in the South where many new universities are linked to older ones in Europe (King, 2009). In fact "the growth of social work as a profession in different countries owes much to international collaboration" (Midgley, 2001: 23). Common forms of collaboration include staff and student exchanges, joint research projects and the launching of joint academic programmes. Most of these collaborations have been criticised for focusing too heavily on the uni-directional "transfer" of capacity from North to South, at the expense of genuine partnership, mutual learning and responsiveness to need (cf. Nakabugo et al., 2010). And yet partnerships present immense benefits to involved institutions and individuals.

The PROSOWO project was jointly implemented by four East African and one Austrian higher education institutions with overall coordination provided by the Carinthia University of Applied Sciences (CUAS) in Austria. The four East African institutions included Makerere University in Uganda, University of Nairobi in Kenya, (National) University of Rwanda and Institute of Social Work in Tanzania. The project benefited from APPEAR's preparatory funding which facilitated the development of a joint proposal that was eventually funded. This article traces the partnership from these early stages and, reflecting on the process and nature of this partnership, highlights its benefits, challenges and lessons. The lessons underscore elements that are considered to have contributed to the success of the partnership from a largely experiential perspective.

Building the partnership
Academic partnerships sometimes begin through informal contacts in conferences or other fora which can be harnessed as opportunities emerge. However, someone usually has to take the initiative. This requires zeal and skilled leadership and coordination. In PROSOWO's case, Professor Helmut Spitzer contacted potential partners and followed this up with visits and meetings at the respective institutions. Once the prospective partners had expressed their willingness to participate, a workshop (made possible through APPEAR's preparatory funding scheme) was held with representatives from all the partner institutions that would be directly involved in the planned project. The workshop turned out to be not just a means to an end (proposal development) but also a milestone as far as laying the foundation for collaboration and partnership was concerned. By the end of the workshop the mutual conviction was that even in the worst case scenario, and the project proposal were not to be considered, the interaction had yielded a very strong basis for individuals and their respective institutions to, in a modest way, begin to collaborate through sharing of resources and materials, consultation and mentorship built around the newly enhanced social relations.

Once the project had been approved for funding, an inception meeting provided a concrete opportunity to further enhance the partnership. This meeting, held in Dares Salam, Tanzania, was intentionally left largely unstructured, which allowed for free interaction between the individuals. Whilst the primary purpose of the meeting was to discuss implementation modalities for the project, retrospectively it served a higher purpose of socialization and enhancement of interpersonal relationships. As argued by Freshwater, Sherwood and Drury (2006), face to face meetings are central in building collegial relationships and thus holding such meetings early in the project was very helpful. Subsequent meetings held at least once a year, coupled with regular electronic communication, became a crucial feature of the partnership and helped to strengthen collaboration.

Benefits from the partnership
Besides the specific outcomes directly related to the particular project, cross-national collaborations are associated with a variety of benefits and will "inevitably broaden a person's horizons, enrich their lives, and provide them with both professional and personal networks for life" (Grathwol 2005, cited in Freshwater et al., 2006: 297). Link and Vogrincic (2012: 343

cited in Healy and Link, 2012) contend that international exchanges promoted through such partnerships are essential for "expanding cultural awareness, sharing ways to implement human rights ... cooperating in the development of curricula, collaborating in fieldwork practicum, and generating relationships among students, faculty, and colleagues in ongoing and sustainable ways." These benefits become apparent as one reflects on what has been experienced and achieved through the PROSOWO project. A few of these benefits are elaborated below.

One of the most significant benefits from the PROSOWO project was the expansion of professional networks. Over the three year period, participation in regional and international professional bodies and events such as conferences has increased tremendously both at the institutional and individual levels. Taking Makerere University's department of Social Work as an example, the department had neither been a member of the regional *Association of Schools of Social Work in Africa* (ASSWA) nor of the *International Association of Schools of Social work* (IASSW) until the launch of the PROSOWO project. However, the department had actively participated in the now defunct ASWEA in the 1970s and early 1980s. Thus the joint project reawakened this innate strength and potential of the oldest school of social work in East Africa to once again take up its position in professional networks and linkages both for her own good and the good of others.

Similarly the partnership provided a springboard for regional networking. Whilst a number of Universities in East Africa have individually collaborated with Universities in the North, regional collaboration or South–South partnerships have not been as common. The plausible excuse relates to resource constraints. And yet, through the PROSOWO partnership, a key lesson has been that such south-south partnerships are essential for peer support and mutual learning from comparable contexts and challenges. The PROSOWO East African partner countries are joined together in a political confederation known as the East African community with numerous shared challenges including poverty, disease, illiteracy, conflict and forced migrations among others as well as shared ideals such as the ethic of *community* and *ubuntu*. The confederation presents opportunities to harness our strengths and resources as social work training institutions. Such regional networks can serve as important stepping stones to additional external resources (Koehn and Dement, 2010).

Academic partnerships beget other partnerships and linkages that can be carefully harnessed for the present and the future. Through the PROSOWO project, there were numerous opportunities for exchange visits through which new linkages have been developed both within Africa and Europe. Guest lecturers, participation in conferences and workshops and invited articles and interviews in the local and international press have opened new frontiers for knowledge and experience sharing crucial for professional and personal growth. The underlying benefits of these also directly relate to the increased visibility of not only our respective institutions but also the social work profession which the project was designed to promote in the first place.

According to Koehn and Dement (2010), building research capacity within collaborating institutions in the South is considered a defining criterion of a successful cross-national academic collaboration. This was one of the major outcomes of the PROSOWO partnership.

When we set goals for the project, capacity development with regards to academic publishing was emphasized, to be achieved through joint publications. As a result, many individuals have acquired tremendous skills and competences in this area, culminating in many jointly or singularly published works including a pioneering publication on social work in East Africa (i.e. Professional Social Work in East Africa: towards social development, poverty reduction and gender equality, edited by H. Spitzer, J. Twikirize and G.G Wairire, 2014). The latent capacity in many individuals – including myself – has been awoken, and by the end of the project, I came to appreciate publishing not only for myself but for the other, for the fact that knowledge is better shared and that we learn more through sharing. A related skill enhanced among many participants in the project has been in the area of public presentations at conferences, workshops and other fora.

Lessons learnt

A few very significant lessons have been learnt that will enhance future partnerships. These range from relationship building to communication, intercultural awareness, and the role of leadership in determining the success of cross-national partnerships.

Probably the most important lesson relates to the centrality of relationships in making cross-national partnerships work. The starting point in developing a partnership is relationship building between institutions and the individuals directly involved in a particular project. In the case of institutions, the technical aspects of signing memoranda of understanding are emphasised; but equally important is the quality of the social relationships that develop between participating individuals. Social relationships are embedded in the concept of partnership which "contains strong personal connotations and implies a form of social interaction that is supposed to entail a considerable degree of equality, mutual trust, shared vision, and mutual benefit among the different entities involved" (Obambaa and Mwema, 2009: 355). Thus relationships, even in the context of academic partnership, must be intentionally developed. In the case of PROSOWO the informal contacts between prospective partners and most especially the early identification of individuals that would directly participate in the project was a starting point in developing not just the project's formal (technical) aspects but also its social relationships. The unstructured discussions that took place during the inception meetings naturally delved into issues of culture, difference and diversity – aspects that directly impacted on the dynamics of the partnership and enabled partners to smoothly work through tensions that would arise in the latter stages of the project (see also Spencer-Oatey, 2013).

Another age-old lesson is the importance of effective communication. Open and consistent communication is crucial for joint ownership of decisions and collective responsibility for the direction and outcomes of the project. Communication enhances trust, reduces tension and gives a sense of togetherness and democratic dealings in academic partnerships. And yet effective communication can be a daunting challenge in cross-national partnerships. Besides the hard-core issues such as access to communication facilities, our different cultural backgrounds, coupled with individual personalities can influence the depth and breadth of our communication, how messages are packaged and/or decoded, as well as how fast feedback is given. In the case of the PROSOWO project, our major medium of communication was email and in the later stages of the project, telephone and Skype calls. Given the multiplicity of cultures, language and educational orientations, words and symbols differed even if the main medium of communication was English. As has been argued by Spencer-Oatey (2013), effective communication in intercultural interaction can be particularly difficult "because people may focus on different clues when inferring meaning and/or they may arrive at different meanings from the same clues" (Spencer-Oatey, Isik-Guler and Stadler, 2011, cited in Spencer-Oatey, 2013: 247). Whilst we all understood English, for example, some minor uses of language were not fully understood. For example, "it's up to you" – a commonly-used phrase in the course of the PROSOWO interactions – can communicate freedom of choice and self-determination, but it can also communicate indifference. Such minute differences in language have the potential to create tensions or even inhibit communication unless they are fully understood in the context of socio-cultural and linguistic diversity.

In order to enhance communication and teamwork, it is crucial for partners to cultivate cross-cultural awareness. Wang (2008) recommends an intercultural dialogue "which understands that interactions between individuals from different cultures entail inherited frameworks infused with different perceptions and values ... [D]ialogue offers possibilities for building emergent understandings and new frameworks rather than submission to imported wisdom. The result is a group of educated practitioners with more sophisticated repertoires than agents from both the indigenous and foreign cultures" (cited in Spencer-Oatey, 2013: 247).

Such interactions are based on respect and not merely tolerance and as argued by UNESCO, "equitable exchange and dialogue among civilizations, cultures and peoples, based on mutual understanding and respect and the equal dignity of all cultures is the essential prerequisite for constructing social cohesion, reconciliation among peoples and peace among nations" (http://www.unesco.org/new/en/culture/themes/dialogue/intercultural-dialogue/). In the case of PROSOWO, there were ongoing efforts to engender such dialogue through open and honest communication but also through deliberate steps to hold meetings in different partner countries. Each consortium meeting included some social event as quotididian as going for a walk through the streets, which to some extent exposed participants to the cultural contexts of their respective partners, and also enhanced their level of bonding. An added advantage was that the European coordinator was effectively conversant with the socio-political context of the East African region through previous visits and field research.

Related to intercultural dialogue is the need to guard against *professional imperialism* (Midgley, 1981), where Western ideas and practices are perpetuated through an education system that is heavily dependent on Western theories and texts and where these ideas and practices are viewed as superior. This tendency is largely rooted in a history of colonialism and economic imperialism. The APPEAR programme dictated that one of the partner institutions had to be from Austria, the donor country, thus presenting a risk of perceived imperialism. Instead of romanticising about the equal partnerships, we acknowledged this possibility and openly and continuously reflected on how well we were guarding against it in the collaboration. Team members openly discussed the merits and dangers associated with this scenario and determined as much as possible to uphold the principles of equality, mutual exchange and learning and to minimize any form of impositions from either direction. A crucial step was to ensure joint problem identification, themes, goal setting and evaluation and to respect all knowledge and contributions irrespective of their originator. Such a partnership may incorporate differences in perspective without implying superiority of knowledge or methods of knowing. Notwithstanding the fact that financial resources are usually from the North, effective partnership requires that even "smaller partners are seen as bringing equal value to the collaboration, through resources such as knowledge and local legitimacy" (Wildridge, et al, 2004: 7). The North-South dichotomy can be minimized when partners espouse the principles of equality and the African philosophical ideal of *Ubuntu*, which in turn creates an environment of mutual benefit and enduring North-South, and South–South academic partnerships, rather than asymmetrical relationships.

A final lesson relates to the critical aspect of leadership. A charismatic, respectful, and democratic team leader has a great influence on the nature and outcomes of a cross-national academic partnership. These ideals were particularly evident in the project decision making. Even where members wanted to cede decisions to the overall coordinator, there was firmness on the part of the coordinator that to the extent possible everyone's views had to be listened to, respected and incorporated or that a consensus should be reached regarding issues large and small. A common phrase from the coordinator was "I want to hear from the southern partner", "thank you but let's wait for our colleagues' views". Most of this was through online communication, and yet notwithstanding the potential delays that democracy can create, it became an indispensable ideal in the partnership as it is for politics and institutional governance.

Concluding remarks

Just like any other cross-national, cross-cultural partnership, the PROSOWO project had its highs and lows but on the whole, it has provided immense opportunities for learning and growth both at the personal and institutional levels. This short article has not delved so much into the difficulties faced but they can be deciphered in the overall lessons and experience shared. Issues of different cultural and academic orientations, personalities, difficulties in communication, different working and social political and economic contexts, administrative bureaucratic procedures are some of the hurdles that had to be overcome in order to make the partnership work. Open communication, strong interpersonal relationships, mutual trust and respect of partners, a satisfactory appreciation of different contexts of partners as well as flexibility all contributed to the success of the project.

References

Freshwater, D./Sherwood, G./Drury, V. (2006): International research collaboration: *Issues, benefits and challenges of the global network. Journal of Research in Nursing* 11(4) 295–303.

King, K. (2009): Higher Education and International Cooperation: The role of academic collaboration in the developing world. In: D. Stephens (ed.): Higher Education and International Capacity Building: Twenty-five years of higher education links. Oxford, Symposium books, Pp. 33-49.

Koehn P. H./Demment, M. W. (2010): *Higher education and sustainable development in Africa: Why partner transnationally?* Background paper for the Ministerial Conference on Higher Education in Agriculture in Africa; Kampala, 16 November 2010.

Link, R. J./Vogrincic, G. C. (2012): Models of international exchange: In: Healy, L./Link, R. J. (Eds.): *Handbook of international social work: Human rights, development, and the global profession*. Oxford: Oxford University Press, Pp. 343–348.

Midgley, J. (2001): Issues in international social work: Resolving critical debates in the profession. 21 *Journal of Social Work* 1(1), 21–31.

Midgley, J. (1981): *Professional imperialism: social work in the third World*. London; Heinemann.

Nakabugo, M. G./Barrett, E./McEvoy, P./Munck R. (2010): Best practice in North-South research relationships in higher education: The Irish-African partnership model. *Policy and practice: A Development Education Review*, 10 (Spring), Pp. 89–98.

Obambaa, M. O./Mwema J. K. (2009): Symmetry and asymmetry: New contours, paradigms, and politics in African academic partnerships. *Higher Education Policy*, 2009 (22), Pp. 349–371.

Spencer-Oatey, H. (2012): Managing interaction processes. Maximizing the benefits of international education collaborations. *Journal of Studies in International Education* 17(3), Pp. 244–261.

UNESCO (undated): Intercultural dialogue. United Nations Educational, Scientific and Cultural Organization. Available at: http://www.unesco.org/new/en/culture/themes/dialogue/intercultural-dialogue

Wildridge, V./Childs, S./Cawthra, L./Madge, B. (2004): How to create successful partnerships – a review of the literature. *Health Information and Libraries Journal* (21), Pp. 3–19.

7.4.3 "Mzungu, how are you?"
Reflections on the human element of North-South partnerships

by Helmut Spitzer

"Intertwined histories": Wazungu and counterparts

I have been involved in various development and research projects in differing East African countries in the past 20 years – as individual researcher and consultant, as a member of research teams and as coordinator of the PROSOWO project (Promotion of Professional Social Work in East Africa). While most projects had a national or regional focus, PROSOWO was designed as a cross-national and cross-cultural venture, with stakeholders from universities, practice fields and policy arenas from various African countries and Austria as the European partner. A common term for a European or "white" person in East Africa is *"mzungu"* (plural *wazungu*). This term can have many connotations. Linguistically, it derives from the Kiswahili term *"kuzungua"* which means "to go around"; hence, etymology tells us that the idiom is associated with people who are on the move. Historically, it became a synonym for light-skinned foreigners who seem to have the common feature of travelling a lot. In my view, the term is not racist, but it is certainly linked to both historical and contemporary relations between "North" and "South", between colonialists and those who were colonized, between Europeans and Africans. In this perspective, *mzungu* can also denote a label for somebody who represents wealth, knowledge and power. Many children who see a stranger like me get excited and automatically start calling *"Mzungu, how are you?"* Even after so many years, I still ask myself what I actually might mean to them. Even colleagues in the academic field sometimes call me *mzungu*, albeit in a rather ironic manner.

Although I personally don't care which skin colour a person has, and although I tend to forget that sometimes I am the only non-African when working in an East African context, I identify myself rather well with the term *mzungu*. It helps me to define my own role and also to be aware of my own capacities and limitations. From a self-critical Eurocentric point of view, it also serves as a constant reminder of the different backgrounds and circumstances between me and my African partners.

In development terminology, our partners in the Global South are sometimes referred to as "counterparts". These counterparts are the ones who represent good-hearted people in former colonized countries, endeavouring to bring about change in their imperialistically shattered, poverty-stricken, neo-liberally corrupted contexts. While our mission is usually time-limited, the counterparts live there on a permanent basis, and although we sometimes don't apprehend (or don't want to apprehend) it, they quite often suffer from the same problems we jointly want to deal with when we try to identify our "target groups" in a research or development project.

When looking back, I realize that what I mainly remember after all these years are my concrete counterparts, or more properly spoken, "significant others". People – women, children and men – who impressed me in one way or the other, and who influenced my way of thinking not only with regard to the perception of realities of African ways of life, but also our interconnectedness in a globalized world, or, in the words of Edward Said (1994), our "intertwined histories" on Earth. Many encounters helped me to reflect on the concept of global citizenship, thus helping me keep in mind that we have an ethical responsibility for the realization of human rights and the common good of humankind. The German philosopher Immanuel Kant's categorical imperative can serve as a guiding principle here: "Act only according to that maxim by which you can, at the same time, will that it should become a universal law." The African equivalent to this can be found in the ethical principles of the concept of *ubuntu*, a term denoting humanity and the interconnectedness and mutual responsibilities between an individual and the community, or even society. In essence, *ubuntu* means that all people are one another's keepers (Munyaka and Motlhabi, 2009, cited in: Murove: 63-84).

I also learned that life is actually like a game of dice; I no longer take for granted the twists of fate that meant my children were born in a relatively well-off context in a highly developed country and not in a slum in Nairobi, a rural village in Eastern Congo or a refugee camp in Darfur. In the face of concrete manifestations of chronic poverty, social exclusion and political violence in contexts such as the African Great Lakes region, one's own privileged position may turn out to serve as a catalyst to explore one's options to take action. One of these options is to engage in cross-cultural research, development efforts and advocacy practice with people on the other side of the globe who share a similar vision. For me, the PROSOWO project turned out to be such an option.

From professional imperialism to horizontal dialogue
In social work, the academic and professional field I mainly work in, theory cautions against prolonged "professional imperialism", a term coined by James Midgley (1981) who introduced it to denote the export of Western theories, knowledge systems and concepts to the countries of the South. In fact, such tendencies can also be observed in psychology, sociology and other fields in humanities and social sciences, and most probably also in other scientific realms. This analysis definitely applies to the East African countries where I usually work; a simple visit to a university or departmental library reveals the abundance of foreign social work literature and the almost non-existence of locally generated publications.

I provide two examples from the PROSOWO project which illustrate the actuality of this process. The first example took place in an African context. On one occasion, a student referred to me after I had given a speech where I tried to reflect on the need to contextualize international social work models with regard to their relevance for African contexts. The student was very excited and told me that I had opened his eyes since he now realized that whatever he had been taught so far actually derived from non-African contexts. He sarcastically put it in a nutshell and said that what he had learned so far are the writings of Karl Marx and the Bible. The second example took place in Austria. I invited some of my East African colleagues to provide a guest lecture at a university. One colleague gave a speech about counselling in African contexts, thus referring to indigenous, culture-specific methods. The students and I were deeply impressed. After the presentation, I asked him whether he also teaches the same methods at his home university. His immediate response was "no" – there he mainly relies on literature from Europe and the United States.

So what is the key challenge in this regard, particularly when it comes to North-South partnerships? Firstly, technology transfer cannot work as one-way traffic. Simple dichotomies of who is the owner of knowledge on the one hand and who is supposed to serve as a mere recipient of this knowledge on the other hand must be deconstructed and finally overcome. Rather, such partnerships should be conceptualized in a way that both sides can learn from each other; hence, technology and knowledge transfer should at best be multi-directional (Ferguson, 2005: 519–535), and perhaps even with the priority on South-North instead of vice versa. As well as good intentions, such a view requires reflective skills on the side of so-called donors and other stakeholders. This is a crucial mental prerequisite in order to tackle more concrete manifestations of unequal power relations and the inherent hegemony in existing partnership programmes. Secondly, there must be mechanisms to "decolonize" mindsets in order to overcome a deeply rooted mentality of inferiority and dependence on the side of the Southern partners. This applies particularly to African elites. In fact, the "big men" in Africa (it is still rather unusual to come across a female version of this species) and the *wazungu* experts too often represent an ominous alliance to defend the anachronisms of paternalistic donor-beneficiary terminologies.

In the PROSOWO project, this danger was also apparent. In virtually all East African countries, social work is still a rather weak and under-recognized profession, and social policy measures are very rudimentary compared to historically developed and relatively well-elaborated systems in many European countries. One might think that there must have been a latent temptation to scrutinize the established welfare system of a highly industrialized country like Austria in order to find out what could be adopted in the counterpart context. But from the very beginning, the involved partners agreed upon their common interest in realizing a project that is truly based in and relevant for the respective cultural, social and economic contexts. Although the East African partners had the chance to get to know some universities and welfare agencies in Austria, we actually never spent a single moment in discussing state-of-the-art social work models in the German-speaking realm.

The underlying philosophy of the PROSOWO project – both in terms of content as well as with regard to management issues – can be found in the idea of "horizontal dialogue" which derives from the Brazilian advocate for a critical pedagogy Paolo Freire (1996). This dialogical principle in international partnership implies mutual trust, reciprocal respect and equal participation in decision-making processes, despite the fact that the involved partners come from different intellectual understandings and resource backgrounds. In fact, such an approach is very compatible with the aforementioned concept of *ubuntu*. In theory, many international development projects claim virtues such as participation and dialogue, though in reality such claims too often turn out to be mere lip service. In practice, they necessitate a constant awareness of underlying (sometimes cultural) misunderstandings, mutual projections and tough institutional realities in the Southern contexts which are not conducive to smooth project implementation and which can only be analysed when they are openly shared in an atmosphere of trust. The true power of horizontal communication between the dialogue partners becomes particularly apparent when it comes to conflicts, delays and deviations, because it challenges oneself to be empathetic, self-critical and flexible at the same time. In conflict resolution processes, stereotyped deliberations must be dealt with sensitivity and combined with a joint endeavour to reach a win-win situation. When handling diversity (which is often the case in the field of social work), it is important to critically reflect on both the counterpart's situation as well as the *mzungu* perspective. In the PROSOWO project, this challenge could be seen with regard to issues of culture, religion and gender.

Controversial issues: Culture, religion and gender

In the efforts towards realizing social work models which are both appropriate and relevant for African contexts, culture becomes a key point of reference. Culturally relevant social work must seek tangible ways to incorporate local knowledge systems of coping, resilience and conflict management in professional training and practice. But culture is not only a key to the liberation and empowerment of people; it can also serve as a means of legitimizing existing power hierarchies and classifying certain groups of people, most prominently under the umbrella of traditional and religious norms and beliefs. Sometimes, arguments based on cultural aspects can even work against the fulfilment of fundamental human rights (e.g. female genital mutilation). This is particularly true with regard to gender relations, where women as a group find themselves in a low social status and an underprivileged economic position in the community and in society. The discussion of such issues turned out to be a constant challenge in the PROSOWO project.

To give one example: While it seemed to be a quite easy task to discuss the relevance of gender equality and gender mainstreaming for social work training and practice in academic discourse, some colleagues (as far as I remember, exclusively male) exposed rather conservative opinions in the context of a casual conversation. The challenge was to critically reflect on one's own cultural bias and historical context on the part of the *mzungu*; and on one's own internalized norms and views on gender roles and sexual orientation on the part of the counterpart. These debates and reflections became even more crucial and contentious pertaining to the issue of homosexuality. At a time when the PROSOWO team was about to plan a big social work conference in Kampala in 2014, the controversial Anti-Homosexuality Bill in Uganda was just in the process of becoming a law. Although sometimes hidden or only expressed in a very latent manner, homophobic attitudes even among social work educators became apparent, and views against people with a homosexual orientation were reinforced with anthropological, religious and cultural arguments. What I really admired in the process of these deliberations is the fact that some colleagues seemed to find a fragile balance between the universal principles of human rights' thinking and a flexible handling of cultural norms - which are, by the way, usually very much influenced by political propaganda.

In some East African contexts I observed that basic professional and ethical principles of social work are very much interwoven with Christian approaches. For example, social workers have a professional mandate to advocate rights of sexual minority groups; at the same time, anti-homosexuality is often justified with the Bible. And although the social work profession promotes respect for diversities, I repeatedly found myself in situations where a common Christian prayer was expected to be exercised despite the fact that at least one colleague was Muslim and another one agnostic.

Ownership and sustainability
The PROSOWO project officially ended in November 2014. Amazingly, apart from some minor aspects, all the project's objectives – which had been over-ambitiously formulated four and a half years before – had been achieved. Social work in the East African region is no longer the same. In my view, the most important factor in the success of this project can be found in the intrinsic motivation of a number of individuals – backed by their respective colleagues and, most notably, by their families. From the very first beginning, the team members got passionately involved, demonstrating a strong will to invest much time and energy to get things going.

A crucial moment in the formulation of the key objectives and planned activities of the project was a joint workshop which took place in Nairobi in 2010 where the team came together and spent an intensive week brainstorming project ideas and writing the draft proposal. This was a precondition for the eventual sense of *ownership* among project staff as well as the beginnings of human relationships in which mutual trust and joint action were able to flourish. From my experience, too many proposals are written in offices far from where they are actually supposed to be implemented, and with little or no communication with those whom they are supposed to target or those responsible for putting the proposals into practice. Under such circumstances, it can be no surprise that even brilliantly written papers can just fade away without making any tangible impact.

I would like to take this opportunity to briefly mention some of the sustainable impacts of the PROSOWO project beyond the actual implementation period. When I started to work on this article, I was still full of impressions from a trip I had just made to some East African countries. In Tanzania, I observed immense progress with regard to the professional status of social work. It seems as if the country is a pioneer with regard to the establishment of a legislative framework and a regulatory body for social work in the region. This is particularly noteworthy since Tanzania (along with Rwanda) only served as partners with a limited budget since they do not constitute official partner countries of the Austrian Development Cooperation. Also, the Tanzanian National Association of Social Workers is struggling to reinforce its capacities and to launch another big social work event in East Africa, this time in Arusha (after the much-praised PROSOWO conference in Kampala in March 2014).

In Burundi, I was even more spellbound. A highly committed team of social work educators, students and practitioners managed to establish the first ever national association of social workers in this politically unstable country. Inspired by the Kampala conference, they were able to launch a large social work conference in the almost total absence of financial means. On World Social Work Day 2015, more than 250 delegates marched on the streets of Bujumbura to celebrate the importance of social work and to promote human dignity and worth.

Finally, in Uganda, social work reached a level of political recognition which could only have been dreamed of just a few years before. Following a series of meetings with the Ministry of Gender, Labour and Social Development, the first ever public dialogue on social work was organized in Kampala on World Social Work Day 2015. The objective of the event was to educate the public about the role of social work in advancing positive social changes for the improved well-being of individuals, families and communities. It was also envisaged to call for public sanction of the social work profession and to trigger targeted discussions for government recognition of the profession as key in advancing social development.

Behind all these efforts and achievements lies the power of human capital – individuals and groups of people who can bring about positive change in their societies, given sufficient resources and a joint vision. Here lies the role of international partnership programmes: to facilitate such noble initiatives without necessarily claiming to know which way is the right one, and without imposing concepts which work in one context but which have the potential to fail or even cause damage in others. To be frank, the Austrian social work community can learn a lot from the developments in East Africa. Maybe the next step is to implement a similar project in Austria and to exchange roles of *wazungu* and counterparts.

References

Ferguson, K. M. (2005): Beyond Indigenization and Reconceptualization. Towards a Global, Multidirectional Model of Technology Transfer. *International Social Work* 48(5), 519–535.

Freire, P. (1996): Pedagogy of the Oppressed. London: Penguin Books.

Midgley, J. (1981): Professional Imperialism: Social Work in the Third World. London: Heinemann.

Munyaka, M./Motlhabi, M. (2009): Ubuntu and its Socio-moral Significance. In: Murove, M. F. (Ed.): African Ethics. An Anthology of Comparative and Applied Ethics. Scottsville: University of KwaZulu-Natal Press, Pp. 63–84.

Said, E. W. (1994): Culture and Imperialism. London: Vintage.

7.4.4 Enumeration of results

- Empirical research on the role of social work in poverty reduction and the realization of MDGs conducted (in total 2,000 respondents).
- Revision (informed by empirical research) of undergraduate social work curricula and new courses to be included in proposed Master of Social Work programmes (Kenya and Uganda only).
- Publication of four national books based on PROSOWO research findings (Kenya, Rwanda, Tanzania, and Uganda).
- Final project publication entitled "Professional Social Work in East Africa: Towards Social Development, Poverty Reduction and Gender Equality", edited by Helmut Spitzer, Janestic Twikirize and Gidraph Wairire.
- In total, approximately 1,000 physical copies of project-related publications disseminated to social work training institutions and other stakeholders in the East African Community.
- Production of a fieldwork manual (Uganda).
- 6 journal articles published.
- 32 conference papers presented at international conferences and symposia (Austria, Kenya, South Africa, Sweden, Uganda, Hong Kong).
- Launch of the international social work conference "Professional Social Work in East Africa" (March 2014 in Uganda).
- Launch of two social work symposia (June 2011 in Kenya, June 2012 in Austria).
- Forum on "Social Policy and Inequality" at the Austrian Development Conference (November 2014).
- Attendance at three scientific writing workshops (Austria, Sweden, Uganda).
- Three grants for PhD studies in Austria (one from Kenya, two from Uganda).
- ASSWA membership for Rwanda, Tanzania and Austria established.
- PROSOWO regional network extended to Burundi with Hope Africa University as an "associated partner".

- Realization of frequent consortium meetings, national and regional stakeholder meetings, dissemination and sensitization workshops.
- Several meetings with government authorities held; initial steps towards the realization of a regulatory body for social work made (Tanzania, Uganda).

Presentation of the PROSOWO-book "Social Work in East Africa. Towards Social Development, Poverty Reduction and Gender Equality" on November 12th 2014 in Vienna

Lively participation of social work students at the "International Social Work March Conference" 2014

7. 4 Promotion of Professional Social Work Towards Social Development

Field research in Ruanda

"International Social Work March" in Kampala, Uganda, on Sunday, March 16th, 2014

"International Social Work March" and "International Social Work Conference" supported by APPEAR

The PROSOWO-team

Janestic Twikirize represented the PROSOWO-team at the APPEAR gender workshop in November 2013

PROSOWO grant holders at the Alpen-Adria-University of Klagenfurt

7.4 Promotion of Professional Social Work Towards Social Development

Team members from Tanzania with project coordinator Helmut Spitzer

PROSOWO team together with Vishanthie Sewpaul, President of ASSWA (second from right)

Marching for social justice and poverty reduction

8 THE CONTEXT OF BURKINA FASO

8.1 Elements for a Burkina Faso National Pharmacopoeia: Monographs Redaction and Quality Control of Endangered Antimalarial Medicinal Plants

Project Coordinator: Aline Lamien-Meda
Coordinating Institution: Institute for Applied Botany and Pharmacognosy, University of Veterinary Medicine Vienna
Partner Institution: Laboratoire de Biochimie & Chimie Appliquées, University of Ouagadougou
Associate Partners: Phytofla Burkina Faso, University of Pretoria, University of Graz, University of Lausanne, University of Oxford, Université libre de Bruxelles, Belgium
Partner Country: Burkina Faso
Project Duration: 1 September 2012 – 31 August 2014

8.1.1 The project - MEAMP

The APPEAR project "Elements for a Burkina Faso National Pharmacopoeia: Monographs Redaction and Quality Control of Endangered Antimalarial Medicinal Plants (MEAMP)" was run by a consortium of two universities. The two collaborating research institutions were the Institute of Animal Nutrition and Functional Plant Compounds (TFP), Veterinary University of Vienna, Austria, and the Laboratoire de Biochimie et Chimie Appliquées (LABIOCA), University of Ouagadougou, Burkina Faso.

The project contributed to the establishment of a national pharmacopoeia in Burkina Faso through the redaction of five monographs and the capacity building of medicinal plants quality control by focusing on endangered antimalarial medicinal plants from Burkina Faso, as malaria constitutes a leading public health concern for both adult and infantile populations. Fieldwork, laboratory and bibliographic investigations have been carried out in a multidisciplinary approach (incorporating microbiology, parasitology, toxicology, phytochemistry, botany and ethnology) through a North–South scientific collaboration.

Burkina Faso is a Sahelian landlocked West African country. The climate is of a Sudanian kind, with a short raining season (July to October) and a longer dry season (November to June). The recrudescence of endemic/epidemic diseases such as malaria (occurring mainly during the raining season) and meningitis (dry season) is associated to the alternating seasons. The country also faces the persistent effects of dryness cycles in a context of climate change and environmental degradation.

According to the "Institut National de la Statistique et de la Démographie", the population of Burkina Faso was estimated at 15.7 million in 2010, with nearly 80% living in rural areas. This population is characterized by its youth (e.g. children under the age of 15 account for 46% of the population) and high growth rate (3.1%). The health situation of the country is related to this socio-economic reality. According to the 2008 annual statistical report of the Ministry of health, malaria was the leading cause of infantile death and constitutes a public health preoccupation for the whole population. Limited access to health services for geographical and financial reasons, combined with the poor quality of these facilities, contribute to the promotion of traditional medicine or pharmacopoeia.

The practice of traditional medicine in Burkina Faso has been consecrated by law since 1994 (Law n° 23/94/ADP of 19 May 1994 establishing the code of public health). Since 2001, traditional medicine has been a key component of the various national health policies, particularly the strategic plans against malaria. For that purpose, in 2002 the ministry of health established a department in charge of the promotion of traditional medicine and a national pharmacopoeia. Moreover, a national policy strategy as regards traditional medicine/pharmacopoeia was adopted in 2004. About 3000 traditional healers and herbalists organized in nearly 30 associations are now officially recognized by the ministry of health while the national availability of ameliorated traditional remedies is increasing.

Ethnobotanical investigations carried out in all regions of Burkina Faso have highlighted more than one hundred antimalarial medicinal plants. Some of these medicinal plants demonstrated efficient *in vitro* and *in vivo* antiplasmodial activities on sensitive or resistant plasmodium strains. Despite the relatively abundant literature on local medicinal plants, supported by an institutional environment in favour of promoting traditional medicine in Burkina Faso, there are no national pharmacopoeia documents or monographs on antimalarial medicinal plants currently available. On the other hand, the quality of medicinal plants sold in local markets, including antimalarial plants materials, is not well documented. Special attention must be paid to endangered medicinal plants in the context of the over-exploitation of natural resources and habitat fragmentation.

Since the WHO is actually promoting the establishment of common medicinal plant monographs and as malaria constitutes a leading public health concern for both adult and infantile populations, the MEAMP project's first research activity was a botanical and ethnopharmacological study of antimalarial medicinal plants in three administrative regions of the country: Cascades (Banfora), Hauts Bassins (Bobo-Dioulasso) and Sud-Ouest (Gaoua). It established a listing of plant species used in these regions for the treatment of malaria and also details of endangered species.

The five most endangered plant species (*Argemone mexicana* L., *Cochlospermum planchonii*, *Pavetta crassipes* , *Securidaca longepedunculata* and *Zanthoxylum xanthoxyloides*) have been sampled from 2 region markets (Ouagadougou and Bobo Dioulasso), and from the field of the three surveyed regions. An interdisciplinary approach (botanical, pharmacological, toxicological, phytochemical, antimalarial and antimicrobial) organized into four research activities, was used to comparatively investigate the quality of the collected medicinal plant samples, and also to establish medicinal plant quality control procedure and methods which were disseminated to the surveyed herbalists and traditional healers.

8.1.2. The project's importance

by Aline Lamien-Meda

The MEAMP project was created by two partner institutions with an existing cooperation background. In fact the project coordinator, now working at the northern partner organization (Vetmeduni, Austria), did her master's and PhD degrees at the southern partner organization (University of Ouagadougou, Burkina Faso). With her research background from the University of Ouagadougou, she undertook diverse short-term projects in charge of phytochemical analysis at the Veterinary university of Vienna, which allowed her to improve her knowledge in the field of phytochemistry. During this time, she continued research activities in collaboration with colleagues from University of Ouagadougou. She was convinced that this APPEAR project would provide an opportunity to establish strong collaborative links and develop a partnership between the LABIOCA of University of Ouagadougou and the Institute of Animal Nutrition and Functional Plant Compounds of Veterinary University of Vienna within the framework of research on medicinal plants in West Africa.

MEAMP's focus on medicinal plants came because traditional medicine remains an important part of the contemporary health-care system in African countries, and according to the WHO 2013 World Malaria Report, "an estimated 207 million cases and 627 000 malaria deaths are estimated to have occurred in 2012. There is an urgent need to increase funding for malaria control and to expand programme coverage, in order to meet international targets for reducing malaria cases and deaths."

The project contributed to the establishment of a national pharmacopoeia in Burkina Faso through the redaction of monographs and the capacity building of medicinal plants quality control. Fieldwork, laboratory and bibliographic investigations have been carried out in a multidisciplinary approach (including microbiology, parasitology, phytochemistry, botany and ethnology) through a north–south scientific collaboration. The project also contributed to the preservation of endangered antimalarial medicinal plants by establishing a listing which could be used by the national authority in charge of biodiversity as evidence for the protection of these plant species.

The MEAMP project was a great opportunity to set up a consortium and strengthen the collaboration between the Institute of Animal Nutrition and Functional Plant compounds of the University Of Veterinary Medicine Of Vienna (Austria) and the Laboratoire de Biochimie et Chimie Appliquées (University of Ouagadougou).

MEAMP contributed to capacity building at the southern institution in the following ways:
- Acquisition of additional scientific equipment for phytochemical and cytotoxicity studies
- Training of two postdoctoral researchers
- Training of one PhD student and one master's student
- Workshop training of students and the training of two staff members
- Development of scientific contacts and collaborations with partners from the North

- Development of local expertise in terms of quality control of herbal medicines
- Development of local expertise regarding the redaction of monographs for further contribution to the national pharmacopoeia of Burkina Faso

The two partner organizations exchanged knowledge of research methodologies and shared research samples:
- Transfer of ethnopharmacological knowledge to the northern institution
- Exchange of phytochemical methods
- Project samples collection and distribution between both partner institutions

Each institution learnt much about the specifics of university administration and budgetary administration of internal and external finance sources during the project implementation. By the project's conclusion, each direct project member had gained experience leading their own work package, and the concomitant schism that often exists between prior expectations and real-world feasibility.

The MEAMP project also contributed to the local health organization in Burkina Faso through a beneficial and positive collaboration with Dr. Zephirin Dakyuo (PHYTOFLA, Banfora, Burkina Faso) in the early stages of the project. When project results were communicated back to the surveyed populations of traditional healers and herbalists, who deal with medicinal plants every day, it was seen as a way of revalorization of traditional medicine. The MEAMP project, at the end of its two years duration, had set up a quality control system for medicinal plants at the partner institution and some methods were resituated in practice to Dr. Dakuyo's "Laboratoires PHYTOFLA". Collaboration is in place for a future clinical trial of a phytomedicine used for malaria treatment in Burkina Faso. Various scientific papers regarding the project results are in preparation and will be published as proof of the efficacy of the plant species selected by the project.

In the early stages of the project, members considered the gender participatory aspect by trying to include female students in project activities to give to them the opportunity to afford a university degree. The team itself included three female scientific members: the project coordinator (Dr. A. Lamien Meda), a master's student (Orokia Traoré), and Prof. O.G. Nacoulma from LABIOCA, University of Ouagadougou. The selection of a female master's student came as an amendment to the project proposal which had called for a PhD student, but which proved impossible as there was no one available at PhD level. At the northern institution, three female and one male diploma students participated in project activities.

Gender participation was also observed during the carrying out of the project survey and the collection of samples. During the ethnobotanical survey, 23% of the surveyed herbalists and traditional healers were women, and when sampling medicinal species in plant markets, around 90% of medicinal plants traders were female. These results showed that women are widely represented among the direct beneficiaries of the project (herbalists, traditional healers and medicinal plants traders). In fact, in Burkina Faso and other African countries, the primary health care of children undertaken mainly by women. Research financed by the Netherlands Organization for Scientific Research (NOW) showed that African mothers switch easily between using modern health care services, traditional herbalists and even the medicinal plants grown in their own back gardens. African women's own knowledge of herbs hence plays a major role in the health of their children and grandchildren.

The quality control procedures developed by the project were also taught to a gender assistant from PHYTOFLA, the project's local medicinal plant pharmaceutical partner, in order to help them to improve their quality control system. The same quality control procedures, along with others regarding good collection, conservation and conservation practices, have been written up in a fact-sheet that uses easily understandable French. These fact sheets are dissemination tools which should be translated into different local languages to facilitate dissemination event to gender population. This should be accompanied by gender language facilitators to avoid any self-expression problems among women in a mixed-gender auditorium.

8.1.3. Complexities of implementation and dissemination challenges

by Martin Kiendrebeogo

MEAMP was the first joint research project between the Institute of Animal Nutrition and Functional Plant Compounds (Veterinary University of Vienna, Austria) and the Laboratoire de Biochimie & Chimie Appliquées (University of Ouagadougou, Burkina Faso). Since it was our first experience in the planning and execution of such a project, some of our expectations were perhaps unrealistically high when compared to the results achieved and the complexities of daily implementation in the southern research group.

Financial and budgetary aspects

The University of Ouagadougou, like most southern universities, do not have the financial autonomy to enable them to advance funds to research projects. Planned activities were hence delayed due to the time needed for the administrative and accounting procedures for the transfer of funds by the northern institution and disbursement by the southern institution. Had we been aware of such an issue at the project's inception, we would have planned activities that do not require a high budget for the first semester of the project, and for the first months of each semester, so that any such delays were minimized.

During the project's financial planning, the budget allocated for fieldwork and staffing costs in the southern institution was too low. During implementation, we were obliged to reallocate funds for the fieldwork but were unable to do the same for the staff. Consequently, the southern partner was unable to fulfil all the biological and chemical activities planned within the project documents. Hence, in future we would pay more attention to the budgetary part of the research proposal and the total working time required for each staff member.

Enrolment of females for PhD training

To take into account the gender perspective, we had planned to involve one male and one female PhD student within the project at the southern partner institution. However, given the under-representation of females in scientific university training, we could not find a suitable candidate at the time of recruitment for the PhD position. Finally, we enrolled one male PhD student and one female master's student. We hence did not successfully contribute to the planned PhD training of a female student. However, on completion of her master's thesis, the female candidate obtained a four year PhD scholarship.

Dissemination challenge for research development projects
The challenge for research development projects like those in the APPEAR programme is to generate deliverables that can significantly impact the day-to-day lives of populations. The key issue here is that of properly disseminating achieved results to potential beneficiaries. To this end, dissemination should take into account some social considerations such as the gender perspective and the linguistic aspect regarding the educational level of final beneficiaries. Dissemination should be sensitive to gender and the social specificity of men and women from beneficiary communities taken into account.

It is very important to consider the educational level of populations in designing dissemination strategies. In African countries, populations are mainly located in rural areas and peoples are mostly uneducated. Radio is hence the most suitable mass-dissemination channel for non-educated rural populations, while newspapers and television are more appropriate for educated urban citizens. Proximity dissemination strategies (meetings, non-formal discussions) with policy makers and key persons of local communities (chiefs, elders, etc.) should also be used for additional impact. In all cases, local languages are more suited for non-educated peoples.

8.1.4. Enumeration of results

MEAMP ended with the following results and output:
- Listing of the endangered antimalarial medicinal plants (based on traditional healers perception) from western part of Burkina Faso
- Pharmacological and phytochemical profiling of the top five endangered antimalarial medicinal plants from western part of Burkina Faso
- Quality control information of the selected 5 medicinal plants
- Five monograph drafted
- Research papers: one published paper (Zerbo et al., 2013), two others in preparation
- Training of students: one master's student, four diploma students, one PhD student, 2 postdocs and one assistant from Phytofla
- Listing of traditional healers and related associations from the western part of Burkina Faso
- Dissemination of the project result to the surveyed herbalists and traditional healers
- Technical note about "Good collection and conservation practice of medicinal plants"
- Four medicinal plants fact sheets
- An exchange of scientific methods and biodiversity of medicinal plants between the 2 institutions
- Project management achieved by the 2 institutions with the coordination managed by a female researcher

- Well established technical cooperation with a local phytomedecine producer (Laboratoire PHYTOFLA, Banfora, Burkina Faso)
- Well established scientific cooperation with international partners (University of Pretoria, University of Graz, University of Lausanne, University of Oxford; Université Libre de Bruxelles; Medical University of Vienna)

Cochlospermum planchonii

Pavetta crassipes

Securidaca longepedunculata

Zanthoxylum zanthoxyloides

Meeting with traditional healers in Hauts-Bassins

8.1 Antimalarial Medicinal Plants   215

Meeting with traditional healers in Cascades

Sampling of medicinal plants sold in market

Sampling of S. longepedunculata roots

MEAMP kick off meeting participants

Visit of Burkina Faso embassy in Vienna with project coordinator Aline Lamien-Meda (third from left).

Project coordinator Aline Lamien-Meda

8.2 Sustainable Management of Water and Fish Resources in Burkina Faso

Project Coordinator: Andreas Helmut Melcher
Coordinating Institution: University of Natural Resources and Life Sciences (BOKU), Vienna, Department of Water, Atmosphere and Environment; Institute of Hydrobiology and Aquatic Ecosystem Management
Partner Institutions: International Institute for Applied Systems Analysis Laxenburg; University of Vienna, Department of African Studies; Ministry of Environment and Sustainable Development, Burkina Faso, General Directorate for Fish Resources; University of Ouagadougou, Laboratory of Animal Ecology and Biology; Polytechnic University of Bobo-Dioulasso, Department of Rural Sociology and Economy, Institute for Health Sciences; International Union for Conservation of Nature, West and Central Africa
Partner Country: Burkina Faso
Project Duration: 15 November 2011 - 14 November 2014
Project Website: http://susfish.boku.ac.at

8.2.1 The project – SUSFISH

Burkina Faso is a Sahelian country located in central West Africa. It is ranked in the bottom five percent of all developing countries by the UN Development Index, which signals an urgent need for sustainable development. But that need is challenged by severe natural (chronic water scarcity and episodes of severe drought) and socio-economic constraints. The latter constrain development in various ways: Burkina Faso has one of the world's highest population growth rates, in a nation that already has 6 times as many people as a century ago and poor access to both financial and human capital. For example, almost half the population lives in poverty and only 31% of children complete primary school. As a result, famine is recurrent and chronic malnutrition affects 44.5% of five-year-old children and 13% of women of childbearing age. Thus, attaining food security is central to national development policies and strategies.

In response to threats of chronic water scarcity and episodes of severe drought, 1400 reservoirs have been created since 1950 to provide a dispersed network of water storage facilities throughout Burkina Faso. As fisheries, these reservoirs have also become important new sources of food. However, the dangers of overfishing, intensive agriculture and sedimentation threaten the services (fish, water quality) these reservoirs provide. To establish the sustainable management of natural and man-made aquatic systems, Burkina Faso requires methods and tools for the standardized assessment of the water quality and ecological status of rivers.

SUSFISH was designed to strengthen in-country capacities for science, policy and practice in order to establish a basis for sustainable fisheries in Burkina Faso. This means building scientific capacity to monitor and assess the dynamics of reservoir services, the educational capacity to train scientists and technicians in these concepts and methods, and institutional capacities in management and policy formulation. SUSFISH was implemented by a consortium of eight institutions with expertise in the areas of research, education and development.

Five of the partner institutions are from Burkina Faso, and the remaining three from Austria (see above). Based on research in the biophysical and social, economic and political sciences, the SUSFISH project has established a foundation of knowledge useful for assessing and realizing the potential of sustainable fisheries in Burkina Faso. The SUSFISH project was founded by natural scientists in academia and government to explore the possibility of analysing and then managing fisheries sustainably based on rigorous biophysical science. However, the long history of otherwise technically-sound natural science projects that have suffered utter failure for social, economic and/or political reasons prompted SUSFISH's most prominent innovation: research that included and integrated both biophysical and non-biophysical factors that might help or hinder the sustainability of fisheries in BF. The research established a transdisciplinary knowledge base with inputs from both the natural and social sciences, as well as from a diversity of non-academic sources both within and beyond BF (businesses, NGOs, fishermen and fish mongers). The research focus was further expanded to look for interactions both within and between biophysical and non-biophysical factors using scenarios and systems analysis. SUSFISH research set out to establish a factual basis for sustainable fisheries.

The SUSFISH project has clearly met its overall goal of providing the scientific basis for the making sustainable of fisheries in Burkina Faso. This has been achieved both in terms of the generation of knowledge and the building of capacity able to apply that knowledge. Capacity building has been achieved through the provision of tools (software for analysis and hardware for fish monitoring) as well as training in the use of those tools. Knowledge has been generated in terms of new concepts and facts about Burkina Faso aquatic ecology and society. This new information will serve as a foundational database capable of informing the formulation and implementation of policy, providing benchmark data from which to measure progress and setting of performance level targets for policy and practice. The practical implications of SUSFISH research is that it provides specific knowledge about the sensitivity of certain fish and benthic invertebrate taxa to specific pressures and/or clusters of pressures that offer the data basis for monitoring the presence and impacts of pressures. Overall, SUSFISH surveys demonstrate that parameters such as fish size, abundance and diversity are related to the quality of fisheries and habitat management. Therefore, both fisheries and water can be better managed based on science that rigorously monitors and manages multiple levels: aquatic taxa, the water column, habitat quality and surrounding land uses, and the human activities that generate pressures impacting these aquatic and terrestrial habitats.

8.2.2 A transdisciplinary approach to the integration of people, fisheries, socio-economic factors and higher education

by Raymond Ouedraogo, Moumini Savadogo, Colette Kabore, Gustave B. Kabre, Adama Oueda, Aimé J. Nianogo, Florian Peloschek, Jan Sendzimir, Gabriele Slezak, Patrice Toe, Henri Zerbo and Andreas H. Melcher

Introduction

Back in 2006, Raymond Ouedraogo (MSc for fisheries management), senior manager of capture fisheries and aquaculture at the General Directorate for Fish Resources (GDFR) of the Ministry of Agriculture, Water and Fish Resources (Burkina Faso) was unable to attend a Symposium run by the European Inland Fisheries Advisory Commission (EIFAC) that took place in Austria. Although the regional office of the Austrian Development Cooperation (ADC) in Ouagadougou was unable to fund conference participation, it did advise him to apply to the Austrian North South PhD scholarship programme.

This broader opportunity to pursue doctoral studies was a great opportunity not only for Raymond but also his supervisors, Andreas Melcher and Stefan Schmutz from the University of Natural Resources and Life Sciences (BOKU) in Vienna. The application process was facilitated by a history of networking and cooperation within Burkina Faso (BF) by fisheries experts from several institutions – particularly the former head of the GDFR, Gustave Kabre of the University of Ouagadougou and Aimé Nianogo, the regional director of the IUCN for Central and Western Africa – who contributed support and advice. Raymond attained his doctoral degree in 2010. His doctoral research in Vienna allowed him to expand the network of scientists interested in African inland fisheries from Burkina Faso to Austria (BOKU, University of Vienna, IIASA Laxenburg and practitioners of Burkinabè-Austrian relations, namely Petra Radeschnig and Gritschi Kerl). This network joined the Universities of Ouagadougou and Bobo Dioulasso to provide a broad base of natural and social scientists to successfully answer the APPEAR programme's first call for preparatory projects in 2010. We are grateful to the APPEAR team for this vital initial funding and also for their frequent helpful technical and practical support in submitting a full project proposal.

The formulation of SUSFISH

A vital point during the preparation phase for SUSFISH was a series of meetings in January 2010 in Burkina Faso. All potential partner institutions met to discuss and formulate the project. From the Austrian side, Stefan Schmutz and Andreas Melcher (Applied Limnologists) of BOKU and Jan Sendzimir (System Ecologist) of IIASA came to meet Raymond Ouedraogo (Fisheries), Mrs Kardiatou Kabore (Fisheries Management), Mrs Colette Kabore (Gender and Fish Expert) and Henri Zerbo (Fisheries Management) of the fisheries department, Aime Nianogo and Moumini Sawadogo (Biologists) of the IUCN, Gustave Kabre and Adama Oueda (Biologists and Ecologists) from the University of Ouagadougou, Patrice Toe (Sociologist) and Léon Blaise Sawadogo (Health Sciences) both of the Polytechnic University of Bobo Dioulasso. It is important to mention that the head of the ADA office, Mrs. Elisabeth Soetz and

Yves Desaille took active part in the discussions. In order for partnership to succeed in such transdisciplinary ventures, it is crucial to establish trust and understanding, and these initial face-to-face meetings offered sufficient time to discuss and mutually forge the project's founding concepts and methods. The Austrian partners benefited from the rare opportunity to visit local reservoirs, rivers, landscape villages and people in order to understand the issues of the Burkinabe water and fisheries. As overall coordinators, Andreas and Raymond played key roles in the formulation of the project. Andreas, because of his expertise in international research cooperation. Raymond, because he was able to consider a diversity of contradictory issues in the Burkinabe sphere of water and fisheries in light of the many questions and expectations posed by the Burkinabè partners. Moreover it was not initially self-evident that the many partners, from their various disciplines and speaking different languages could write a consensual document.

Project partners and important team (building) work
Although SUSFISH officially started in November 2011, for administrative reasons related to financial management, the kick-off meeting took place in March 2012. The group visited sampling sites around Ouagadougou and Bobo Dioulasso and visited all partner institutions.

The SUSFISH project united a diverse spectrum of students, experts, stakeholders and organizations. In total more than 100 scientists, students, experts, fishermen and others were directly involved in SUSFISH. This included more than 25 students in Burkina and in Austria and more than 20 researchers from Austria, Burkina, Benin and France, as well as five traditional fishermen, ten drivers and others who became directly involved through attending meetings, training sessions or lectures, doing applied research, participating in the sampling of fish, macro-invertebrates and environmental parameters, driving people for field trips, or by contributing to the accountancy and coordination of the project. Everybody showed great commitment to working together and to sharing knowledge and resources. The coordination between all institutions was effective thanks to planning meetings, annual reports, trimestral meetings of coordinators, two public symposia (one in Austria and one in Burkina), as well as both virtual and face-to-face communication.

Meaningful cooperation took place between all SUSFISH partners in three main dimensions: As well as the obligatory North-South and South-North partnerships there was also a fruitful exchange between Southern partner institutions and the Northern partners. It was the first time that all institutions in the North and the South had worked together in this constellation and we grew to be more than just project partners, to become trusted friends.

A very good illustration of the close cooperation between the Ministry, the UO and BOKU is when four Austrian students stayed in Burkina after the rainy season in 2012 in order to work with colleagues of UO. A basis for this cooperation was the newly installed Memorandum of Understanding between UO and BOKU. The students were sent by a BOKU (KUWI) scholarship to Burkina to sample fish, benthic invertebrates and environmental parameters for their master's theses and to train Burkinabe students in standardized sampling methods and analyses. Consequently the Ministry granted the sampling team a car and a fishing machine free of charge for their field trips for data collection. The Southern partners assisted each other in implementing activities. For instance, in 2012 four Austrian students from BOKU stayed in Burkina for about three months to work under the supervision of the UO. Because the UO had a scarcity of means of transportation, the GDFR allocated them a car free-of-charge, with SUSFISH only having to meet the fuel, insurance and technical costs (which came to less than 200 Euros altogether). Without this contribution, the UO would have had to rent a car for 75-100 Euros per day. In addition, the UO was granted access to the electric fishing equipment and other materials of the Ministry.

Partner institutions often cooperate in study design and implementation. This was the case between (1) the GDFR, the Department of Rural Sociology and Economy (University of Bobo-Dioulasso) and the UO and (2) the UO and the Institute for Health Sciences of the University of Bobo Dioulasso. The cooperation was enlarged to include other APPEAR-funded projects, like MEAMP in Burkina Faso and other institutions. In so doing, the national coordinator took part in the workshop to launch the second project and in the workshop to formulate a third project where he gave a presentation on the difficulties encountered by SUSFISH and the solutions the project had found. SUSFISH was an opportunity to strengthen relationships between the French IRD, the French cultural centres in Vienna and in Ouagadougou, the University of d'Abomey-Calavi (Benin) and many Embassies (of Burkina in Vienna, of France in Vienna and in Burkina).

The wide range of project partners also became a resource in terms of technical questions regarding project implementation. The acceptance of differences and the sharing of capacity allowed SUSFISH to overcome serious obstacles. For example, for administrative reasons it was not possible to comply with rules for projects managed by governmental institutions. This administrative constraint was overcome thanks to the contributions of all partners. In the beginning SUSFISH was designed to be fully managed by the GDFR. However, administrative constraints meant this was not possible if the project were to follow the governmental rules for project management. As a solution, the management was shared between the IUCN (mainly responsible for finances) and the GDFR (mainly responsible for administration). Later on, the national coordinator, Raymond, left the GDFR to join the Institute for Environment and Agriculture Research (INERA) but continued to fulfil his project functions. Each partner institution took decisions according to the requirements of their domain of expertise and the administrative procedure with which they were confronted. Where decisions regarding the broad direction of the entire project had to be made, however, the two coordinators conducted direct discussions. From time to time, communication and understanding suffered for reasons all-too familiar in Africa and especially Burkina: poor telephone and internet networks making it difficult to reach people and exchange documents. In one case, it took a week to have a Skype meeting.

Understanding requires taking into consideration partners' respective communicative needs. In addition to differences in disciplines, levels of education and in cultural and administrative backgrounds, SUSFISH also had to overcome obstacles in communication. English only partly served as the language of scientific cooperation and research. In practice, Burkina Faso's official language of French, as well as Moore and Jula were important modes of communication. This multilingual context meant that translation and interpretation played a major role in facilitating understanding. Equally, however, the openness and flexibility of all team members to work in a context of changing linguistic priorities contributed largely to the successful progress of SUSFISH.

The transdisciplinary team & disparate levels of understanding
SUSFISH was formulated and implemented by a transdisciplinary team that included senior and junior scientists (ecologists, sociologists, experts in health and nutrition and gender experts), stakeholders in fisheries management, as well as practitioners such as fishermen and fish processors. Each expert was fully responsible for the organisation of their work according to what was developed in the contract that was signed. In each discipline, the team members showed various levels of research and working experience and they referred to a wide range of scientific and expert knowledge. In order to integrate all these different approaches and perspectives, SUSFISH encouraged peer-to-peer learning in the field. The aim was to give consideration to the other's perspectives and to explain their own. In so doing, the team members shared their disparate, sometimes even conflicting ways of understand-

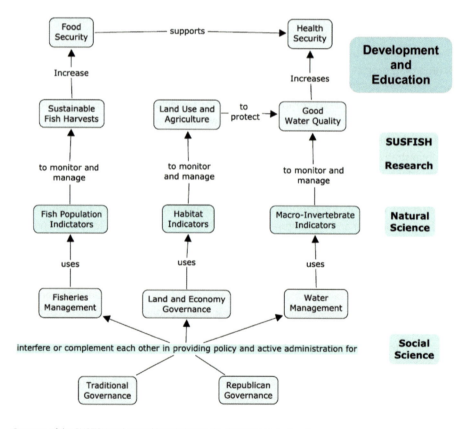

Structure of the SUSFISH project and its relation to development and education

ing. This became particularly important when sampling fish in changing water bodies. While local practitioners such as fishermen focus on catching the biggest fish, their assessment of appropriate species and sampling places diverged from the aims of the participating fish ecologists, who worked under the premises of standardized field collection. It was the responsibility of every member to explain and understand how the strategies of data collection could impact the results.

To acknowledge such special efforts, the team created a special SUSFISH Award in July 2014 for the excellent work of junior scientists within the project. The funding was organized through redistribution of an Austrian prize for the best thesis in fresh water ecology, and the prize aimed to promote the continuing research of early-career scientists in their respective disciplines. A SUSFISH team of junior and senior scientists jointly developed an application process and a set of evaluation criteria linked to the SUSFISH's transdisciplinary aims. A scientific committee evaluated the applications. The award ceremony was held in Ouagadougou during the final symposium in July 2014 and showed SUSFISH's commitment to applied research: eight laureates were honoured in all disciplines. Level of academic achievement was not the only criteria to define excellent contributions: at the final symposium in Ouagadougou (15-16 July 2014) a scientific committee recognised the excellent contribution of the fisherman "Doum Doum" with the SUSFISH Award in the category "best field work".

Gender perspective

At all career levels, the low level of participation of women in ecological science remains a challenge for research projects such as SUSFISH. Following the results of the SUSFISH project's evaluation workshop (March 2013), a workshop was organized between the project members to analyse socio-structural factors and consequences of gender imbalances within SUSFISH. During the last project year activities were carried out to focus on a gender-sensitive analysis of structural and social causes of disparities in the fisheries, both on a practice as well as a management level. Our case study findings highlighted the importance of women as players in the management of financial and natural resources management within this sector. But this importance is restricted only to the local level, as the interests and needs of women are hardly represented at regional or national level.

In order to contribute to a gender-sensitive research agenda in ecological sciences SUSFISH focused on two main areas:

- Providing information about gender disparities in socio-ecological research linked to the formal Burkinabe education system (e.g. primary and secondary education). In this context we note the cooperation with the ministry for women and gender to develop a strategy to integrate gender issues in curricula development.
- Continuing to strengthen the participation of female researchers in research practice at the project level.

Efforts and concrete measures were implemented to integrate a gender perspective into the project in both areas. At the conceptual level, an expert in gender was part of the SUSFISH staff and guided such project activities as research protocol development, data processing, reports and thesis writing. To increase the awareness of SUSFISH staff regarding gender, we organised a special workshop in June 2014. This was also the start of a new Gender Strategy submitted to the Ministry. The success of this strategy can be clearly seen in female participation in SUSFISH events: In the kick-off workshop in 2012 the number of female applications was very low. However, in 2014 six female students graduated successfully within the framework of SUSFISH, and at the final symposium of Ouagadougou 24 presentations were given by female researchers. In addition, because of the SUSFISH project's research focus on integrating gender issues into our research agenda, SUSFISH staff worked closely with important stakeholders for women's affairs in fisheries and water management. As a result the presentation of project results to the public in July 2014 attracted a wide range of female actors and decision makers, e.g. the President of the national union of fish processors was present.

Conclusions and outlook

SUSFISH allowed the production of reliable information that will be used to improve the governance of water and fish. For illustration, the listing of fish species is a legal and technical requirement that had never been fulfilled, and SUSFISH proposed a list of species. The development of the Red List of fish will give insight for diversity conservation, not only for fish but for other species as well. The consideration of local communities' opinions in fisheries will be improved via the process of decentralisation that started one and half decades ago. As for education, networking and future cooperation, the memorandum of understanding signed with BOKU is an important asset. Moreover, the equipment purchased by SUSFISH will continue to be used by the Burkinabe institutions. SUSFISH results on food security and nutrition were used to develop training manuals on the use of fish in diet and to train women in the Sindou, Banfora. In addition, finally more than 200 fishermen, more than 50 female processors of fish and about 75 local and national fisheries staff gave their time to be interviewed and hundreds more interested persons and experts attended SUSFISH events, discussions, meetings, workshops and symposia in Burkina and Austria. All these advances in concepts, data, skills acquisition and equipment serve as a solid foundation for the re-establishment of the sustainable governance of fisheries and aquatic ecosystems as a post-revolutionary government takes shape in the coming years.

8.2.3 Joint research and scientific exchange for higher education

by Gabriele Slezak, Adama Oueda, Philippe Cecchi, Gustave B. Kabre, Otto Moog, Raymond Ouedraogo, Florian Peloschek, Léon G. Blaise Savadogo, Stefan Schmutz, Jan Sendzimir, Patrice Toe, Herwig Waidbacher and Andreas H. Melcher

Introduction

To participate as a scholar in an applied research study is an important experience in a student's career. That is especially so if one can contribute actively to a greater transdisciplinary research project that explores the methodological and technical frontiers of applied science. In aiming to develop an innovative and adaptive assessment of the integrity and long-term sustainability of water quality and fisheries in Burkina Faso, SUSFISH presented this peculiar opportunity to more than 20 students from Burkina Faso and Austria. While conducting data collection in the field as an integral component of the project, students learned to work in teams with junior and senior researchers in diverse study areas all over the country. They conducted their own field research assisted by the team members and supervising staff. Finally, as shown in the concluding symposium in July 2014 in Ouagadougou, all these case studies from junior researchers constituted an important contribution to the broader project results. Because both natural and social science issues were examined in a wide range of examples from all over the country, it was possible to shed light on the complexity of natural resource management in Burkina Faso.

Practice in field work

The SUSFISH project required students to improve their skills in developing and applying social and natural scientific methods in the field. Multiple field trips over the project's duration offered ample opportunities to gain practical experience in data collection on fish and benthic macro-invertebrate species freshwater habitats, governance of water resources and social practices. This meant intensive training in data collection and analysing methods as well as developing an approach for measuring techniques adapted to the socio-ecological environment of reservoirs in Burkina Faso. For instance, existing protocols were adjusted to the local conditions and requirements so as to develop field protocols that are sensitive to specific Burkinabè characteristics.

Ecological and biodiversity approaches

In natural sciences scholars at various levels were trained to undertake surveys of fish and benthic macro-invertebrates all over the country. This included training on standardized field collection techniques and sampling gears, species identification and enumeration methods as well as on analyses using aggregated biological attributes or quantification of the numbers of key species. Furthermore the field work was embedded in joint preparatory activities and data processing measures after collection, such as laboratory work to identify and control quality for fish and macro-invertebrates taxonomy. On-site activities were linked to workshops on the utilization of Red List criteria and categories in order to contribute to the evaluation of the conservation status of fish species at the national level for the first time ever in Burkina Faso. Thus SUSFISH students contributed significantly to (a) the development of standardized sampling and new assessment methods, (b) capacity building for applied ecology education based on peer-to-peer learning, (c) capacity building in monitoring of the fish and benthic invertebrates assemblage as an integral component for biodiversity studies and of water management in Burkina Faso.

Socio-political approaches
In the social sciences, students got the opportunity to work on issues of fisheries management, governance, society and local fishing as well as fish processing practices within the larger framework of the institutional cooperation of several university departments and the ministerial body GDFA – the General Directorate for Fisheries & Aquaculture of Burkina Faso. In terms of research practice they experienced transdisciplinary and explorative approaches in social, economic and political science by developing a set of quantitative and qualitative data collection methods, and subsequently by coordinating and adjusting data analysis to the team's focal research interests. SUSFISH partners from various academic and political institutions provided flexible supervision in accordance with the particular implications and dynamics of the applied participatory approach. For instance, gender expertise was integrated in the research agenda in the form of workshops for junior and senior scientists. This included training on gender-sensitive field collection techniques, identification methods of factors for gender imbalances, implementation of participatory- and awareness-raising strategies in field work as well as on focusing on gender issues in data analyses. As a result SUSFISH field studies featured a noteworthy emphasis on gender issues in fisheries, nutrition, health and natural resource management, which contributed generally to applied gender research in Burkina Faso.

Ways of knowledge sharing and dissemination
During SUSFISH, much effort was spent sharing knowledge between team members as well as between SUSFISH partners and others. At the beginning of the project, many methodological workshops were organized to formalise the methodology.

During the kick-off meetings in Ouagadougou and Bobo-Dioulasso in March 2012, experiences from Burkinabe and Austrian experts guided the final choices of study sites and the calibration of sampling methodology and study design as well. Austrian lecturers then offered theoretical and practical courses in scientific methods for assessing the ecological status of bodies of water and applied statistical analyses to all interested students. These courses were given whenever Northern partners visited Burkina. In addition the SUSFISH team and students attended statistical (SPSS) workshops organized by our APPEAR partner project MEAMP (Elements for a Burkina Faso national pharmacopoeia: monographs redaction and quality control of endangered antimalarial medicinal plants). To give support to all these (indoor) courses, field training was also given during March and November 2012 by the Austrian and the Burkinabe partners.

From October to December 2012, four master students and junior lecturers, funded by an additional BOKU KUWI scholarship, arrived from BOKU to support and train Burkinabe students in practical fieldwork, study design and data management. This was an opportunity for students to engage in peer-to-peer knowledge exchange. Both groups of students shared knowledge in order to widen their grasp of international standards in limnology and aquatic sciences, especially as they apply to the semi-arid conditions in Burkina Faso. It was and is very important that the Burkinabe PhD students were additionally trained in scientific thinking and writing by English native speakers and scientists from US, France and Austria, implemented through additional advanced courses, proof-reading and co-authorship. Scientific working visits to museums and universities in Vienna and elsewhere in Europe gave opportunities to strengthen scientific networks and the capacities of SUSFISH partners. The students shared knowledge with taxonomic experts (e.g. fish, mollusca, hemiptera and coleoptrera) and were trained in species identification, preservation & sample storage and labelling approaches. Through the implementation of SUSFISH, workshops, conferences and meetings provided a framework within which to share experiences, views and knowledge. Those meetings were a way to share information with other national and international partners external to SUSFISH, stakeholders and policy makers. For the broader dissemination of SUSFISH results, conferences were organized on topics such as "Water and Fisheries Management in Burkina Faso" and "Gender Perspective in Fisheries". Journalists, national radio and television were also present at the symposium in Ouagadougou 2014 which resulted in the wide dissemination of SUSFISH results to a nationwide audience.

Partnership and collaboration

Proper but flexible management of SUSFISH made the wide range of partners an asset in adapting to changing conditions and in developing a comprehensive overview of BF fisheries that embraced both natural and social sciences. SUSFISH started with seven full partner institutions and a further two became associated during implementation (the national office of IRD, the University Abomey-Calavi of Benin, the Natural History Museum in Vienna, the Africa Museum in Tervuren Belgium and the Centre for Systems Solutions in Wroclaw, Poland). Wherever possible there was also intensive exchange between the two Burkinabe APPEAR projects SUSFISH and MEAMP. These partnerships led to a network that crossed disciplinary boundaries at various levels (scientists-scientists, scientists-politicians, scientists-practitioners, administrative officers-development workers). This network became more fully integrated during the implementation process than had been originally planned at the beginning of the project. A good example of this is the institute LBEA at UO, which established new relations or strengthened existing ones with the Burkinabe partner institutions. Such ties arose from the need to co-supervise students (UPB, BOKU) across disciplines or to share material or competences (DGRH, UPB, IUCN). By the project's completion, cooperation had been strengthened in many ways: between SUSFISH Austrian partners and Burkinabe partners, between SUSFISH national partners (Burkina Faso), between SUSFISH partners and other Burkinabe institution, between SUSFISH partners and other international (European) institutions between SUSFISH national partners (Austria). These strong partnerships resulted in significant career development at several academic levels: 17 MA theses, two PhD projects and one *veniadocendi* (*aggregation* or habilitation) for our colleague, Dr. Leon Savadogo at UPB. SUSFISH cooperative research and its results contributed to the latter explicitly by facilitating scientific publishing, training, participation in research projects, presentations at scientific conferences and symposia, partnerships, as well as the supervision of students' theses and dissertations.

Transcultural research practice

To work as a student or researcher in the field of development research requires training in understanding complexity. But how do we approach complex and changing systems? In natural sciences we examine patterns of behaviour (trends, statistics), mechanisms or inter-relations that hypothetically explain that behaviour, and potential development pathways, dynamics that illustrate the implications of our assumptions about those mechanisms and patterns. In social sciences we analyse the different actors along their social interactions and representations. But in both approaches the personal involvement of the researcher is crucial to the whole process. The SUSFISH team of experts understands research to be an interactive process, which is – in addition to interactions in the field – crucially shaped by the researchers' personal factors such as biography, languages, social class, nationality and gender. Therefore at all levels of cooperation we encouraged the exchange of ideas and debate in order to negotiate the meaning of the terminologies inherent in the various scientific disciplines or trainings present in the team.

This aim was initially significantly reinforced by the students' preparedness to participate in foreign research contexts. The two PhD-students from Burkina Faso, who are partly studying in Austria and the four Austrian MA students who studied in Burkina Faso as well as the 13 Burkinabe MA students in Burkina formed a group of young scholars who wanted to reflect different research contexts. Together they had the opportunity to experience practical constraints and learn how to integrate this transcultural experience into the research process. It resulted in a joint data corpus as a basis for several new research questions on bio-assessment and the management of Burkinabè water bodies and fisheries. At the end of SUSFISH, the first generation of publications and theses demonstrates an impressive contribution from junior scientists based on the data jointly collected during field work. This aim was fully reinforced at the conclusion of SUSFISH in exercises of scenario development and conceptual mapping that integrated observations from all project partners.

System analysis – room for discussion

In this respect SUSFISH applied participatory research methods to develop scenarios as ways for experts and partners to examine the dynamic implications of the facts and questions generated by the project. Such exercises allowed participants to reconsider their assumptions and questions in light of the dynamics that they anticipated, and it further allowed elaboration of what particular variables and parameters ought to be measured to better understand how the system is changing. As such, these exercises will inform future research agendas. Our research focus was further expanded to look for interactions both within and between biophysical and non-biophysical factors using scenarios and systems analysis. Self-evidently, the group discussions on results from natural and social sciences as well as from a diversity of non-academic sources (businesses, NGOs, fishermen and fish mongers) were intensive and lasted several days, but they helped us to establish a transdisciplinary knowledge base for sustainable fisheries. By using conceptual mapping exercises we examined the possible structures of relations that might underlie the dynamics. These efforts were important to identify how some partners imagine concepts or patterns of relations and how they would propose to analyse them in the future. In short, these participatory methods enhanced our ability to reflect upon ourselves as parts of a transdisciplinary team.

Conclusion

One of the most important lessons learnt was that communication in meetings, workshops and symposia is very important to strengthen partnerships and encourage the sharing of resources. In particular, student exchanges should be highly promoted in such transdisciplinary research projects because they lead to effective sharing of knowledge, resources and experience and also contribute to the reinforcement of local institutions' capacities. Further, another important lesson we learned was that a project's design should adequately consider joint research activities for junior (and senior) scientists, allocating adequate financial resources and flexibility in terms of time and coordination for joint and continuous supervision. It is obvious that these efforts should be embedded in a greater process of discussion and with the involvement of the whole project team. To conclude, system analysis should be a core element of project design as it facilitates the integration of diverging and even conflicting research results and moreover enables a clearer overview and summary of the project achievements for the partners themselves.

8.2.4 Enumeration of results

- More than 75 fish species and 61 families of macro-invertebrates have been identified and their spatial distribution described in Burkina Faso's first common list. Auchenoglanis gen. and Hydrocynus gen could be used as sentinel genera. Clariassp and Sarothorodonsp increase with pressures, unlike other species, e.g. Alestessp and Schilbesp., which are sensitive and decrease in number as pressures arise.
- The first time pressures on aquatic ecosystems were classified and recorded in a scientific database located at the University of Ouagadougou. Fish and benthic invertebrates based assessment methods for waters under human pressure are under development.
- Discovered important differences between the communities of benthic invertebrates in rivers and reservoirs. Water plant habitats exhibit a higher richness and diversity of taxa than sedimentary habitats.
- Showed biological assessment of bodies of water in Burkina Faso to be feasible. Two possible ways were considered: 1) adapting an existing method, or 2) developing an original methodology.
- Definition of reference sites in typologically similar rivers and areas. Ascertained that a

larger dataset comprising good, moderate and bad sites in different areas is necessary for future investigations.
- Showed that habitat and human pressures influence biodiversity.
- Increased knowledge about fish and benthic invertebrates – sampling method, taxonomy, distribution, ecology, and conservation status. Adaptation of determination keys for BF.
- Development and implementation of a standardized monitoring system is necessary to protect waters and the environment.
- A national metadatabase with information on fish, fisheries and aquatic environment is developed: virtual and physical databases and libraries were identified. A minimum of 205 references were recorded, covering fish, fisheries, legislation, gender, aquatic biodiversity and red lists of fish and macro-invertebrates. More than 13 000 individual fish were sampled and stored.
- Adequate biological assessment methods enabling policy makers and managers to enforce appropriate management plans will help to raise public awareness for the protection of water sources.
- An official (IUCN red) list of fish species and invertebrates and a national database of metainformation on existing biophysical characteristics of fisheries, the diversity and conservation status of fish species and benthic invertebrates, the pressures on fish populations and methods of water assessment based on fish and macro invertebrates are under development.
- The population of direct fisheries stakeholders is estimated at about 32,700 persons (14% are women and 82 % men), 3,000 fishmongers (54% are woman). Between groups of stakeholders some disparities in the access to fish resources are noticeable: man vs. women, allochthon vs autochthons, and youth vs. elderly. As a consequence preliminary results show unequal representation in decision-making committees and restricted access to information about laws, regulations and rights in the fisheries among those groups of society.
- The SUSFISH project aimed to integrate gender issues at all stages of research. This approach required new networks, new forms of cooperation to accord equal status to both genders, and target women explicitly as important actors. During the reporting period the project team decided to focus on this challenge and to use gender sensitivity in order to contribute to a better understanding of social practice, complex interrelations of power relations and strategies of inclusion and exclusion in the fisheries and water sectors.
- The results of social science research show first, that macro-level policies and legislation are not known at regional and local levels. The national organization in charge of fisheries is unknown as well because no tangible activity is undertaken in the field or to target the direct stakeholders. The field police fisheries officers (foresters) are not inclined to work on fisheries in the areas of monitoring, surveillance and control. As a result, prohibited fishing methods are increasingly used. Second, both "republican" e.g. European democratic, and traditional institutions make relatively important contribu-

tions to the governance of water and fish resources. But the two systems have to be harmonized.
- Fisheries management report submitted to the government (e.g. fisheries undertakings and their negative consequences like stocking are not known at regional, provincial and local level, meaning that an adjustment of policies, legislation and institutions must be undertaken towards sustainability in fisheries management).
- The stakeholders are organized in familial units of production and processing, and organized in local, provincial, regional and national association.
- Strategy for the integration of gender in the fisheries and water management was developed and submitted to the ministry (e.g. role of men and women in fisheries and fish processing, economic activities of women like loans to fisherman, trading).
- Women who fish and process fish earn 464,966.67 F (709 Euros) per year, which represents 84.5% of their total income. More than half of the money is used to feed the family. Women involvement in fisheries contributes to improving the diet quality and especially to reduce the number months where the household is in food insecurity.
- For the first time SUSFISH analysed the income situation in fisheries. Fishermen have usually several economic activities, from fishing a fisherman earns about 7.7 Euros/day.
- Poor hygienic conditions surround fish products. Consequently at microbiological level, Staphylococcusaureusis abundant mainly on smoked fish, faecal coliforms and fungus. We also found Shigellasp., E. coli, and Salmonella sp. in some fish. Fried and toasted fish were not contaminated by parasites, but we noticed a massive presence of Mucidae larva on smoked fish, trematoda and some nematoda on fresh fish.
- Biological, social and economic implications due to the creation of reservoirs.
- Two dualistic frames are met in the management of natural resources: the republican system that is legal and the traditional one that is legitimised.
- Strengthening cooperation between partners institutions within Burkina and International (e.g. Benin, Ivory Coast, Belgium, France CIRAD, USA and Austria)
- We observed that in Burkina Faso, fish intake contributes to improving food and nutrition security. Income from fish sales also helps improve the household food and nutrition security.
- As for capacity building and education strengthening, about 23 students (2 doctoral) and more than 20 masters) have been involved in SUSFISH. Several others are expected to be assisted.

Wetlands around the city of Dori in the Northern part of Burkina Faso. A fisherman is collecting fish from his nets while his wife with their baby on the back is washing carpets on the shore

Big elephants having a rest at a reservoir in the protected ranch of Nazinga close to the border with Ghana

A young fisherman proudly presents an impressive and endangered African tiger fish (Hydrocynus vittatus) on a tributary of the Nakanbè river

Frozen rare giant fish, called "aba aba" (Gymnarchus niloticus) at a fish market in Ouagadougou

Fresh rare giant fish, called "aba aba" (Gymnarchus niloticus) at a fish market in Bobo Dioulasso

The SUSFISH students take a shower at the waterfalls close to Banfora in the Western part of Burkina Faso

Around the area of Bobo Dioulasso the African catfish (Clarias gariepinus) are waiting to be fed. They are protected, because they are considered a holy species

Burkinabe and Austrian students are trained to sample fish. They are implementing the so far unknown electric fishing method in Burkina Faso

Traditional cast net fishing for commercial purposes at one of the big reservoirs in Koubri, south of Ouagadougou

Traditional cast net fishing for scientific habitat assessment purposes at one of the free-flowing river sections below Koubri, south of Ouagadougou

Local fishermen in their hand-made wooden traditional canoes casting their nets after the rainy season at one of the big reservoirs in Koubri, south of Ouagadougou

A Burkinabe student is trained by the national SUSFISH coordinator Raymond Ouedraogo in how to sample fish. They are implementing the so far unknown electric fishing method in Burkina Faso

SUSFISH excursion in Austria 2013, visiting the Danube Hydropower station at Ybbs: K. Kabore, P. Toe, A. Oueda, G. Kerl, K., Mano, L. Savadogo, K. Krieger, R. Ouedraogo, F. Peloschek, M. Savadogo, H. Zerbo, J. Sendzimir, A. H. Melcher, J.L. Steffan, I. Kabore

A local fisherman and two Austrian students on the road to sample fish at the protected Nazinga ranch, close to the border with Ghana

SUSFISH final symposium in Ouagadougou July 2014: SUSFISH PÉCHE – EAU, Sustainable Management of Water and Fish Resources in Burkina Faso

Women cutting fish and preparing them to be sold at the local market close to Bagre

Women and children are washing clothes in the ancient city centre of Bobo Dioulasso

The Austrian SUSFISH team, the local SUSFISH coordinator, the president and representatives of the provincial fisheries association from Lake Bam in Kongussi

Project coordinator Andreas Melcher and the Naba (chef de village at Lake Bam) during a discussion about fisheries and impacts on livelihood

Raymond Ouedraogo and Gabriele Slezak discussing with an eighty-year-old fisherman about changes over time at Lake Bam

Visiting the holy crocodiles 20 km west from Ouagadougou

At the final symposium 2014, Adama Oueda from the University of Ouagadougou, his students and Raymond Ouedraogo from the Ministry of Science are honouring the local fisherman "Doum Doum" for his fantastic support during all sampling seasons

8.2 Sustainable Management of Water and Fish Resources in Burkina Faso

Students from the University of Ouagadougou are sampling fish in Koubri, using electric devices

With the support of Prof. Otto Moog students from the University of Ouagadougou and the BOKU are sampling benthic invertebrates and adapting their field protocol

A local fisherman is controlling his net in a small reservoir not far from Bagre

9 THE ETHIOPIAN CONTEXT

9.1 Academic Partnership on Legal and Human Rights Education

Project Coordinator: Wolfgang Benedek
Coordinating Institution: University of Graz, Institute of International Law and International Relations
Partner Institutions: Ethiopian Civil Service University, Institute of Federalism and Legal Studies, Addis Ababa University, Center for Human Rights
Partner Country: Ethiopia
Project Duration: 1 October 2011 – 30 September 2013

9.1.1 The project - APLHRE

The number of universities in Ethiopia has dramatically increased in recent years. This has brought new opportunities as well as challenges. In particular, the new universities are in urgent need of qualified staff as well as infrastructure for the various study programmes they offer.

Cognizant of this, the project "Academic Partnership on Legal and Human Rights Education", or APLHRE, was developed as a partnership between the Ethiopian partner institutions and the Universtiy of Graz, Austria, to cover the following five academic core activities:

- Short Term Exchange Visits (co-teaching of guest professors from Graz in the South and mutual short-term research visits)
- Assistance in Curriculum Development
- Organization of two Legal and Human Rights Academies
- Problem-oriented joint research and publication of research results
- Supervision of Ethiopian PhD candidates at the University of Graz

The wider objective of the project was to improve the academic, research and management capacities of the Ethiopian partners in the field of legal and human rights education. This coincided with the implementation of the Democratic Republic of Ethiopia's latest Five-Year Development Plan, which gave special attention to the development of the education sector.

Initially, the project was to run for two years, from 01 October 2011 until 30 September 2013, but it was extended for a third year, until 30 September 2014, at the request of the partner institutions, in order to enable them to implement the entire range of planned activities, including those which could not be finalized during the initial phase of the project.

9.1.2 The project and its people

by Christian Pippan

Context

Ethiopia, arguably East Africa's political and (together with Kenya) economic powerhouse, is struggling to maintain the momentum of transformation more than twenty years into its journey from repressive dictatorship to democratic rule. Well-minded cooperation partners in the West and elsewhere, who are serious about supporting Ethiopia and its people in realizing the promises of political transition and reform, are thus called upon to reinforce their contribution to domestic efforts at capacity and institution building, particularly in the field of human rights and good (democratic) governance. Indeed, while much can be said about the elusiveness of the concept as such, the overall objective of "good governance" is intrinsically linked to the legal framing and practical application of individual human rights and freedoms and has become a matter of course in contemporary political, developmental and legal discourses. The United Nations, for example, have repeatedly recognized a transparent, responsible, accountable and participatory government, responsive to the needs and aspirations of the people, as a *sine qua non* for the full realization of "all human rights for all" (and vice versa).

In national settings, therefore, any enterprise working on the promotion and protection of human rights will also need to systematically analyse the respective roles of the rule of law, popular participation, accountability, transparency and so on, not only as mutually reinforcing principles and norms, but also as a set of performance standards against which the actions of key players in society are evaluated. Such an approach is all the more imperative in Ethiopia, where governance priorities are now formally concentrated on the promotion of human rights and freedoms, as well as on entrenching national policies that endeavour to curtail over-centralization of state power, enhance the accountability of leadership, consolidate democratic institutions and strengthen people-centred processes. Among the various recent socio-economic and political reform initiatives of the Ethiopian Government, one of the most promising with regard to sustainable good governance concerns the effective quality enhancement of the domestic higher education sector, which is marked by a steady growth in the number of public universities (since the mid-1990s the number has increased tenfold to more than 20 universities today). With the adoption by the government of a 5-year Growth and Transformation Plan (GTP) in 2011, Ethiopian universities and other higher education institutions have been encouraged to critically assess and, as a result, improve to the extent possible their contribution to the national vision – set out in the GTP – of developing Ethiopia into "a country where democratic rule, good governance, and social justice reigns".

The project

Organized under the general topic "Academic Partnership on Legal and Human Rights Education", the recently concluded project was initiated and formulated in response to the specific partnership demands of two renowned academic institutions in Ethiopia: The Center for Human Rights (CHR) of Addis Ababa University (AAU) and the Institute of Federalism and Legal Studies (IFLS) of the Ethiopian Civil Service University (ECSU). The Institute of International Law and International Relations (IILIR) at the University of Graz (KFUG) served as the coordinating organization in Austria under the OeAD's APPEAR programme. From the outset, the project targeted the prevalent gaps and needs regarding (international) law-based human rights studies at Ethiopian universities and other relevant stake-holding institutions and was guided by the overall goal of delivering positive inputs to Ethiopia's governance and human rights discourse, *inter alia*, by revealing the connection between relevant good governance parameters and the realization of internationally and domestically recognized human rights norms.

APLHRE eventually became a 3-year project, running from Autumn 2011 to Autumn 2014 (including a one-year, no-cost extension). In operational terms, the academic partnership aimed to address the acute teaching, research and management challenges of the two Ethiopian partner universities through five core activities: (1) facilitation of short-term exchanges in teaching and research, (2) implementation of problem-oriented joint research, (3) organization of (two) summer schools (entitled "Legal and Human Rights Academies") for selected students and local staff, (4) assistance in curriculum development at AAU and ECSU, and (5) facilitating the PhD studies of Ethiopian junior staff at KFU Graz. Taken together, these activities aspired to enhance the academic (research and/or training) capacities of the southern partners, thereby aiming to contribute to their efforts in meeting the above mentioned public demands regarding the implementation of national development strategies.

At the time of the formal completion of the project at the end of September 2014, eight teaching visits (4 to ECSU-IFLS; 4 to AAU-CHR), based on a co-teaching methodology whenever possible, had successfully taken place. Nine researchers from the partner institutions in Ethiopia (4 from ECSU-IFLS; 5 from AAU-CHR) conducted research visits at the University of Graz during the project period (each of them having been in residence at KFUG for one month). Two Human Rights Academies, involving (in total) more than 50 participating academics, students and practitioners, were jointly organized by the project partners and carried out at the premises of AAU-CHR in September/October 2012 and September/October 2013, respectively. Likewise, two problem-oriented legal and human rights research workshops were jointly conceived and implemented at the premises of ECSU-IFLS (each for one week) in October 2012 and October 2013, respectively. The papers presented at these workshops were developed into a book entitled "Ethiopian and Wider African Perspectives on Human Rights and Good Governance" (edited by Benedek, Pippan, Woldetsadik and Yimer), which was eventually published by Neuer Wissenschaftlicher Verlag, Vienna in 2014. Additionally, a number of MA and LLM curricula (all of which include courses on human rights) have been reviewed and revised during the project period (4 LLM curricula and one MA at AAU, two LLM and one MA at ECSU), using relevant input from IILIR-KFUG as appropriate. Finally, complementing the above mentioned core project activities, two staff members (Kalkidan Negash Obse and Wondemagegn Tadesse) of one of the partner universities

(AAU) have successfully enrolled as PhD candidates and are currently pursuing their studies at the University of Graz.

The people

All partners perceive the project to have been exceptionally successful, but none of the above mentioned project outcomes would have been possible without the engagement, flexibility and oft-tested willingness to go the extra mile of all the people involved at the various stages of project implementation. At the beginning of it all stood the idea of two Ethiopian postgraduate students – Mohammud Abdulahi (then PhD candidate at IILIR) and Mesfin Ayele (an LLM candidate in KFUG's Diversity Management and Governance programme) – to apply for funding under the Austrian Agency for International Cooperation in Education and Research's (OeAD) APPEAR programme. Univ.-Prof. Wolfgang Benedek, Head of the IILIR at KFU Graz, took up the initiative and, following the proposal's acceptance in June 2011, served as the responsible Project Coordinator for the full duration of the project. He was assisted in his role by the author of these lines, who served as Assistant Project Coordinator, as well as by several part-time (student) assistants occasionally designated to perform specific project-related tasks (Reinmar Nindler, of IILIR, deserves special mention here due to his extremely important contribution to budgetary aspects of the project).

Ethiopian universities are very dynamic in their staff recruitment – the person in charge of a project at one point may no longer be available at another. This happened within the framework of the present project, particularly in the early phase of its implementation. Thus, the initial coordinator for AAU-CHR left the university and was replaced by a new coordinator, Tadesse Kassa Woldetsadik, in 2012; likewise, ECSU-IFLS's director was replaced, also in 2012, by the Institute's current director and local coordinator, Solomon Abay Yimer. However, none of these changes had any fundamental effects on the partnership. Early on, the two southern partners distributed lead role responsibilities between themselves and committed to implementing all project activities on the basis of a joint implementation agreement. Accordingly, they carried out all activities and covered all project costs in close co-operation with each other and in liaison with the coordinating institution at KFU Graz. In practice, all matters for decision were communicated and decided jointly between the three partners, either via email or directly in coordinator meetings in Graz (during the kick-off event at KFUG or subsequent research visits) and Addis Ababa (during teaching visits, the HR academies and/or the research workshops). From the point of view of the project coordinators in "the North", the working environment has been outstandingly cooperative and constructive during the entire life span of the project, which was greatly advanced by repeated personal contact and the friendly, welcoming and professional attitude of our Southern partner institutions and their respective staff.

9.1.3 The importance of the cooperation

by Tadesse Kassa Woldetsadik

Context

The national educational system of Ethiopia has long been fraught with complex problems relating to relevance, quality and equity. Against such a background, the Education and Training Policy of the Federal Democratic Republic of Ethiopia (1994) featured as one of its objectives the enhancement of education with the aim of strengthening the individual's and society's problem-solving capacity, ability and culture, and of integrating education and training with development, mainly by focusing on research. Successive educational sector development programmes have since been applied and, quite recently, Ethiopia's Growth and Transformation Plan has resolutely concentrated on how to bring about qualitative and quantitative change in the education system.

The overall strategy followed in this regard has been to provide good quality higher education to larger numbers of students, equitably but with diminishing dependence on public resources in the longer term. Higher education has been conceived as a key component of the national capacity-building programme, which emphasizes human resource development, the improvement of working systems and institutions in order to facilitate decentralization, democratization and the overall development of the country. In the past two decades, sustained investment in higher education infrastructure and the dramatic expansion of public universities offering legal and human rights education have been justified on the basis of such broader considerations.

Among other measures, this has required careful coordination at various levels of implementing institutions, the provision of continuous capacity development training both locally and abroad and the establishment of exchanges and partnerships with patron organizations and foreign academic institutions that command resources, expertise and experience in educational leadership, management and governance. It was within this broader context that the idea of instituting a project that assists the initiatives of public universities in Ethiopia was conceived and a specific proposal submitted to the Austrian Government. Coincidentally, since 2010, the Austrian Government has been implementing, through its Development Cooperation schemes, a new strategy to support demand driven higher education, research and management partnerships between Austrian universities and academic institutions in selected priority countries from the South.

Focusing on complex thematic issues involving human rights and good governance in national and regional contexts and the particular roles of higher education institutions in this regard, this current North-South cooperation was initiated and formulated in response to specific partnership requests from two academic institutions in Ethiopia, namely the Institute of Federalism and Legal Studies (Ethiopian Civil Service University) and the Center for Human Rights (Addis Ababa University) in collaboration with the Institute of International Law and International Relations (University of Graz).

Factors that prompted the partnership
Despite the welcome expansion of such higher education institutions in Ethiopia (with no less than twenty universities today offering legal and human rights education or running various forms of clinical and legal aid programmes) and in spite of the national policy's clear direction with regard to the role of education in deepening democratic and human rights values and in accelerating overall development, the educational system remains beset by multifaceted problems. The absence of effective planning, management, resource allocation and utilization capacity within academic institutions has been pervasive; professionals possessing deeper insight and qualifications in the subject matters of human rights curricula have been in short supply; opportunities for significant research capable of impacting national policy frameworks and thinking have been very scarce; appropriate professional development programmes for academic staff have been poorly organized; and, in many cases, the minimum level of human and financial resources required to achieve the stated objectives of national policy have been lacking.

In such a context, the realization of one of the key objectives of the educational sector development programmes and the GTP itself – making Ethiopia a country where "democratic governance, human rights and social justice reigns through the free will and involvement of its people" – becomes an uphill undertaking. Comprehensive and concrete measures need to be adopted to enhance the organizational and academic competence of higher education institutions in the country. The crucial role of academic and research partnerships with northern institutions, which in the past have served as vital platforms to kick-start and vitalize Ethiopia's higher educational system, continues to constitute a fundamental mark of "intervention", helping address some of the above stated limitations.

Project rationale and organization
These shortcomings of the educational system led the APLHRE partners to design a project that would contribute to the southern partners' transformation into national centres of excellence in legal and human rights education, enhance their capacity in human rights education, training and research, improve their research and publication competence relevant to the national developmental enterprise and, most importantly, draw on the professional and physical resources of the northern partner, made accessible through the implementation of a formal partnership arrangement.

In light of these considerations, areas of collaboration were clearly identified, with each point of partnership intervention fulfilling a specific set of objectives.

- Short Term Exchange Visits: this scheme entailed visiting professors from the University of Graz co-teaching in the master's and PhD programmes of southern institutions. It also involved short-term research visits by academic staff from the southern partnering institutions to the University of Graz.

This activity presented two notable advantages. Firstly, it created a platform for sharing the extensive teaching and research experience of professors from Graz with their often junior counterparts at ECSU and AAU. Secondly, the research visits of Ethiopian academic staff to Graz enabled the former to benefit from the conductive research facilities at the University of Graz, enabling junior staff from the Southern partners to further their research free from the overwhelming routines of administrative responsibility that they are expected to handle in tandem with academic functions at their home universities.

- Legal and Human Rights Academy and Research Workshop: the need to include this constituent in the proposed project was prompted by the necessity of providing high end intensive training on a variety of issues relevant to human rights and good governance for Ethiopian junior academics, teaching in public universities and other stake-holding organizations (both governmental and non-governmental). This forum was meant to acquaint participants with contemporary developments in the field of human rights and good governance and, hence, to extend their academic and research competences in these fields. By involving a small number of Austrian students in the academy, the cultural dimension and international networking objectives of the scheme were also adequately taken into consideration.

On the other hand, the research workshop was expected to engage young academics based in the two southern partner institutions and other Ethiopian universities in supervised research on the overall theme of "Ethiopian and Wider African Perspectives on Human Rights and Good Governance". The resulting research output was subjected to rigorous review by competent professors from Graz, ECSU and AAU, published internationally and distributed to all stake-holding institutions, both domestic and abroad. This problem-oriented research undertaking was meant not only to augment the research skills of Ethiopian academics, but it was also anticipated that the final product would have an influence on relevant national and regional policy discourse and, hence, contribute in one way or another to Ethiopia's long-term development in the field of good governance, human rights and rule of law.

- Admitting Ethiopian PhD candidates at the University of Graz: this component of the project aimed at creating an opportunity for academics in the two southern institutions to enrol in PhD programmes at the University of Graz and hence assist in the key intervention area of capacity development. Given that ECSU and AAU have together been entrusted with the unique national responsibility of proffering graduate programmes that contribute to the realization of Ethiopia's multifaceted developmental objectives, staff capacity development at the institutions themselves has become an inevitable prerequisite in this regard.
- Finally, the curriculum development component of the project has helped to revise and update, with the assistance of the University of Graz, three curricula (two LLM and one MA) at ECSU as well as five curricula (four LLM and one MA) at AAU. This further contributed to APLHRE's general vision of enhancing the Southern partners' capacity in the field of legal and human rights education.

9.1.4. Enumeration of results

The project has achieved the following main results:
- Two members of AAU-CHR are enrolled for their PhDs at the University of Graz. They are successfully pursuing their studies.
- Eight co-teaching visits were conducted which contributed to the project's overall capacity building objective. Four were conducted at ECSU-IFLS and four at AAU-CHR. They have benefited 112 students at ECSU-IFLS and 29 students at AAU-CHR, while the teaching capacities of 6 local co-teachers have been enhanced.
- Nine research visits by academics from the Ethiopian partner institutions (four from ECSU-IFLS and five from AAU-CHR) were carried out at the University of Graz during the project period.
- Two Human Rights Academies were organized and fifty-one academics, students and practitioners were trained. Forty of the trainees were young Ethiopian academics, students and practitioners from fifteen universities (including the two Southern partners) and from four legal and human rights practicing institutions in Ethiopia; eleven were Austrian students from the Law Faculty of the University of Graz.
- Two one-week Legal and Human Rights Research Workshops were jointly organized and successfully held in Addis Ababa during the time of the Human Rights Academies.
- One book (jointly edited by project partners) and one human rights training manual have been produced, published and disseminated.
- The book, entitled "Ethiopian and Wider African Perspectives on Human Rights and Good Governance" (edited by Benedek, Pippan, Woldetsadik and Yimer; Wien 2014), represents the research outcome of the project and was published by Neuer Wissenschaftlicher Verlag (http://www.nwv.at/). 250 copies of the book were distributed to libraries of Ethiopian universities which have law schools and/or human rights centres and to several practicing and research institutions in the country.
- The training manual is being printed in Ethiopia in and will be made available to users at the AAU-CHR, the ECSU-IFLS and a wide range of academic and practicing institutions.
- Eight existing curricula for MA and LLM programmes on or including human rights have been revised. Three are curricula for MA and LLM programmes including human rights at ECSU-IFLS; five are curricula for MA and LLM programmes on or including human rights at AAU-CHR and AAU School of Law.
- The teaching, research and management capacities of more than fifty junior and senior academics at various Ethiopian universities have been enhanced as a result of the project. They have acted in several capacities: as co-teachers in the co-teaching visits; as trainees and trainers in the academies; as presenters and discussants in the research workshops; as contributors and co-editors of the published book; as contributors, reviewers and editors of the human rights training manual; as organizers of the various project activities; and as co-managers of the overall project.

Team meeting at the beginning of the project activities

Legal and Human Rights Academy at the Addis Ababa University

Lecturers and students of the Academy

Dr. Heinz Habertheuer from the Austrian Embassy in Addis Ababa welcomes the participants of the final workshop

Project coordinator Prof. Wolfgang Benedek (left) passes the attendance certificates of the Human Rights Academy

9.2 Strengthening Rural Transformation Competences of Higher Education and Research Institutions in the Amhara Region, Ethiopia

Project Coordinator: Michael Hauser
Coordinating Institution: University of Natural Resources and Life Sciences, Vienna (BOKU), Centre for Development Research (CDR)
Partner Institutions: Bahir Dar University, University of Gondar, Amhara Region Agricultural Research Institute
Associate Partner: Sustainable Natural Resource Development Programme in North Gondar
Partner Country: Ethiopia
Project Duration: 1 February 2011 - 31 January 2014
Project Website: http://transact-ethiopia.com

9.2.1 The project - TRANSACT

The TRANSACT project is a joint initiative of two Ethiopian universities, one agricultural research organization, one Austrian-funded rural development program and one Austrian university. The main objective of the project was to strengthen the transformation competences of the Ethiopian consortium partners in research and training. Such transformation competences demand institutional capacities that translate into new partnerships and learning alliances, allowing higher education and research to become more effective development partner and community service providers in North Gondar.

This is important, because in North Gondar there is an untapped potential for social, economic and technical transformation that would gradually improve the lives and livelihoods of farmers. Potential changes include technical improvements in agricultural and natural resource management and the realisation of new income opportunities, which could lead to a transformation from socially unjust rural worlds where farmers live in poverty to a rural society of equality and prosperity. The realisation of this potential requires public and private actors to join forces with rural communities.

In realizing the importance of science and technology for the transformation of the country and its people, who are of largely rural and poor, the Government of Ethiopia has uncompromisingly expanded higher education and research institutions in the country. Higher education and research institutions, however, have met serious capacity constraints in their efforts to meet the expectations of the government. They lack the essential human and institutional capacities required to conceptually and methodologically address research, training and especially communication of research findings that might reach the rural communities. Primarily, their training and research approach is disciplinary, while farmers are subsistent smallholders running all sorts of agricultural activities including crops, livestock, horticulture, forest plantation, natural resources management and marketing, under the same unit of management with very limited land-holdings of less than a hectare each. In addition, the agro-ecologies within which smallholder farmers manage their various agricultural activities are extremely diverse and variable. The experiences, insights and priorities of farmers remain divorced from higher education and research, while farmers and rural communities do not actively participate in such higher education and research systems.

In order to be good development partners for the government and to become effective contributors to agricultural development and rural transformation, higher education and research institutions, and especially the local partner institutions, critically require new capacity in the field of rural transformation competences. The TRANSACT project helps universities to respond more effectively to transformation opportunities among farmers in complex and risk-prone rural areas. A particular emphasis of was placed on learning and human behaviour, as well as communication and collective action, especially in connection with societal interactions that mediate change. This foregrounds capabilities to coach farmers during transformation processes. Hence, the project created much more effective linkages between research, higher education and extension. Its specific objectives were:

- To adapt existing methodologies and develop new ones for inter- and transdisciplinary research, training and outreach that can facilitate institutional learning and rural transformation.
- To develop the human and institutional capacity of Gondar University, Bahir Dar University and ARARI (Amhara Region Agricultural Research Institute) in education, research and outreach, enabling them to facilitate intended transformation in rural areas.
- To generate knowledge for understanding and facilitating institutional learning, rural-transformation and change in the Amhara region.
- To institutionalize self-reflective learning procedures and methodologies across disciplines, as well as units both within and beyond partner institutions, in order to sustain transdisciplinary academic partnerships.

The project was coordinated and managed by a team of contact persons from the partner institutions. Similarly, interdisciplinary teams made up of members from all the partner institutions implemented the project activities. In its planning, the project was anchored by the following innovative participatory aspects: the development of interdisciplinary skills, enhancement of transdisciplinary skills, putting research-into-use and adoption of a territorial approach to learning. During implementation, the project consortium tackled challenges using a participatory approach.

The concepts of multi-stakeholder participation and interdisciplinary and transdisciplinary cooperation in international academic capacity building were new for all partners. Regarding the terms of inter- and transdisciplinarity, the project followed definitions used in the academic context of Central Europe, though even there these terms are often defined differingly by differing institutions, or even by differing departments, faculties and disciplines within the same institution. This confusion also exists in African institutions. However a lot of emphasis was given to those terms (e.g. Transformation Reader, linkages work shop, several key notes, and so on) throughout the project. Cooperation across a large number of institutions with different epistemological and working cultures creates multiple opportunities for mutual learning experiences. TRANSACT provided experts from the participating universities and research institutions with an opportunity to realize concepts of stakeholder integration, transdisciplinarity and interdisciplinarity. Although understanding of these concepts may still differ, the last 18 months of TRANSACT achieved major progress.

Intercultural cooperation across two continents is not possible without some friction. Indeed, intercultural competences and sensitivity accrue from experiences made in partnership projects as TRANSACT. It has to be admitted that several quarrels arose among the consortium on thematic orientation, management issues, team composition, budget allocation and others. For the team, consisting of Ethiopians and Austrians with highly diverse personal backgrounds, these situations were critical. In February 2013 TRANSACT reached a critical juncture; it was precisely at this point that everybody in TRANSACT closed ranks and managed a turn-around in the project's fortunes. Nonetheless the project achieved cooperation across a large number of institutions with different epistemological and working cultures, creating multiple opportunities for mutual learning experiences and increasing intercultural competences.

Transformation was the project's main theme, but to reach a common understanding of transformation is actually a long-term process. It requires a change of thinking, behaviour and action that is hard to achieve in a multi-partnership project of short duration. Nevertheless, debates about the term's meaning and the manifold activities of TRANSACT had a profound impact on how many consortium members think about transformation. For many the change in how they worked together was huge, and it is highly appreciated that TRANSACT enabled this.

9.2.2 Ensuring sustainable agricultural development, enhancing transdisciplinary skills and developing interdisciplinary competences

by Kibrom Mengistu Feleke

Background
Ethiopia is one of the poorest countries in the world, heavily struggling to combat poverty and attain food security. Agriculture is the mainstay of Ethiopia's economy, contributing about 56% of the country's GDP, over 90% of export earnings and accounting for more than 83% of employment, input for agro-processing industries. As a result, sustainable agricultural development receives special attention from the Ethiopian Government. The agriculture sector is characterized by the following features: a high dependency on natural rainfall; a subsistence type of production; high population pressure on agricultural land; shrinking plot sizes; soil degradation and nutrient loss which appears to lead to low productivity; minimum use of productivity enhancing inputs; limited innovation in agricultural technology, and; inadequate participation from the private sector.

In sum, the sound performance of the agricultural sector is fundamental for food security, for social and economic stability in Ethiopia and hence agricultural production is an extremely sensitive issue. A key to the development of Ethiopian economy, therefore, lies in the transformation of the rural sector in general and the agricultural sector in particular. Rural transformation is all about changing the overall quality of life in rural areas, necessitating investments in pro-poor sectors such as: education, health services, and physical rural infrastructure; access to rural financial services; formulation of policies that uphold greater gender equity and the empowerment of the rural people through safety-net programmes; and improving input-output market access to smallholder farmers and strengthening their participation in product value chain. In general, rural transformation must address core issues that include: reducing poverty and inequalities created by previous policy decisions and social structures; ensuring food security; rural economic diversification; strengthening rural-urban linkages; universal access to basic public services; and wider access to efficient and sustainable financial services, without which the benefits of the rural transformation cannot be fully realized.

Understanding the rural sector's multidimensional problems, the Ethiopian government has invested considerable effort in boosting agricultural productivity through several consistent policies and strategies since 1994. The policy framework is largely based on *Agricultural Development-Led Industrialization* (ADLI), the central pillar of Ethiopia's development vision since the 1990s. In order to improve the performance of the agricultural sector, ADLI introduced a menu-based extension package and expanded access to rural credit, infrastructure building, as well as other development initiatives. Next came the five year Growth and Transformation Plan (2011-2015), which introduced the *Agricultural Transformation Plan* (ATP). The strategic directions of ATP focus largely on smallholder farmers and pastoralists who need to efficiently use available modern agricultural technologies to increase productivity and production. With the goal of expanding Ethiopia's international exports, ATP also encourages the private sector to increase its share of investment in agriculture. The government has also pursued a national policy of particularly promoting participatory watershed development to enhance watershed-based agricultural production.

Despite the previously mentioned challenges, there has been promising progress in the agricultural sector performance at least since 2003 (~10% AGDP growth 2003- 2011). The economy has grown on average by 11% per annum since 2003; the average annual growth rate of AGDP exceeds by far the CAADP target of 6% and agricultural investment as a share of total government expenditure is above 15%, to take just two example indicators. Such achievements in the last decade have mainly resulted from high level government commitment, coordinated efforts from development partners, attractive prices for food and cash commodities and new institutional arrangements. However, more must be done in order to improve agricultural productivity and ensure the transformation of the agricultural sector.

As part of a country that faces natural resource quality decline, chronic food shortages and malnutrition, universities and research institutions are required to support rural transformation and develop future management and policy scenarios in preparation for forthcoming changes that are likely to take place in rural areas. Over the past 15 years, higher education, agricultural research and extension has expanded enormously in Ethiopia. Following decentralization, regional agricultural research institutes, centres and stations have also flourished across the country. Similarly, agricultural extension has been structured from the national to the local village level and, at least in theory, reaches farmers and resources users effectively. In practice, however, the following three observations must be made:

- Despite their huge expansion, higher education and research have not yet brought any marked differences in agricultural productivity or improvements in the livelihoods of poor small-scale farmers.
- Undergraduate training is conducted along disciplinary lines, with little attention given to the integration of different disciplines.
- Universities and research institutions have been slow to adopt appropriate reforms, which prolongs the gap between academia and practice.

Anticipating likely changes is conceptually and methodologically challenging, yet it is the only way to adequately prepare and plan for an unlikely future. At this point in time, universities in the Amhara region are ill-equipped with the necessary transformation competences to provide meaningful management and policy advice to regional government development programmes.

The concept

In this project, the concept of rural transformation is perceived as a design for the improvement of the economic and social conditions of rural inhabitants within the watersheds, which must involve integrated strategies for extending the benefits of the development to the rural majority. Such transformation brings about improvements in the living conditions of the farmers and the rural community. Rural transformation, therefore, necessitates multidimensional and simultaneous societal change, including crop production, livestock production, demography, soil and water resources, alternative sources of income and institutional aspects of the community. For all this to happen, it is necessary to have an integrated framework and to ensure effective institutions and extension services are in place to provide continuous and need-based support for farmers. Realizing the importance of rural transformation in the watersheds, the TRANSACT project has, since February 2011, been engaged in implementing capacity building for higher education and research institutions in the Amhara region related with rural transformation in three watersheds of the North Gondar Administrative Zone. The project basically aims to strengthen the rural transformation competences of the Ethiopian consortium partners in research and training. Such transformation competences demand institutional capacities that translate into new partnerships and learning alliances allowing higher education and research to become more effective development partner and community service providers.

In this regard, Activity 3.3 of the project was designed to develop integrated scenarios relevant for rural transformation in the selected watersheds. This is important, because in North Gondar, there is an untapped potential for social, economic and technical transformation that would gradually improve the lives and livelihoods of farmers. As said above, potential changes include technical improvements in agricultural and natural resource management and the realisation of new income opportunities, which could lead to a transformation from socially unjust rural worlds where farmers live in poverty to a rural society of equality and prosperity. The realization of this potential requires public and private actors to join forces with rural communities through inter- and transdisciplinary methods.

Despite the Amhara region's huge and untapped potential for wide social, economic and technical transformations that would gradually improve the lives and livelihoods of farmers, higher education and research institutions of the region have not been sufficiently responsive to this potential. This is due to a common constraint: a lack of the essential human and institutional capacities needed to conceptually and methodologically address rural transformation through knowledge generation, training and communication of research findings that can reach deep into rural communities. At the same time, very few of the experiences, insights and priorities of farmers and rural communities diffuse into the higher education and research systems. This widens the gap between academia and practice.

Undoubtedly, therefore, the overall objectives and focus areas of the project are in line with the policy directions and needs of the agricultural sector in Ethiopia. In this regard, TRANSACT has significantly helped to strengthen the rural transformation competences of Gondar University (GU), Bahir Dar University (BDU) and the Amhara Region Agricultural Research Institute (ARARI) in research and training. Such transformation competences allow higher education and research institutions to become more effective development partner and community service providers in the specific watersheds and beyond.

The project has also significantly contributed towards developing the human and institutional capacity of Gondar University, Bahir Dar University and ARARI in areas of education and research that help the facilitation of intended transformation in rural areas.

The project has also led to a better and more systemic understanding of rural transformation processes. In this regard, the project helps lecturers and researchers in the target higher education and research institutions to respond more effectively to transformation opportunities among farmers in complex and risk-prone rural areas.

As a result of the professional experiences acquired by the project, coordinated linkages across different disciplines have been established. By working closely with experts from various academic background, this project contributed to the evolution of research and training methodologies drawn from different disciplines.

The project adapted existing methodologies and developed new ones for inter- and transdisciplinary research, training and outreach that facilitate institutional learning and rural transformation. Moreover, the project cleared the way for joint learning, research and problem-solving at a local level and in the three micro-watersheds. Through this project, therefore, much more effective linkages between research, higher education and extension have been realized.

The project created partnerships and collaboration among partner institutions for joint curriculum development, training opportunities, further education as well as capacity building. As a result of launching the TRANSACT project, many ARARI, BDU and GU academic staff were given the opportunity to pursue their MSc and PhD studies at BOKU with the support of ADC. Furthermore, insights gained through cooperation efforts could be incorporated into educational material.

The project was useful in that it has provided skills necessary to plan for an uncertain future. The project has also introduced new modes of collaboration between science and local actors and better and more context-specific results that have a higher societal impact.

In general the TRANSACT project was important because the project focuses mainly on boosting agricultural productivity in order to ensure sustainable agricultural development and ultimately bring rural transformation. The project was also important in its emphasis on capacity building in rural transformation competences within higher education and research institutes in the region. Moreover, the project was helpful in enhancing transdisciplinary skills and in developing interdisciplinary competences of experts and farmers.

9.2.3 Transforming research? A critical reflection

by Birgit Habermann

After many years of pondering about a suitable way to take the cooperation of the BOKU and her Ethiopian partners to a higher level, the APPEAR programme finally offered an adequate framework in 2010. I was in Ethiopia at that time for my thesis research, and I was happy to hear that there was an opportunity to strengthen our partnership network. After some initial brain-storming we organized a small mini-workshop in Gondar. At that stage the partnership had already been expanded due to the initiative of our main Ethiopian counterpart, and we now had three partners instead of one. This constellation would later contribute to overcoming some of the enormous complexities the project faced. One or two representatives from each partner institution attended the mini-workshop. It was already a small group, but the actual idea of TRANSACT was brought forth by just two participants, who got very excited about a shared vision: the transformation of higher education and research institutes towards a more holistic, transdisciplinary, and fair cooperation with farmers. A different kind of research and training approach should be developed and adopted by this project in order to achieve sustainable change for rural transformation.

While preparing the proposal, we unwittingly created several challenges for the project. One challenge came from outside: the fact that the Ethiopian Government launched the Growth and Transformation Plan (GTP) after we had already submitted the proposal. Most of our Ethiopian partners mistook the project for something that followed, rather than predated, the development idea of the GTP because of the massive media campaign for the GTP. The impressive launch of the project had already indicated that this project would be expected to make a substantial contribution to the transformation of the Ethiopian economy. This was of course way beyond its scope. However, these ambiguities nevertheless triggered an interesting debate about the topic "transformation" and other terms used by the project such as "interdisciplinarity" and "transdisciplinarity" at an early stage. As the project went on, our understanding of these terms went through interesting developments. While the diversity of the interpretations of those terms at the outset prepared the ground for stimulating theoretical debates, the final consensus on the definitions towards the end of the project was evidence that these debates had continued and thrived throughout the project. I personally enjoyed these debates and felt that they were in themselves an important outcome of TRANSACT.

The second challenge was that we selected watersheds as geographic units for the research sites. This happened because it seemed to us the most logical and common way of proceeding. Because of our epistemological background and the perception of BOKU as a natural science university, most of our partners perceived TRANSACT as a kind of integrated watershed management project. They hence placed TRANSACT inside departments dealing with agriculture, forestry and the like rather than social science units. The project was already well underway when we realized that we had teams full of agronomists, microbiologists, soil scientists and foresters, rather than sociologists, anthropologists, psychologists and so on. However, as I will describe later on, in spite of the huge challenge this presented us with, this also prepared the ground for institutional learning. Linkages were created to other departments, and new theories and methods were discussed that led to a mindshift within the project consortium.

The third challenge was that CDR accepted the task of project coordination. In my view, it would have been more correct to place the management in Ethiopia, but due to problematic relationships among the Ethiopian partners at that stage, that this was considered inappropriate. This later had an effect on the entire project network – during Focus Group Discussions (FGDs) it became clear that the Ethiopian partners perceived CDR only as coordinator, not partner. The perception of the Ethiopian partners was that they were responsible for operationalizing the project while CDR's tasks were ones of coordination and maintaining donor relations. On the one hand, this had the advantage that the network between the Ethiopian partners became stronger. Although it was at times a bumpy ride, at the project's final stage the partners agreed that their relations had improved and that they were now cooperating at a different level. On the other hand, though, this created a minefield of tensions for CDR. Although CDR had suggested a large number of potential partners and team members at the proposal stage, their involvement did not happen. Only a few CDR researchers became actively engaged in the project.

In the first year, I had the advantage of being on-site most of the time, which made it much easier for me to engage with partners. In the final year, several BOKU staff members were involved in teaching and training; however, this again reinforced the perception of CDR as coordinator and supervisor. Of course in the last 15 years this has been the primary role of BOKU staff members cooperating with partners in Ethiopia, for example when supervising Ethiopian students. However, TRANSACT's motivating ideas included the transformation of this relationship and a significant expansion of the concept of capacity development. The persistence of these pre-conceived roles in TRANSACT has shown very clearly how difficult it is to move away from such stereotypes. In the FGDs there were heated debates about this. One example was email correspondence. While BOKU staff members complained that their comments and recommendations were not responded to or misunderstood – sometimes with harsh and offensive feedback – the staff members of the Ethiopian partners complained that they felt belittled. They complained that BOKU staff either took too long in responding or responded with offensive criticism. For some Ethiopian partners, BOKU staff members contributed nothing except criticism, and they felt this to be patronizing. More input into the research in the actual activity teams was desired, but through direct and on-site engagement, not just in the form of often delayed feedback on texts sent via email in the manner of a supervisor. This perceived lack of direct input and engagement from BOKU members also led to considerable confusion at the outset of the project, as many of the activity team-leaders and team-members were not clear about the aims and objectives of the activities assigned to them.

As most of them were natural scientists, and the tasks in the activities were more of a social scientific nature, it was of course a challenge for them to further develop the ideas and concepts sketched out in the proposal and the at first consortium meeting, and then later on taken over by the project management at CDR. However, CDR was as much as a learning partner in this project as the Ethiopian partners. Repeated visits by the project leader and coordinator from CDR helped to resolve such issues, many of which were resolved through a reorganization of the teams to partner with researchers from other departments at the Ethiopian partner institutes and by seeking advice from CDR partners at BOKU. Through this, the concept of "scenario management" became an essential part of TRANSACT's research activities. In spite of all the difficulties, it was exactly this challenge that eventually led to one of the most substantial outcomes of TRANSACT, an in-depth engagement of natural scientists with trans- and interdisciplinary research approaches as well as social science theory and methods. One of the most important outcomes of this was a report and manual on such methods that was developed jointly by a team of Ethiopian and CDR researchers.

There were other challenges in the project, such as: the overambitious objectives we had designed; the persistent lack of gender equity; different interpretations of the concept of "participation" between the Austrian and Ethiopian partners; methodological challenges when implementing scenario management in the field, and; the different framings of knowledge and capacities of farmers. However, the most important lesson I have learned from this project was that misunderstandings between researchers who believe that they are talking about the same subject can be really quite striking. It was crucial for TRANSACT to carry out an activity on institutional learning as a kind of self-monitoring mechanism because, as a result, the consortium became aware of many issues hampering the research progress at an early stage. Having such mechanisms for feedback and reflection seemed crucial. In addition, I feel that more on-site presence and joint field research activities undertaken by all partners are essential if a common understanding of the issues at hand is to be reached, also from a methodological point of view. It is inappropriate and inadequate for the foreign partner to merely act as supervisor, even though this may be have been the exact role that Ethiopian partners themselves would have assigned to CDR at the outset.

9.2.4 Enumeration of results

In order to be good development partners for the Ethiopian government and become effective contributors towards agricultural development and rural transformation, the partnering higher education and research institutions critically required capacity building in the area of rural transformation competences. The TRANSACT project helped universities to respond more effectively to transformation opportunities among farmers in complex and risk-prone rural areas. A particular emphasis of this project was placed on learning and human behaviour as well as communication and collective action, especially in connection with societal interactions that mediate change. 14 activities were planned and implemented, serially numbered according to the 4 expected results:

1. *Adapting existing methodologies and developing new ones for inter- and transdisciplinary research, training and outreach that facilitate institutional learning and rural transformation.*
2. *Develop the human and institutional capacity of Gondar University, Bahir Dar University and ARARI in education, research and outreach enabling them to become facilitators of intended transformation in rural areas.*
3. *Generating knowledge for understanding and facilitating institutional learning, rural transformation and change in the Amhara region.*
4. *Institutionalizing self-reflective learning procedures and methodologies across disciplines, units within and beyond partner institutions for sustaining trans disciplinary academic partnerships.*

(1.1) Conducting a baseline survey and training needs assessment led to one report and four publications in the journals Agricultural Sciences and Educational Research. The publications analyzed the factors in establishing inter- and transdisciplinary research in Ethiopia. (1.2) Development and testing of new inter- and transdisciplinary research methodologies were summarized in one manual on applications and procedures for inter- and transdisciplinary research. (1.3) Designing training manuals and teaching materials and (2.2) developing and delivering tailor-made short courses will sustain the project with five manuals and five short courses tailor-made for higher research and education institutions. (2.1) Developing curricula for joint inter- and transdisciplinary doctoral/MSc/MA study programmes has finally resulted in a joint MSc curriculum "Rural Transformation and Innovation System Management RUTISM" for UoG and BDU. (2.3) Organizing learning and experience exchanges for students and staff originated in two sensitization training sessions in Bahir Dar and Gondar. (2.4) Developing web-based information and communication technologies established a one-stop information centre, www.transact-ethiopia.com. (3.1) Identifying the three pilot micro-watersheds of Wujarabe, Mezege, Godinge in North Amhara was done in the first months of TRANSACT. (3.2) Conducting joint research planning to identify thematic research areas followed and provided three doctoral students and three master students from Ethiopia with scholarships to enroll at BOKU. (3.3) Joint research activities were implemented, with scenario planning as tool for future development interventions. (3.4) Sharing experiences across sites occurred via farmer experience-sharing tours in North Amhara. (4.1) Organizing six bi-annual consortium meetings, one exposure and learning visit, one closing conference and 30 field visits by BOKU team members created a strong network. (4.2) Developing joint development-oriented "transformation research" projects created two proposals for follow-on projects, subject to future funding. (4.3) Documenting institutional learning and impact of TRANSACT with and across participating institutions provided the consortium with feedback throughout the project duration and fed into a comprehensive project report.

Meeting farmers in Mezega

Meeting farmers in Wujaraba

3rd consortium meeting at ARARI, Ethiopian Institute of Agricultural Research, February 2012

Linkages workshop

Scenario training, September 2012

The Blue Nile Falls known as Tis Abay in Amharic, meaning "smoking water" and situated about 30 km downstream from the town of Bahir Dar and Lake Tana

Signing of Memorandum of Understanding between Bahir Dar University and University of Natural Ressources and Life Sciences (BOKU), February 2013: (from right to left) Dr. Fentahun Mengistu, Director General, Ethiopian Institute of Agricultural Research, Prof. DI. Dr. mul. Martin Gerzabek, Rector of the BOKU, President Dr. Baylie Damtie, Bahir Dar University, Dr. Heinz Habertheuer, Austrian Embassy, Prof. Dr. Andreas J. Obrecht, APPEAR programme, Dr. Soloman Abrha, Vice-rector University of Gondar, Dr. Yinager Dessie, State Minister for Foreign Affairs

On the shores of Lake Tana near Bahir Dar

9.2 Strengthening Rural Transformation Competences 263

Workshop with farmers in Wuja-raba, February 2013

Scenario transfer

Closing conference, June 2014

9.3   Responding to Poverty and Disability through Higher Education and Research

Project Coordinator: Gottfried Biewer
Coordinating Institution: University of Vienna, Department of Education
Partner Institution: Addis Ababa University, Department of Special Needs Education
Partner Country: Ethiopia
Project Duration: 1 October 2011 – 30 September 2014
Project Website: http://respond-her.univie.ac.at

9.3.1 The project - RESPOND-HER

The project "Responding to Poverty and Disability through Higher Education and Research (RESPOND-HER)" is based on an academic cooperation between the Department of Special Needs Education of Addis Ababa University (AAU) and the Department of Education of the University of Vienna (UV). First steps towards collaboration occurred in 2007, when a student from AAU obtained a PhD scholarship in the field of Special Needs Education within the North-South Dialogue programme of Austrian Development Cooperation (ADC). The project "Classifications of Disabilities in the Field of Education (CLASDISA)", begun in 2010 and financed by the Austrian Science Fund (FWF), also involved staff members from the Department of Special Needs Education of AAU in basic research at an international and competitive level. This project focused on the educational situation of school-age children with disabilities in three countries: Austria, Thailand and Ethiopia.

The main focus of RESPOND-HER was the educational and employment situation of persons with disabilities who had studied or were studying at universities in Ethiopia. Given the exponential rise of the number of universities in Ethiopia, eleven of these universities were chosen as research sites to assess the current situation of university students and graduates with disabilities. As one of the most marginalized and disadvantaged groups within Ethiopian society, persons with disabilities face a considerably higher risk of poverty. The interrelatedness of poverty and disability presents a pivotal nexus that comprises a global phenomenon that has been elaborated in a number of publications. Poor people face a higher risk of having or acquiring a disability, and people with disabilities are among the poorest (Mitra et al. 2011).

The project focused particularly on students with disabilities' rights to education and employment, as these are not sufficiently known due to institutional barriers. The project sought to explore the details, and create data-backed descriptions, of the lives of students with disabilities, their university studies and work conditions as these had not been systematically explored before. In Ethiopia, less than 5% of children with disabilities have access to primary universal education. Over 95 % of school-age children have no access to education, which is one of the most powerful tools for mobilizing people's potential and overcoming poverty. Education is pivotal in addressing this crucial issue, to break the vicious circle of disability and poverty and transform the lives of persons with disabilities. In Ethiopia, in spite of the low enrolment rate of children with disabilities in primary universal education, policy documents such as the FDRE Constitution (1995) article 41(5), The Education Training Policy (1995), the Education Sector Development Program IV (2010-2015) and the Growth and Transformation Plan of the Government (2010-2015) underline the right to education of persons with disabilities in the country. The Proclamation of Higher Education (2009) clearly stipulates that the needs of students with disabilities should be accommodated and addressed accordingly. The Country's Proclamation (No.568/2008) has fully rectified the rights of persons with disabilities regarding their employment in the labour market. However, policies are often not reflected in practice and hence university students with disabilities across the higher education sector still face attitudinal, academic, economic and social challenges in the course of their education, as well as employment problems following graduation.

The RESPOND-HER project had two complementary main objectives:

- By developing, conducting and reflecting high quality research on disabilities and by fostering the teaching skills of academic staff from AAU in the course of mutual staff exchange, the project aimed to develop sustainable professional academic capacities for all researchers involved. In the long run, this process will facilitate the development and establishment of training for professionals at non-university institutions.
- The project tried to facilitate students with disabilities' access to higher education and to the labour market by targeting institutional barriers in cooperation with stakeholders (such as representatives of different universities and ministries as well as members of NGOs and disabled people's organizations) from all regions of the country.

As female students with disabilities face an additional level of discrimination due to their gender-attributed roles, the project aimed to pay specific attention to the challenges they face.

Additionally, the consideration of non-academics in curriculum development at AAU is one that has been begun but shall require further attention in future research activities. In particular, the question of whether Community Rehabilitation Workers (CRWs) should be considered in further education planning is an oft-discussed issue.

9.3.2 Reflections on mutual learning experiences

by Tirussew Teferra and Yirgashewa Bekele

Sharing of professional experience
The University of Vienna research team and the Addis Ababa University team were able to successfully carry out their professional responsibilities and have learnt a lot from the project's research undertakings and exchange programmes. They were able to closely connect, get to know each other and learn from sharing professional and cultural experiences. The project opened several avenues for formal and informal interactions among the researchers which led to pertinent and cherished memories on all sides. The project's innovative twin-track approach of teaching courses and participating in international conferences has opened up opportunities for scientific enquiry, long-lasting friendships and future profes-

sional development. The twin-track approach, employed throughout the course of the project, brought two researchers from the north and south to work on related topics or areas of interest, to teach courses and present conference papers. The teaching was arranged in such a way that a researcher from Addis Ababa University or the University of Vienna had the opportunity to travel and stay two weeks in their counterpart country and deliver lectures for the students of the counterpart university. Similarly, researchers had to pair up to jointly write and present scientific papers at international conferences. Common papers were presented by Ethiopian and Austrian staff members at the following international conferences:

- American Educational Research Association Conference (AERA), Vancouver, Canada
- European Conference on Educational Research (ECER), Cadiz, Spain
- European Conference on Educational Research (ECER), Istanbul, Turkey
- World Educational Research Association (WERA) Focal Meeting, Sydney, Australia
- African Conference on Social Work, Kampala, Uganda

To develop the skills and competences of staff members, the Ethiopian team became involved in the joint research project "Classifications of Disabilities in the Field of Education (CLASDISA)", where both research and conference participation were among the target activities of the project. Furthermore, the cooperation placed heavy emphasis on female participation in all project activities and so female staff members and project participants played active roles throughout the project work.

Furthermore, several consultative meetings among the researchers served as a ground for sharing responsibility, developing a culture of team work, as well as learning from one another. The process of collecting field data and organizing, interpreting and finalizing the write-up was a challenging experience from which much was learnt. Generally the RESPOND-HER project involved close cooperation, clearly-stated shared goals and responsibilities, achieved through the close involvement of team members from both countries. As a result, the cooperation has ultimately benefited both countries by enabling the sharing of knowledge, skills, experience, working cultures and resources.

Concluding remarks

The studies undertaken by the Ethiopian team are the first in the country to generate valuable empirical findings on the present status of the higher education of students and the employability of graduates with disabilities in Ethiopia. The research reports have also come up with practical suggestions as well as manuals to improve the quality of education and employability of graduate students with disability in the country. The research reports have wide-reaching implications for policy as well as the quality of support services provided for persons with disabilities. For instance, the study on the situation of students with disabilities necessitates revisiting and revising policies, legislation and the quality of services delivered for students with disabilities in higher education institutions.

What is more, the project's contribution to the capacity building of staff at both universities, particularly of young scholars, must be emphasized. The staff exchange, joint field research, local workshops and conference paper presentation programmes have not only enhanced the knowledge and skill of the staff in the field but have also elevated the confidence of the staff. This in turn has served to check the quality and standard of the programme of the Department of Special Needs Education at Addis Ababa University. It is also important to note that this project has given a scholarship to one young Ethiopian scholar to pursue his doctoral education at the University of Vienna.

Last but not least, the joint research and capacity building project venture has been valuable for the socio-cultural transaction between the researchers of the two collaborating universities. The mutual understanding, respect and commitment demonstrated by the researchers have laid a solid foundation for future cooperation in this field.

9.3.3 Lessons learnt from the Austrian perspective

by Gottfried Biewer and Michelle Proyer

Reflecting upon the mutual learning experiences in the academic cooperation underlying RESPOND-HER makes one think back to the early stages of the project's inception. In the case of the RESPOND-HER project, collaboration emerged in several steps over some years. Starting with the doctoral study of an AAU graduate in Vienna, the Austrian team became acquainted with educational issues in Ethiopia. This led to the involvement of AAU in the basic research project CLASDISA and the visiting professorship of Professor Tirussew Teferra at the University of Vienna in 2009. It was at this time that the main objectives for a common collaborative project to investigate the situation of university students and graduates with disabilities were suggested by the Ethiopian side.

Members of the team working on the project proposal at the University of Vienna were very excited about becoming involved in further collaborative measures with AAU. Following a highly positive experience working on the ongoing CLASDISA project, the idea of being involved in something ground breaking was an exciting prospect. Providing baseline data on the situation of students with disabilities in Ethiopia, where heretofore there had not been much of a data base on the topic of education for persons with disabilities as such and even less beyond primary and secondary education, sounded like every researcher's dream, involving an exploration of the unknown and potentially leading to sustainable change. The perspective of applied research seemed to be complementary to the basic research aims of the ongoing project CLASDISA. In accordance with the profile of the Special Needs and Inclusive Education research unit of the Department of Education at University of Vienna, the engagement in research activities with an international and development focus is crucial.

The idea of working with researchers from a different continent and producing knowledge beyond borders was another issue that got many of us highly involved. Perhaps in this excitement, the research team in Vienna overlooked the challenges and opportunities intercultural research on the academic level might incorporate. Intercultural exchange is hard work and requires a range of capacities, though this fact is too often ignored during the planning stage of international collaboration. The following list aims at highlighting some facts to illustrate that. Mutual learning involves hard work that in the end, sometimes after travelling on a bumpy road, leads to success and unforgettable experiences. As will be seen, many of the areas described below are interrelated.

Encounters and reflections among the team members: Tales of gender and beyond
Bringing a relatively high number of researchers together on both sides of the cooperation involved getting to know each other and our specific approaches to work and research. Not only did we quickly encounter differences in communication (to be discussed below) and research practices (the Austrian team focusing on qualitative approaches and the Ethiopian team focusing mainly on quantitative ones), we also found that the composition of the teams interesting. The initial research team at AAU consisted of two women and six men, whereas the Austrian team in its original composition consisted of two male researchers, one being the head of the research activities, and apart from that only females (adding up to 5 members). Considering that gender-related issues were of the utmost importance in the structure and assessment of the APPEAR project structure, we pointed out from the beginning that the reference to females with disabilities needed to be kept in focus at all levels of research.

Communication: Converging perspectives
Another striking aspect that became evident right away was the different approaches to responsibility. The Austrian team followed a specific division of labour and responsibility involving direct communication with those in charge of certain tasks. If one researcher from Vienna was, for example, travelling to Addis Ababa to hold a lecture, he or she was appointed to organize all related necessities such as booking of flights and coordinating activities with the Ethiopian partners. Decision-making was mostly based on decisions made among the team.

The Ethiopian team, on the other hand, operated according to what the Austrian team described as a more hierarchized line of responsibility. Thereby, the leadership of the Ethiopian team was involved in large parts of the communication and decision-making. Merely understanding these different approaches, and still less discussing them, was not easy for either team, but although it took time, in the end a high level of transparency in communication processes was enabled. Over time, communication improved as the differing management structures became clearer to both sides. Additionally, responsibilities in Ethiopia were adapted in accordance with the necessity to identify work packages and nominate managers and co-workers for these accordingly.

Another issue related to communication that underlay some less productive phases of the cooperation was that of unanswered emails. A number of explanations (such as power-cuts and migrated mailboxes) took time to emerge but again enhanced the level of understanding. It showed how resources such as constant Internet access or electricity were taken for granted by the Austrian partner. Only when power-cuts or Internet outages are experienced first-hand do such considerations for communication become clear.

Gender and involvement of CRWs: Crossing the borders of academy
Reading the feedback from one of our project application's reviewers, we acknowledged the importance of considering the needs of non-university stakeholders in order to gain a fuller picture of the living conditions of students with disabilities and their environment. Although both project partners were willing in this respect, perceptions of urgency and modes of involvement differed. It was important to acknowledge a long history of cooperation or non-cooperation between AAU and stakeholders that took time to become comprehensive for us. The successful involvement of different stakeholders in the course of a workshop on the educational needs of community rehabilitation workers proved successful and paved the way for future work on the establishment of higher education programmes for this group. It also underlined the importance of the Austrian partner's efforts to work towards a more inclusive research agenda.

The implicit need to consider gender at every level of the research cooperation was acknowledged on both sides, but again it took time for this to become clear as ways of talking about its importance differed. Approaches to a common understanding worked especially well on the level of collaborative measures between individuals. This enabled more openness and the realization of a workshop that gave females with disabilities the possibility to share their experiences and get in touch with each other. Such perfectly functioning collaboration improved the overall collaborative structure.

Teaching exchange: New experiences for all
The advantages of teaching exchange have already been very well elaborated by our colleagues above. Approaches to teaching were varied but the impact on students from both partner institutions was remarkable. For the Austrian participants, engaging in teaching made it necessary to cope with unexpected challenges (such as power-cuts) on the one hand (which of course absolutely does not imply that technical equipment at the University of Vienna always works well) but also to lecture to an incredibly engaged audience. The AAU students' obvious wish to learn and their critical and challenging attitude were extremely striking for the Austrian teachers. Being able to cope with and teach in diverse settings is a valuable asset.

Concluding remarks
Following the (far from comprehensive) list of points above, we can conclude that the cooperation held a multitude of challenges and surprises in store. Most of the time, problems were solved through good organization and spontaneous innovation, such as was the case when one Austrian participant arrived at AAU just recently having learned that their partner for a collaborative measure had had to travel to another city on short notice. Although the absent partner had appointed a replacement, due to the short notice this person had not had a chance to learn what was planned or what the initial partner had been asked to organize. Surprisingly, a room for a lecture on the following day was set up immediately and a number of students were called to inform others about this opportunity. Unexpectedly, more than 80 participants attended and made the session an unforgettable one.

One was tempted to compare this institutional practice with the one back home in Vienna. Similar spontaneity was most likely unheard of in such a rigid, sometimes over-organized context and a spontaneous lecture like that at AAU would have been unlikely to have taken place given the need to allocate most rooms at the University of Vienna months in advance. Local circumstances must be considered, but this rather plain example shows the simple way in which intercultural experience can lead one to question what one is used to and whether a given practice is the right one. This collaborative project taught us to think beyond prejudice and to be more patient, mostly with ourselves and our perceptions of how communication should work or how effective collaboration can be defined beyond counting answered emails. Hence, this project had an impact beyond its important contribution to research on higher education of persons with disabilities in Ethiopia: it also led to unforgettable experiences and memories.

We would therefore like to take this as an opportunity to thank our research partners for their involvement and this extraordinary opportunity to learn from each other!

9.3.4 Enumeration of results

The following lists the results and products of the research activities, organized according to certain themes. The points are partly overlapping but will be mentioned more than once if applicable. This is to underline the overall consistency of the research activities.

Research activities:
- Publication of the "Baseline survey on GWDs' (Graduates with Disabilities) access to the labour market"

This document comprises a report on the employability of graduate students with disabilities in Ethiopia as assessed at 5 universities from across the country: Addis Ababa, Hawassa, Adama, Bahir Dar and Mekelle. It was carried out by the research partners from AAU at the beginning of the project in order to illustrate and, for the first time, give a detailed account of students with disabilities. Students, graduates, employers and representatives of disabled people's organizations were interviewed in focus group discussions or surveyed via questionnaires.[1]

- Publication of the "Assessment of the Situation of Students with Disabilities in the Ethiopian Universities"

The research for this report was conducted by the Ethiopian research partners and focused on data collected in 11 universities: Adama Science and Technology University, Addis Ababa University, Aksum University, Bahir Dar University, Dilla University, Jigjiga University, Haro-

---

[1] URL: http://respond-her.univie.ac.at/fileadmin/user_upload/p_respond_her/Employability_Final_July_9_2013_Research_Report.pdf

maya University, Hawassa University, Mekelle University, Gondar University and Samara University. More than 400 students, student deans and vice presidents were involved in the study in order to assess the actual situation of students with disabilities and the state of service provision.[2]

- Focused research on females with disabilities at AAU involving a workshop with 25 students and additional interviews with two students (publication in progress)

Dissemination:
- Development of manuals for universities and employers on students and graduates with disabilities. A draft version had been discussed with stakeholders. The reports were printed and distributed.
- Research reports
- Attendance at five international conferences and provision of a national conference and regional workshops to disseminate the findings of the project around Ethiopia and the participating universities
- Project website to update interested audience on latest developments: http://respond-her.univie.ac.at/home/
- Work on a publication related to females with disabilities

Capacity building:
- Nine mutual teaching and learning exchanges and various guest lectures and workshops
- Capacity building for external stakeholders and females with disabilities
- International and national exchange among professionals from higher education by involving different locations all over the country

Gender-related issues:
- Consideration of gender-related issues and consideration of the topic at any stage of the research
- Empowerment workshop for females with disabilities

---

[2] URL: http://respond-her.univie.ac.at/fileadmin/user_upload/p_respond_her/students_with_disabilities_ethiopian_universities_16_11_2014.pdf

Disability is a reality for me but a possibility for everyone! A sign in front of Addis Ababa University library referring to students with disabilities

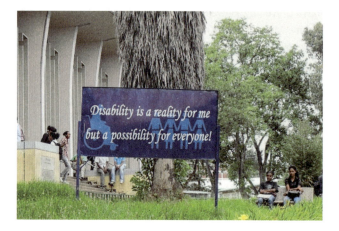

International day of persons with disabilities in December 2013

The research team during the first meeting at Addis Ababa University in 2011

9.3 Responding to Poverty and Disability 273

Entrance to the campus of Hawassa University

Meeting at Bahir Dar University in December 2013

Project coordinator Gottfried Biewer exchanges ideas with members of club of students with disabilities at Jigjiga University

Center for Students with Disability at Addis Ababa University

Limited accessibility of the newly built library of Jigjiga University

Yeshitla Mulat, Gertraud Kremsner and Sandra Schuetz visited a local school during their teaching exchange in November 2014

10 STUDENT MOBILITY

10.1 The Second Component of APPEAR

10.1.1 Scholarships within the new framework

by Elke Stinnig

Background

At an informal meeting in January 2010, our team brainstormed the most fitting name for our new programme. After hours of discussion and playing with letters and catchwords to find an interesting, catchy acronym, we got excited when the name APPEAR appeared. The acronym stands for Austrian Partnership Programme in Higher Education and Research for Development, signalling a new instrument for the funding of cooperative projects in higher education. APPEAR emerged as a response to two main issues which have been prevalent in the discourse around international development since 2000: (1) the increased focus on higher education as a driving factor for societal change; (2) criticism that individual scholarship programmes have not been effective enough in contributing to institutional capacity development.

Responding to such issues, in 2009 the Austrian Development Cooperation (ADC) introduced its new strategy on "Higher Education and Scientific Cooperation". The APPEAR programme is based on this strategy, and consists of two main components: (1) the newly introduced academic partnerships and scholarships (see also Chapter 2); (2) the continuation of the North-South-Dialogue Scholarship Programme that had been implemented by the OeAD on behalf of ADC since 1984. Within this new framework, the focus has shifted to scholarships that are linked to existing APPEAR projects, and which promise to have a stronger impact on institutional capacity-building and the improvement of higher education and research in the collaborating countries.

Objective, benefits and figures of the scholarship component

APPEAR's scholarship component aims to enable students and professionals employed at a higher education institution in the eligible countries to complete a master's or PhD programme at an Austrian higher education institution. The studies are expected to be in line with the programme's thematic focus and also with the regional and national development strategies of the respective countries, thereby contributing to poverty reduction. The relevance of capacity development for the home institution has to be clearly outlined in the ap-

APPEAR scholarship holders in the OeAD house

plication and confirmed by the respective human resources manager. As field research work must be undertaken in the student's home country, the financial and/or technical support of their institution is also requested. The applicant further confirms their readiness to return to the home country after completion of the studies to resume employment, in order to pursue an appropriate development-related assignment. Another understandable requirement is that the student must be admitted at a respective Austrian University. For a PhD application, a confirmation letter from an Austrian scientific supervisor must be submitted, while for master's studies, a letter from the master's programme manager must be provided. The APPEAR selection board then decides the award of the scholarship based on an applicant's academic qualifications and professional experience, as well as the relevance of the research topic for the home institution and for the countries' development. The monthly scholarship rate for a PhD amounts to EUR 940 (with an average duration of 36 months) and for a master's it amounts to EUR 880 (with an average duration of 24 months). The scholarship is also paid during field work undertaken in the students' respective home countries. Additional grants include financial support for travel, German courses, conference participation and publishing the study results.

Since APPEAR's inception, a total of 128 scholarships have been financed, of which 68 were integrated from the previous North-South-Dialogue Scholarship Programme, 39 were individual scholarships, and 21 scholarships were linked to APPEAR projects. 23% of the scholars pursued master's degrees and 77% PhD study. 70% of scholarship holders came from Sub-Saharan Africa, with Ethiopia having the biggest share (60%), a consequence of its long-held status as a priority ADC partner country in higher education. 44% of scholarship holders studied agricultural sciences, 21% social sciences, 27% natural sciences and 8% technical sciences. APPEAR has a strong commitment to gender issues, and women are particularly encouraged to apply. One of our gender mainstreaming measures is to give prefer-

Female scholarship holders from Uganda, Ethiopia and Nicaragua

ence to female applicants when all requested academic standards are equal to those of the male applicants. Unfortunately, the programme has to date received too few applications from women, meaning that women are still under-represented among scholarship holders (29%). This is largely attributed to traditional conceptions of family and gender roles, as well as structural barriers that limit equal access and the promotion of women in higher education in their respective countries.

The new focus on embedding scholarships in APPEAR projects was initially not reflected by the number of submitted applications. This was probably due to a lack of emphasis thereon in the initial programme publicity, as well as the fact that the concept's novelty meant that it was sometimes too early for project applicants to find suitable scholarship candidates during the project proposal phase. Therefore, in order to increase the number of project-related scholarships, two separate calls were made, strictly for possible candidates from existing APPEAR projects. This added 21 scholars who were directly involved in the existing APPEAR partnerships.

In the last 5 years, 102 scholarship holders have achieved masters' or doctoral degrees. The APPEAR team is pleased with the success rate of the scholarship programme. So far, only two scholarships have had to be cancelled during studies; one due to personal issues and one due to a lack of academic performance. Six persons who had been awarded a scholarship cancelled their study before coming to Austria.

Becoming and being a scholarship holder

Being APPEAR's scholarship officer, I have seen the faces of many happy, proud and relieved students holding master's or PhD degrees in their hands, eager to return home to their families and resume work at their home institutions, as well as looking forward to future academic careers and professional advancement. However, before the start of their studies in Austria, our potential scholars must face many different and sometimes unexpected challenges. In the case of a potential student deciding to come to Austria for PhD study, for instance (some steps are also applicable for potential master's students), a lot of preparation work must first be completed. This includes developing a doctoral proposal, searching for a scientific supervisor in Austria, and submitting a complete scholarship application within the required timeframe. Only when all the formal and content-related requirements have been fulfilled, and if enough funds are available in APPEAR, can a student be selected for the opportunity. The applicants, when receiving the good news of being awarded a scholarship, often cannot imagine that such a long process still lies ahead before their arrival in Austria to finally begin their studies.

The second step following the award of a scholarship is the preparation for the studies in Austria, starting with the application for admission at the Austrian higher education institution. This process is easier if somebody has already obtained an Austrian university degree, but can be long and tedious if one has studied elsewhere and the respective university system differs substantially from Austria's. If not already in German or English, a student's international certificates and documents must all be translated into one of those languages by an officially registered and certified translator. In addition, the certificates have to be certified or legalised where the documents were issued. My experience is that the legislation process is long and frustrating for prospective students.

The next step in the application process is the application for a residence permit for "special cases of gainful employment". The name "residence permit" already gives one the feeling of a pitiless bureaucracy. The application for the residence permit must be submitted in person at the Austrian representative authority before travelling to Austria. Since Austria does not maintain embassies in all APPEAR partner countries, however, potential scholars from countries such as Burkina Faso, for example, have to go to Dakar in Senegal, while scholars from Uganda must travel to Addis Ababa, Ethiopia to apply. This whole process is overly-bureaucratic, time-consuming and costly. While our programme supports travel costs in such cases, that may not be enough to meet the unforeseeable inconveniences experienced by the student.

Normally, after all the required documents have been forwarded and processed by the relevant authorities in Austria, applicants are notified about their being granted of a residence permit. Only then one can apply for an entry visa to Austria. Luckily, due to OeAD's long experience in implementing such scholarship programmes, we are able to provide essential information and (legal) guidance during this arduous application process. Students must be well organised, perseverant and self-reliant in order to get through this pre-study phase.

After clearing these administrative hurdles, potential students must say goodbye to their families and take leave from their home institutions. Once in Austria, OeAD provides a monthly subsistence scholarship (financed by ADC), as well as the required guidance and advice in study and legal related issues, on issues such as university enrolment, taking out health and accident insurance and registering at the "Meldeamt" (Office of Registration). Once students are settled into their study programmes, OeAD is there to help whenever scholars encounter problems within or outside university life. In our experience, the first phase after settling down to the real academic work in Austria is usually crucial for the success of the entire study. This phase consists of working out the details of the doctoral proposal, specifying the research question, discussing the theoretical and methodological framework, elaborating a detailed work- and time-plan, following the academic courses that are required by the host university and learning discipline-specific research skills as per the project requirements.

In my opinion, as well as sufficient academic titles, it is vital that PhD or master's candidates possess high levels of commitment and perseverance, as well as good organisational skills, in order to successfully attain their degrees. Additionally, the supervisor's role is pivotal. Good supervisors give guidance throughout the duration of the research by discussing relevant theories, methods and approaches, as well as providing detailed feedback in order to improve the PhD thesis itself. The relationship between supervisors and students must remain respectful, trustful and open to criticism. From my own experience, students can encounter a multitude of academic and personal problems during their studies. However, with close collaboration between students and supervisors, practical solutions can always be found.

Dealing with the language barrier, integrating into a new environment, getting acquainted to Austrian lifestyles, finding new friends, as well as working at an Austrian institution can be at times very challenging for scholarship holders. This situation makes some students, modern communication technologies notwithstanding, feel homesick and to miss their friends, families and home environment. To help in this respect, OeAD conducts regular trips, excursions and extra-curricular educational activities for students to help with the integration process. This not only helps them to find out more about Austrian culture and history, but also allows them to meet colleagues and network amongst themselves. For our newcomers, the APPEAR team also organises workshops on interculturality, with the aim of transforming social skills into intercultural competences. In the frame of these workshops, concepts of interculturality, including cultural impacts on people's behaviour and ways to understand differences and similarities, are discussed, so that the students can get an increased understanding of various cultures. From my experience, these workshops have made students reflect more about their own cultural backgrounds, explore cultural and social aspects of their personal and professional lives and share experiences about critical incidents and challenges of working and living in a multicultural setting with other students. Besides, the students also get a chance to discuss solutions and strategies for current or future collaboration with people from different cultural and academic backgrounds. These skills and strategies are generally needed when working on international projects.

Scholarship holders at the workshop "Conflicts: Causes - Dynamics – Solutions" jointly organised with the Afro-Asian Institute in Salzburg

Our programme is "klein aber fein" (small but beautiful) as we say in German. We therefore aim at facilitating intensive communication and close collaboration with our students. Over the last few years, I have helped with some of the serious unforeseen personal life-events that our students have had to cope with, such as serious sickness, loss of family members back home or the pregnancy and birth of a child while being in Austria. On an academic level, students have been hampered by difficulties such as delays in data collection or lab analysis, a change of supervisor or long review processes. I am sometimes amazed to see how our scholars deal with all kind of challenges, an especially with how some of our female scholars have dealt with pregnancy while continuing their PhD studies. Here, I would like to mention one exceptional case. One pregnant student, who had formally organised to return to Uganda for the delivery of her twins, unexpectedly and prematurely gave birth to two girls while still in Vienna. Fortunately the girls and their mother were well and healthy. While the babies had to stay in hospital, the mother somehow found time to continue with her studies at the university. Due to her supervisor's tremendous assistance, as well as organisational and administrative help from various colleagues, she was able to find a new apartment, find baby equipment and succeed in organising a passport (via the competent Ugandan embassy in Berlin). However, when the infants were finally able to travel, we re-

Elijah Ndung'u and Ronald Luwangula among other scholarship holders during the workshop "Conflicts: Causes - Dynamics – Solutions"

During an excursion to the Schallaburg, Lower Austria

alised that it is not possible to fly alone in an aircraft with two babies. Fortunately, another Ugandan scholar who was leaving to undertake field work stepped in and accompanied the young family. The flexibility of our programme, the support of the supervisor and colleagues and of course the commitment of this scholar made it possible for her to continue her studies long-distance while in Uganda. Her successful defence took place in March this year.

A constantly challenging area for APPEAR is immigration law, including the seemingly interminable standard visa and residence permit application processes, as well as those cases where students had to leave Austria for field work. The whole process can be time-consuming and cause delays in starting the scholarship or returning to Austria. Another important aspect of our programme is conducting field work in the home countries. PhD candidates usually start with this work after twelve months in Austria. The duration and the number of field work trips depend on the respective research project, with some students going up to three times. Besides their academic necessity, field studies are important for the students since they allow them to meet their families and maintain links with their home institutions.

Following an international trend (especially in the natural sciences), PhD candidates and their supervisors often prefer to publish a cumulative thesis rather than a monographic dissertation. A cumulative thesis is a collection of scientific articles which have been published in peer-reviewed and recognized journals. In addition to the publications, a summary that describes the objective of the research, the theoretical and methodological approach, reviews of the papers and a discussion of the most important scientific findings have to be included. Generally, with a cumulative thesis the research findings are more accessible, a greater level of dissemination can be reached, and the students are better prepared for the publish or perish academic routine. As the review process involves a critical examination of the publications by reviewers, and the integration of this feedback by the students, managing a cumulative thesis can be time-consuming and, where major adjustments are required, very frustrating. Scholarship holders have at times had to take a break from their scholarship, return to their home country and wait for the decision of the review process. We have observed that this last phase of the PhD can be very difficult for the students and requires a lot of patience and energy.

Role and visibility of students from developing countries
One of the basic principles of APPEAR is to follow an open-minded concept of knowledge, science and empirical research. One-sided "knowledge transfer" usually preserves the predominance – which is often seen as sign of arrogance – of "western science" and "western interests". Our students bring new perspectives from their diverse backgrounds, thereby enabling a fair exchange of scientific knowledge and information. This gives an opportunity for Austrian institutions and scientists to gain new perspectives upon various scientific and development issues from the local knowledge and practices of their students. Data collected by the students during their field studies, and its analysis thereafter, increases knowledge and allows the formation of a global perspective on problem solution. The idea is that such global development research can help to address problems like climate change or food security which often do not respect national or regional borders.

Bhutanese scholarship holders after watching the movie "What Happiness Is"

Based on our selection criteria and through our personal interaction with scholarship holders, we know that we have very qualified international students who also contribute to the internationalisation of Austrian higher education institutions. Besides bringing in knowledge and experiences from different cultural backgrounds, sometimes the students also work as tutors or are invited as guest lecturers in various fora. The APPEAR team also works to increase the visibility of scholarship holders' academic achievements in various ways and seeks to involve them in development-related activities. We provide information about different research activities on our website and also try to tap the experiences of our scholars by inviting them to give presentations or recommending them for relevant panel discussions.

For example, we screened the movie "What Happiness Is", about gross national happiness in the kingdom of Bhutan by the Austrian filmmaker Harald Friedl. Afterwards, Harald Friedl joined a discussion about the movie together with one of our Bhutanese scholars Dorji Rabten, who is a Forestry Officer at the Ministry of Agriculture and Forests in Bhutan and was at the time of the screening studying on the master's programme in Mountain Forestry at the University of Natural Resources and Life Sciences (BOKU). Hence the audience not only got insights on the concept of "happiness" and current development efforts and progress in Bhutan from the perspective of the film maker but also from the actual perspective of Dorji Rabten and other present Bhutanese scholars.

Kalkidan Obse explains the Rights-Based Approach

Another successful example in this regard was our cooperation with Amnesty International. We jointly organised two workshops on the theme of: "You are powerful. Become an active agent for human rights". In addition to providing an understanding of human rights and the Rights-Based Approach (RBA) applicable in present-day society we also aimed at linking up national and international students. The general concept of human rights, the history of the human rights movement and major (international) legal frameworks on human rights were introduced by Amnesty International. Then Kalkidan Obse, a PhD candidate at the University of Graz (see Chapter 9.1.), discussed the practical application of RBA in the context of small NGOs and community-based organizations such as student networks. The presentation sought to familiarise participants with the values, principles and approaches associated with RBA and their application in practice. Inspired by the activities of the Amnesty International Students Network the participants then took part in interactive group-work discussions, sharing examples of joint activities and measures on how to become active agents of human rights from various countries.

Beyond the scholarship
Current and former scholars have excellent knowledge of potential areas for cooperation between their home higher education institutions and those in Austria. They act as cultural intermediators, are multipliers of information, knowledge and ideas, and they initiate and/

Wossen Argaw Tegegn representing the perspective of female scholarship holders at the Gender workshop in Vienna

or build up future cooperation projects in science and research. As already described above the working relationship between students and supervisors is usually close and provides an excellent basis for the elaboration and implementation of projects. Upon return to their home institutions they are professionals and experts in their field, and usually they receive promotion to higher positions. Looking at different international evaluation reports, the impact of scholarships cannot always be directly and easily assessed. So called tracer studies can often be biased, since successful alumni are generally more represented and because having benefitted from (and presumably appreciating) the scholarship, they are likely to give positive feedback. With regard to the lack of qualified staff in most developing countries, capacity-building measures and their impact are always valued highly at an institutional level. In order to measure their impact at a national level with regard to the overall objective of poverty reduction, a baseline study on factors that might lead to societal change would be required. Despite this, strong indicators for the impact of our scholarships are available in the high number of alumni follow-up activities, including joint publications, signed Memoranda of Understanding (MoUs), nomination and support of potential students for scholarships, as well as submitted and/or implemented proposals. The results of the APPEAR calls show that former scholarship holders (alumni) play a crucial role as multipliers, partners and coordinators in APPEAR projects. All in all, 134 applications for preparatory funding and 109 applications for academic partnership funding were submitted via four calls. Current or former scholarship holders were involved in 36% of all submitted proposals in various roles: links and multipliers between Austrian institutions of higher education and the institutions in the eligible countries, overall or national coordinator or team member. Current or former

Discussion during the AlumniTalks with Rhoda Birech

scholarship holders were involved in 41% of the accepted proposals for preparatory funding and academic partnership. In 21% of the accepted proposals current or former scholarship holders were the link between the involved institutions, 58% were the national coordinator, 8% the overall coordinator and 13% the team member. In addition we would like to highlight that also students from the eligible countries who studied at Austrian higher education institutions were involved in seven preparatory funding submissions and in five academic partnership submissions.

OeAD regularly organises AlumniTalks, where personal and professional experiences during and after studying in Austria are presented and discussed in order to harness the experience of former scholarship holders and to encourage current scholarship holders to look for future cooperation possibilities. As one excellent example, we recently invited Dr. Rhoda Birech to talk about "How to build-up successful partnerships" between the university and development partners, private sector, government, manufactures and related institutions aiming at enhancing the contribution of academia to national development. Dr. Rhoda Birech completed her PhD at the BOKU and is now working as a senior lecturer and University-Industry Liaison Officer at Egerton University in Kenya. In addition, she was the Kenyan coordinator of the APPEAR project "Strengthening Universities' Capacities for Mitigating Climate Change Induced Water Vulnerabilities in East Africa, WATERCAP" (see Chapter 7.2.). Dr. Birech has kept in close contact with her former host institution, and was in Vienna on the occasion of a project presentation during film festival "Film Days 2014 – "Eat.Drink.Live", organised for the third time in cooperation with the Commission for Development Research (KEF). The key topics were agro-ecology and food sovereignty, climate

Alumni meeting at the event "Ugandan-Austrian University Cooperation" at Makerere University

Alumni with the Austrian Ambassador to Kenya, MA Christian Hasenbichler

change and water vulnerabilities and socio-cultural aspects of health. Each evening focussed on a different central theme and was accompanied by a project presentation and matching movies or documentaries.

Also, in the context of APPEAR project monitoring visits, we organised for the first time an alumni meeting at Makerere University Kampala, Uganda and at Kenyatta University in Nairobi, Kenya, to showcase the importance of institutionalised cooperation between Austria, Uganda and Kenya. The event addressed current and former scholarship holders, but was also open to university staff, lecturers and researchers, and other stakeholders interested in current and future cooperation with Austria. The objectives were to discuss the multifarious challenges and advantages of Ugandan/Kenyan-Austrian university cooperation and to spark ideas regarding potential opportunities for future projects. In organising the events, we worked closely with former scholarship holders in Uganda, with Dr. Helen Nakimbugwe, a member of the APPEAR Steering Committee, and in Kenya with Dr. Pamela Ngugi and Dr. Luke Olang, the coordinator of a research project recently financed by the Commission for Development Research (KEF).

Application of knowledge

Higher education and research will only contribute to societal development and positive change if the acquired scientific knowledge, methods and skills are relevant and applicable in a local context and put into practice in their respective environment. Therefore, the development orientation of a proposed study is one of the main selection criteria for the award of a scholarship. In addition, priority is given to scholarships that are linked to APPEAR projects. For example, TRANSACT, a project to strengthen rural transformation competences among Ethiopian consortium partners in research and training in the Amhara Region, Ethiopia (see Chapter 9.2.), integrated three doctoral students – Ms Atsede Desta, Mr Kumela Gudeta and Mr Asaminew Tassew. They conducted their research on demography, livestock production and non-farm livelihoods in the same study area, they used the same methodology (scenario planning) and they collected data in a coordinated manner. Reports about the different themes were presented in the project. Finally the doctoral students also participated in the integration of the scientific findings in the same conceptual framework. This approach has several advantages (even though the whole process requires additional time and resources for coordination and preparation). The doctoral students' research on a development-oriented topic, they receive feedback from different supervisors, stakeholders and their fellow colleagues, they get support during their field studies and they learn to work in an international, inter- and transdisciplinary project. This joint approach contributed directly to the success of the project by helping in the analysis of the system and transformation processes in the study area with regard to the respective disciplines. After the completion of their PhDs, Ms Atsede Desta, Mr Kumela Gudeta and Mr Asaminew Tassew will return to the Amhara region with new skills and capacities that are valuable for their respective home institutions.

APPEAR is only effective if the sponsored scholars successfully complete their studies. Therefore we would like to thank our scholarship holders for their commitment and hard work, as well as their scientific supervisors for their dedicated support and guidance. We look forward to staying in touch and to receiving project proposals from our current and former scholarship holders.

TRANSACT project partners and scholarship holders at the event "Linking-up Ethiopian APPEAR projects"

Introduction to the following articles
Unfortunately, not all 126 appear scholarship holders could send a reflection about the experiences they gathered during their APPEAR scholarships for this volume. The following contributions, however, will give an impression about the diversity of our students with regard to countries, professional background and academic disciplines.

- *Ronald Luwangula and Elijah Ndung'u:* Both scholarship holders are pursuing their PhDs within the project "Promotion of Professional Social Work towards Social Development and Poverty Reduction in East Africa, PROSOWO" (see Chapter 7.4.). The two students have worked as project research assistants and presented their scientific findings at the International Social Work conference in Kampala in 2014. Ronald co-authored a Chapter in the PROSOWO book publication and Elijah co-authored the book "The Role of Social Work in Poverty Reduction and the Realization of Millenniums Development Goals in Tanzania".
- *Wossen Argaw Tegegn:* Gender sensitivity is one of the basic principles of APPEAR. In order to build upon the experiences of women working in higher education research in the ADC key regions in general, and upon the gender mainstreaming experiences of the current projects in particular, in 2013 we organized a gender workshop. In addition to APPEAR project partners we also invited Wossen to represent female scholarship holders. Wossen was the founder of the Gender Equity Office at her home university, has long experience in gender issues in the higher education system and pursued her PhD on the topic of "Gendered Exclusion in a Technology University, Ethiopia: Institutional Culture as a Barrier for Participation" at the University of Vienna. She was super-

vised by Social and Cultural Anthroplogist Marie-France Chevron, whose contribution on "What does it mean to be a scientific supervisor within the APPEAR Scholarship Programme?" can be found in the following Chapter.
- *Sarah Ayeri Ogalleh:* Sarah is an environmental scientist by training and was a PhD candidate at Centre for Development Research (CDR), University of Natural Resources and Life Sciences, Vienna (BOKU). As part of the Friday lectures she was invited for the Roundtable Discussion on "Teaching in English? Preconditions, Advantages, Problems". The objective of the Friday lectures was to present the multidimensional strategy "internationalization 'at home' and ways of integrating intercultural, international and global dimensions into the curricula and teaching/learning processes at the universities".
- *Kalkidan Obse:* Kalkidan is pursuing his PhD within the "Academic Partnership on Legal and Human Rights Education, APLHRE" at the University of Graz in Austria (see Chapter 9.1.). Human rights are a central topic in our programme; therefore we have on several occasions asked Kalkidan to share his expertise. As mentioned before, he explained the Rights Based Approach in the two workshops on human rights for international students, he wrote an article about the reciprocity between human rights and development, with a particular focus on Ethiopia for the ADC journal "Weltnachrichten" and he presented the project ALPHRE during the event "Linking-up Ethiopian APPEAR projects" in Vienna.

10.2 Perspectives from Students and a Supervisor

10.2.1 Experiences of scholarship holders

by Ronald Luwangula and Elijah Macharia Ndung'u

Introduction

From April 2012 to March 2015 we were privileged and honoured to be welcomed into the APPEAR family as PhD scholarship holders within the PROSOWO project (see Chapter 7.4). Our tenure throughout has been marked by a series of unforgettable experiences in Austria and our respective countries (Uganda and Kenya). Our PhD studies in Psychology touch upon the domains of psychosocial development, social work, and poverty alleviation, which are key focus areas of the PROSOWO project. Our PhDs are titled:

- *Towards Rewriting Children's Bondage in Poverty and Vulnerability: Underscoring the Fundamentals to Realizing Children's Social Protection Rights in Uganda* (Ronald Luwangula)
- *The Role of Social Workers in Addressing Trauma of Poverty: A Kenyan Perspective* (Elijah Macharia Ndung'u)

Our experiences

Our first encounter with APPEAR and PROSOWO took place months before our arrival in Austria (i.e. before the start of our PhD studies), when we were given the opportunity to participate in pioneering social work research in East Africa. At that time we had yet to secure scholarships and little did we know that this research project would set the ball rolling for our future and further involvement with APPEAR and PROSOWO.

Our experience of the culture of the OeAD will remain alive in our memories and hearts forever. After securing scholarships and eventually arriving in Austria, it was very pleasing to be part of the welcome meetings organized by OeAD for its scholars. In addition, the OeAD not only kept us continuously updated regarding new initiatives relevant to scholarship and international development, but also facilitated our engagement in a number of these activities and development discourses in Austria. The countless invitations from the OeAD to take part in and contribute to workshops, conferences, get-togethers and tours in Vienna and Salzburg were very much appreciated. The most recent, and also perhaps among the most insightful of these, were the PROSOWO book launch/presentation in Vienna (APPEAR in Practice 5) and the 6th Austrian Development Conference in Salzburg.

Yet another dimension of the OeAD's work is the opportunity accorded to scholars to participate in extra-curricular social activities such as excursions. We very much enjoyed our trips to Italy, Vienna, Salzburg and Klagenfurt. Involvement in these numerous academic and extra-curricular activities really gave us the comforting feeling of being "home away from home". We felt APPEAR appreciated that being PhD scholars is not only about academics;

we also felt integrated and were thankful for the opportunity to become familiar with Austria's cultural, geographical, political, historical, religious, social, architectural art, and rich natural heritage.

We have had invaluable opportunities to take part in PROSOWO activities both in Austria and East Africa. Besides taking part in data collection and analysis, we also actively participated in:

- The 26th June, 2012 Symposium at Carinthia University of Applied Science (CUAS), Feldkirchen
- The International Social Work Conference held in Kampala (16th–18th March, 2014) during which we presented the following papers: *Negotiating between Reuniting "Missing Children" with their Families and Protecting them in the Process: The Dilemmas of CFPUs (Child and Family Protection Units) of Police, Kampala* (Ronald Luwangula) and *Role of Social Workers in Addressing Trauma of Poverty in Kenya* (Elijah Macharia Ndung'u)
- The 6th Austrian Development Conference at Salzburg University (14th-16th November 2014) where we together presented a conference paper entitled *Embracing New Dimensions in Social Development: Role of Social Workers in Addressing Trauma of Poverty in Kenya*
- PROSOWO book presentation at CUAS on 17th November 2014
- Ronald Luwangula co-authored a chapter in the PROSOWO book publication[3]
- Elijah M. Ndung'u co-authored a book about Social Work in Tanzania[4]

Our report would be lacking if we did not mention the qualities and nature of our Professors Klaus Ottomeyer (our primary supervisor) and Helmut Spitzer (overall PROSOWO project coordinator). Anecdotal reports about the way supervisors treat their supervisees back home meant we arrived in Austria with scepticism, angst and some sense of powerlessness in expectation of similar treatment. We are very glad to say that the two Austrian professors' care and kindness dispelled our fears from the very start. The communication, mentorship and working relationships were supportive and less hierarchical and less bureaucratic than our experiences back home. We felt involved and empowered and that our professors regarded us more as colleagues than students.

Another pillar of support came in the form of APPEAR team member Ms Elke Stinnig, whose motherly yet professional care and guidance cannot be overstated – especially in our complex dealings with the Immigration Department in Klagenfurt. We also cannot forget Dr. Franklin Adegeye, who has since sadly passed away, and Ms Sabrina Riedl for their support where the language barrier was a problem. The duo separately, on different occasions, left their comfort zones to come to our rescue. The OeAD Regional Office in Klagenfurt was

---

3   Luwangula, R./Riedl, S. (2014): Integrating Social Work Services into Schools: A Case for School Social Work in Uganda. In Spitzer, H./Twikirize, J. M./Wairire, G. G. (Eds.): Professional Social Work in East Africa: Towards Social Development, Poverty Reduction and Gender Equality. 1st Ed. Kampala, Fountain Publishers. Pp. 315–332.

4   Mabeyo, Z.M./Ndung'u., E.M./Riedl, S. (2014): The Role of Social Work in Poverty Reduction and The Realization of Millennium Development Goals in Tanzania. Kampala, Fountain Publishers

inevitably a blessing for us, as Ms Ulrike Wallenko and Dr. Franklin Adegeye were never tired of our endless questions and unannounced knocks on their doors.

It is gratifying to be able to acknowledge the assistance afforded to us as part of the PROSOWO project, as well as to know that our PhD studies contributed to such an important project. Right from the start, when first conceptualising our PhD topics, it was forefront in our minds that we needed to remain focussed on and relevant to the broader project framework while simultaneously contributing to scholarly and development discourses. We are happy to note that Elijah's focus on the social workers' role in addressing the trauma of poverty in Kenya and Ronald's emphasis on children's social protection rights in Uganda affirm the PROSOWO agenda.

On another promising note, the PROSOWO project added greatly to our professional, scholarly, and social work experience. We have gained a greater appreciation for international social work, social work practices in different contexts, as well as local approaches (some of which we had taken too long for granted) and professional and social networks. The PROSOWO book publication was very timely and its different book chapters are very relevant to our PhD dissertations, so much so that it is something of a "one-stop shop" of material relevant to our PhD dissertations. In our view, the book is a social work handbook in its own right.

Our involvement with APPEAR and the PROSOWO project helped us develop professionally, academically and in our practical abilities and perspectives. We doubt if we could have had any more rewarding, enriching and worthwhile opportunity than we had under APPEAR in general and PROSOWO in particular.

10.2.2 From Kenya to Austria – key lessons learnt

by Sarah Ayeri Ogalleh

Researchers and beneficiaries

This doctoral research was funded by APPEAR. I was an APPEAR grant holder affiliated to the Centre for Training and Integrated Research in Arid and Semi-Arid Lands Development (CETRAD), which has been working in this area for over 3 decades in Kenya. While in Austria, I was affiliated to the Centre for Development Research (CDR) at the University of Natural Resources and Life Sciences (BOKU), Vienna. The project was conducted in Laikipia County of Kenya, in Umande and Muhonia. The project's beneficiaries were the small scale farmers (smallholders), who are experiencing agricultural challenges as a result of climate change and climate variability. With scientific research findings validated by the local communities, the findings can be used by scientists and development agents to tailor their localized agricultural programmes to the needs of farmers, taking into consideration the challenges posed by climate variability and changes to agriculture. In this way, adaptation options that are feasible, practical and attractive to farmers can be supported and sustained by scientific innovations which work together with smallholders' local indigenous knowledge.

Project rationale and results
According to the Intergovernmental Panel on Climate Change's (IPCC) 4th Assessment Report, in the future drier areas will be affected by more droughts while the rainfall regime in general will become rougher and unpredictable in these areas. In Sub-Saharan Africa, and Kenya in particular, agriculture is the main source of livelihood for the majority of resource-poor farmers. Specifically in Laikipia County, located in the arid regions of Mount Kenya, agriculture-dependent communities continue to expand into more marginal, arid ecosystems, where rainfall quantities and distributions crucially impact the natural resources on which agriculture depends. Climate change and climate variability will complicate this situation, particularly for the resource-poorest farmers (of whom the majority are female). Thus, the vulnerability of livelihoods reliant on agriculture is increased and most likely exacerbated and accelerated by climate change and variability.

Localized adaptations by farmers have been seen as a means of empowering these resource-poor farmers to cope with climate variability and climate change. It is therefore important that this research – which focusses on what local farmers can do to cushion themselves against the impacts of climate change while also taking into account local rainfall and temperature data and the farmers' own perceptions – reflects the scientific data, to show how localized knowledge can be instrumental to the research process and successfully integrated with science to inform adaptation practices. Science can provide incentives to farmers by supporting and promoting local, socially-feasible adaptations. Sustainable adaptations at local levels not only support livelihoods but also contribute to efficient stewardship of the environment and to the sustainability of agricultural livelihoods. Our research was conducted in Kenya's Laikipia County, in the sub-locations of Umande and Muhonia, where 288 farmers participated through quantitative data collecting instruments (questionnaire), while about 200 farmers participated via qualitative data gathering methods such as focus group discussions, key informant interviews and participant observation.

Project results
Farmers' perceptions mirror the observed climatic data (rainfall and temperature) for the past 47 years, suggesting that the onset of the rainy season has been shifting later, from March to April, in recent decades, while rainfall intensity and total rainfall have both also changed drastically in that period, hence interfering with farming practices. Farmers term such climatic changes '*majimbo*', meaning that rainfall has become unpredictable and is not to be depended upon as before. Farmers have accumulated a wealth of knowledge about adaptations that help them cope with the impacts of climate change, including early planting, using early maturing and late maturing seeds, continuous planting to increase the chances of a successful harvest and mulching, among other practices. Female and male farmers seem to have different preferences for adaptations. Women farmers are keener to make small shallow wells around plants as a means of saving and prolonging the rain water for the plants, for instance. In regards to livestock, the majority of farmers are actively reducing their livestock numbers, as well as storing grass and maize stalks for future use during dry and drought seasons.

The research's practical contribution is tied to its technical and practical relevance to the adaptation agenda of small-scale agriculture, which in turn helps the long-term sustainability of agriculture as a critical economic sector in Kenya and contributes to the maintenance of livelihoods in Kenya. Indeed, understanding local farmers' adaptations is key to a better stewardship of both the environment and the agricultural sector, and is a critical element in advancing the environmental, social and economic growth.

Personal perspectives from Austria
Travelling and living in an unfamiliar culture can be incredibly exciting, but it can also present significant challenges. Some of the key differences that were very clear to me from the moment I landed in Austria in October 2009 included the German language (in contrast to my English-speaking background), clothing (I arrived in Autumn and the temperatures were so cold for me – I was amazed at how I had to wear several clothes to feel warm), and new systems of working at the university (where in Kenya one registers face-to-face with lecturers and professors, at BOKU everything was online – complications which led me to miss some courses). Yet these cultural differences were key to my recognition of, and interest in, the beauty of being in a foreign country and the beautiful landscape of Austria, which inspired my need to explore the country. I must say that I was immediately impressed by Austria's efficient transport network. I felt so relieved to be able to travel from place to place without feeling stressed (silence in the public transport being contra to what am used to back in Kenya). Some of the key lessons I took from my experience of living in Austria include:

- Life is good and it can always be better anywhere in the world as long as you have the right company with you. At my institute (CDR), I met a young, energetic team, with whom I cooked, ate, partied, sledged and even swam in the Danube. I met a lot of nice people in Austria through many meetings (both planned and spontaneous), with whom I remain in contact even now. The power of integrating with other people bore great fruits of friendships, love and trust.
- The recognition that every meal shared is an opportune moment to be with good friends which should never be taken for granted. I appreciate sharing meals more than before and enjoy them every day even back here in Kenya. I have come to realize that in Africa we take a lot of moments with our relatives and friends for granted. In Austria, where everything involved planning and commitment, I learned that only those who make time for you will be there out of choice, and that it's not automatic for someone to be there just because you need them.
- The ability to question anything without feeling guilty for doing so. From my African background I am familiar with not being allowed to question many things, especially when they came from guardians, parents, professors, lecturers and so on. In Austria, it was a totally different scenario. Sitting in a mixed class of students proved to me that you can always share your opinion and that although many people may be of a different mind, in the long run we are working towards common goals.

10.2.3 Gains, deeds and suggestions: A personal reflection on PhD study

by Wossen Argaw Tegegn

Experiences and achievements

When I look back to the time I spent doing my PhD in Vienna, I find it to have been hugely fulfilling. During my stay there I enjoyed exposure to the international academic environment. Beyond my academic experiences in the regular PhD programme at Vienna University, I had the pleasure of occasionally attending public lectures and seminars on a wide range of topics and of having the chance to travel internationally to participate in seminars and workshops. I am particularly grateful to the open-mindedness and flexibility shown by my academic supervisor and the OeAD in supporting me to undertake a rewarding academic experience as a resident scholar in the USA from September 2011 to February 2012. This experience has certainly boosted my potential as a woman in academia to give back my knowledge and skills to the society from which I came and to the world at large. Beyond the academic gains, I should mention the worthy rewards I enjoyed socially and spiritually. My stay abroad enabled me to meet wonderful, spiritually nourishing people from various cultures. I have always loved meeting new people and having fulfilling conversations about real-life issues and personal human experiences, about families and dreams. In short, my stay abroad has had a hugely positive impact upon my professional and personal life.

I was able to experience all this because of my individual scholarship application to APPEAR. I think such individual applications for scholarships should be encouraged because they offer chances to potential candidates who might for a number of factors not otherwise be selected for project-based scholarships. Moreover, this scheme allows APPEAR to fund unique and interesting smaller-scale research proposal topics from individual applicants.

The PhD research

The impetus for doing PhD research on a gender topic came from my years of experience as the first woman hired in the university where the case study was undertaken. I was the founding head of the Gender Equity Office in 2003 and also served in other administrative positions. I took part in task-forces and committees. My day-to-day encounters with female students and administrative colleagues gave me the opportunity to hear about the overt and covert practices that undermine and disempower women. Discrimination, prejudice and harassment were some of the problems the Gender Equity Office grappled with. There were many administrative and cultural challenges that impeded the ethical handling of gender problems. Our day-to-day interactional and administrative challenges were tremendous. Along with other (volunteer) staff members, I invested long hours in helping female students and staff resolve their troubles. Such problems indicated the pressing need for a sound intellectual analysis of the possible solutions. My experience has helped me to perceive the gendered nature of behaviours, norms and practices within the academy.

These insights led me to initiate an advocacy-oriented research project that investigated gender from the perspective of institutional culture. Studying gender from this perspective enabled the explication of the often unspoken or hidden forms of inequality that exist between what people say and what they do. The research specifically looked at the extent to which Ethiopian universities of technology are different from or mirror the gender assumptions, expectations and stereotypes that exist in the broader society. It investigated gendered institutional norms, roles, and expectations, with attention to both micro- and macro-cultural processes. The research mainly employed a qualitative approach; however, some quantitative data was also used to demonstrate obvious institutional gender disparities as well as to illustrate the importance of exploring the stories that lie behind numerical descriptions.

The results show there are some societally-gendered assumptions, expectations and stereotypes that stay unchallenged in the technological university. My research demonstrated the ways in which women in technological subjects are consistently marginalised by dominant gendered norms, assumptions, expectations and habitual, seemingly natural practices and interactions. The study also showed how women in universities negotiate domination within the oft-unaccommodating "university culture" and actively create strategies for survival. By way of addressing the major problem, the study looked at the institutional gender equality initiatives being exercised in Ethiopian universities and suggested some new perspectives based upon a democratic pedagogy which could introduce transformational change to advance gender equality, social justice and democracy at institutions of higher learning in Ethiopia.

The way forward for scholarship holders

I believe other scholarship holders had similarly rewarding experiences like the one's mentioned above. APPEAR has been encouraging scholarship holders to initiate cooperative projects and build professional networks. Cooperative projects and professional networks are important in bringing about richer, more comprehensive and innovative research results. Scholarship holders can also serve as ambassadors for such wonderful initiatives and need to be proactive contact persons and initiators for future collaboration projects.

10.2.4 What does it mean to be a scientific supervisor within the APPEAR Scholarship Programme? My experience of supervising the doctoral thesis of Wossen Argaw Tegegn

by Marie-France Chevron

Wossen Argaw Tegegn received a doctorate with distinction at the University of Vienna, Faculty of Social Sciences, in November 2013. She wrote her doctoral thesis on "Gendered Exclusion in a Technology University, Ethiopia: Institutional Culture as a Barrier for Participation". The thesis was written with the support of the APPEAR Scholarship Programme and a fellowship at the SAR (School for Advanced Research in Santa Fe, USA).

Wossen came from Adama University (Ethiopia) to Vienna as a scholarship holder in November 2009. Wossen's supervisor was a colleague of mine within the Department for Social and Cultural Anthropology, University of Vienna. Unfortunately, however, this colleague fell seriously ill at the time Wossen came to Austria. Hence, Wossen came to me in February

2010, after several months without support to prepare her dissertation proposal, which must be completed before doctoral studies can begin at our University.

I supported Wossen in the preparation of the proposal and research design of her dissertation. It was a very intensive time as Wossen had to learn a lot about social and cultural anthropology. During our sessions it was necessary to identify her research questions and for me as a supervisor it was a big challenge to find some shortcuts which helped explain complex ideas and theoretical approaches. At this time Wossen had relatively concrete ideas and objectives but not yet the well-grounded education in methodology she would need for her project. It was interesting and exciting to help her to find her way and formulate these research questions according to a socio-cultural anthropological approach.

As the date of the next possible deadline for the presentation was at the end of June 2010, Wossen had to submit her proposal at the end of May 2010. The aforementioned delay caused some difficulties later, but Wossen is a very "tough" young woman (as tough as the women she studied in her doctoral thesis!) and she was able to catch-up. There was, however, only a little time left to actually prepare her fieldwork. Wossen was already scheduled to travel to Ethiopia in June 2010 to start her field research at her home university, which was to run until the end of February 2011. For this reason we pre-scheduled a couple of meetings before her departure and decided that I would continue to support and supervise her by email during her fieldwork. I would have preferred that she delayed her fieldwork but Wossen was eager to start as soon as possible. In the end the APPEAR team and I agreed because we had complete faith in her. It was really impressive to witness her progress.

At the end of 2010, Wossen was granted a 6-month fieldwork extension, during which I continued to supervise via email, answering questions and discussing the methodological problems of gathering and analysing data for such a project. It had been planned that Wossen would return to Vienna in the 2011/2012 winter term in order to discuss issues with her fieldwork, but instead Wossen received a unique opportunity to continue her research abroad. She received a scholarship from the US School for Advanced Research (SAR) to take part in a programme for the support and supervision of young doctoral fellows from developing countries. I find her SAR scholarship, earned as a result of her own efforts and qualities, commendable. It made sense to support her in achieving her goals.

It was important that I get a detailed picture of the progress of her work and of what she would need in the future. A presentation of her research at the SAR allowed Wossen to focus on revising her methodological considerations and the research steps necessary to answer her research questions. I had intensive contact with Dr. Brooks, head of SAR, to prepare the ground for Wossen's stay at this renowned school. There she would require further support in the areas of fieldwork methodology, data analysis and interpretation as well as the anthropological approach at large. For me, it was very important to work on these topics right from the beginning of my supervision.

At this time it was not really easy for Wossen and I to balance our competing duties. One of the biggest difficulties in the supervision of scientific work is to make clear the research question's importance and how every research step helps answer it. While at SAR, it was more important that Wossen understands how to approach well-known problems from a scientific perspective and how to write about them. Through our email contact and meetings in Vienna, however, I tried to impress upon Wossen the importance of reflecting upon the wider structure within such enquiry proceeds.

Despite the fact that Wossen had been in Vienna since November 2009, she was not able to take any university courses until spring 2010 for the above mentioned reasons. For doctoral candidates in Social and Cultural Anthropology, it is not always easy to submit the necessary evidence of academic achievement at the correct times, as they must spend many months (sometimes 12 months or more) in the field. Because of family-related factors – Wossen´s prolonged fieldwork stay was not only a necessity from a scientific point of view – we had to think about the best way to help her in observing the necessities of the programme. Thanks to the support of the APPEAR team, it was always possible to find out solutions in keeping with the goals of the programme. Hence, despite difficulties, we were able to keep to the work schedule and timetable for the scholarship period.

Following my recommendation, Wossen selected several doctoral seminars in my department about "The Engine of Anthropological Field Work" as well as two seminars in other departments: in African Studies on "African Gender Studies" and in Sociology on "Gender and Science". During the 2012 winter semester, Wossen attended a research laboratory on "Global Entanglements and Multi-sited Ethnography" and a methodology seminar on "Ethnographic Methods" at the Department of Social and Cultural Anthropology and of Methodology of the Faculty for Social Sciences.

Additionally, as an APPEAR scholarship holder, Wossen received financial support to attend academic conferences in Switzerland and in USA. She also presented her research at a conference at Adama University in her home country. After Wossen had passed the required PhD seminars and courses, she needed to deal exclusively with the write-up of her dissertation during spring and summer 2013. From May/April until the end of August we had regular meetings and intensive discussions about her PhD thesis and the writing process.

As already stated, Wossen's thesis examined gender inequality in a technology university in Ethiopia. All areas of the university were considered, including the university as a world of its own, but also as part of Ethiopian society. Therefore Wossen explored the institutional and cultural factors that either facilitate or hinder the participation (access and degree) of female students in technological studies in Ethiopia. Selected works from cultural philosophers such as Bourdieu and Foucault were important in helping the thesis examine the university as a cultural and social phenomenon.

Studying women and gender in a broader societal and traditional context was a huge challenge which resulted from the need to scientifically explore what is a highly controversial topic, politically and socially, for Ethiopian society. The main task herein was to describe the hegemonic gender norms, assumptions and expectations in Ethiopian society which were also to be found in the university. The aim was to understand the ways gendered norms and ideologies are (re)produced or challenged in such a setting and to find new ideas how to change them.

The thesis presents political measures which aim to diminish gender inequality and to improve the status of female students in the education system in Ethiopia, as well as critical remarks about measures facilitating the access of women to universities. Although the research employed a qualitative methodology, a lot of statistics are used in the thesis to point out in which areas and at which levels there are inequalities at the university. Using this approach, Wossen was attempting to show how statistics are suggestive of one specific view of reality and how the observed reality differs from this. "Looking behind the aggregate numbers," one of the main phenomena which could be pointed out was the powerlessness of the people and the superiority of the institution. This idea is the red thread running through the thesis.

The thesis' methodology is in turn an important research outcome. Rather than espousing one doctrinal line, the thesis is a level-headed and well-reasoned attempt to find ways and means of identifying and embracing the observed phenomena. The large amounts of missing data make clear how difficult it is to get more exact information on the distribution of male and female staff and students at the different levels of the university. The figures also helped to address the invisibility of women in society.

The results of the qualitative research made it possible to explicate the characteristics of the institutional culture in the Ethiopian university and to show how behaviour can be explained by their expectations and opinions, as well as social norms. The results of the participant observation and interviews enabled the pointing out of the symbolic and mental mechanisms which delimit technology as "tough", and hence as a male field of action. The thesis' qualitative methods also helped explicate the hidden problems in the relationships between male and female students and staff members.

The ethnographic fieldwork made it possible to consider and study everyday actions and interactions. The everyday typical situations in the laboratories of the case study university made clear how traditional, social and cultural behaviours are reproduced in new contexts. During her scholarship, Wossen and I both learned a lot. One of the main goals of research and inquiry in the humanities and sciences is to describe, understand and change things. Wossen Argaw Tegegn is a very talented young woman who demonstrates that women are indeed "tough" enough to effect change in society.

10.2.5 Of PhD, beer and Redbull: My student life

by Kalkidan Obse

I hardly knew anything about Austria a few years ago, and much less did I imagine I would end up studying here. It was while working as a lecturer at the Center for Human Rights at Addis Ababa University, which I had helped to establish as its first acting director, that I had the initial opportunity to meet my current supervisor Professor Wolfgang Benedek in July 2011. Prof. Benedek happened to be in Addis Ababa for a consultation on a proposed project partnership in the context of the APPEAR programme. The project brought together three partner institutions, namely the Institute of International Law at the University of Graz, our Center for Human Rights and the Institute of Federalism and Legal Studies of the Ethiopian Civil Service University. The tripartite project sought to support the rule of law and human rights education in Ethiopia through joint teaching and research programmes involving Austrian and Ethiopian academic staff associated with the partner institutions. The partnership also envisaged the possibility for staff from the Center to pursue postgraduate education at the University of Graz. Prof. Benedek took the occasion to discuss a separate collaborative project between the European Training and Research Centre on Human Rights and Democracy (ETC-Graz) and our Center for Human Rights to organize a regional human rights education workshop for human rights professionals working in East Africa. The successful collaborative workshop ultimately took place in March 2012, drawing participants from various parts of Ethiopia as well as East African countries including Uganda, Kenya and Tanzania.

I and another colleague from the Center for Human Rights arrived in Austria in April 2012 to commence doctoral study at the University of Graz. We were both enrolled in the doctoral programme in international law and both had Professor Benedek as principal supervisor. Although we were to undertake our studies in English, it became quickly apparent that we needed to understand some German to "survive" in Graz. I initially attempted to learn the language, but later abandoned it after I found it to be an onerous undertaking. I quickly developed the necessary "survival" mechanisms to live without the language as I found myself a small network of Austrian and international students with whom I could readily communicate in English. Of course, I knew how to order "one big beer" (ein großes Bier, bitte!) and say "prost!" at parties. Nevertheless, that did not help me avoid the embarrassment I sometimes felt having to admit that I didn't speak the language in spite of living in Austria for quite some time. The list of excuses I used over time included: "You know I am doing my studies in English", "My Austrian friends talk to me in English", "I am not staying here all the time", and "Who said every African wants to learn your language and take your job?" (I didn't actually use this one, but I felt like it when I met some annoying people who took offence at my inability to speak their language).

However, I certainly liked Austria and its people. In my estimation, Austrians may not be particularly keen to befriend strangers at first, but they turn out great friends once they are introduced to foreigners in proper contexts. I was impressed by the genuine effort Austrians made to pronounce people's names properly and understand how they are spelled. One of the first culture shocks I experienced was to realize how perfectly normal it is for Austrians to enquire how old you are upon your first introduction to them. I also found it interesting that an Austrian could explicitly say "I wanna buy you a drink because you bought me one last time" in stark contrast to the culture in Ethiopia where reciprocation operates in more subtle forms. Many Austrians know Ethiopia as a country of runners, so they might ask you to run with them sometimes when they know that you are from Ethiopia. I must say Austrian cities are particularly suited for running and cycling. I did develop a particular fondness for cycling and (occasionally) hiking, although my aversion to the cold climate didn't permit me to take part in the nationally popular winter sports of skiing and ice skating.

As a doctoral student at the University of Graz, I am working on a research project titled: "The Emerging Regional Regulation of Domestic Constitutional Law in Africa: The Quest for a Theory of International Constitutional Law". The project studies the emerging normative standards of the African Union (AU) which purport to regulate key aspects of domestic constitutional law and analyzes the implications thereof, in theory and practice. The dissertation investigates the topic in light of the discourse on global constitutionalism (international constitutional law) and a myriad of contemporary developments in the field of international law. While the research findings emphasise the progressive nature of the recent normative initiatives of the African Union, the research also identifies key conceptual limitations of the existing normative framework as well as the institutional and practical and challenges to the promotion of constitutionalism in Africa. The dissertation concludes by providing appropriate recommendations and proposals aimed at linking AU's recent adventurism in constitutionalism with a corresponding emphasis on institutional legitimacy and accountability of the regional organization.

My stay in Austria has provided me ample opportunity to learn about the country, its people and political culture. I was struck by the parallels that I observed between Austria and Ethiopia as much as by the stark differences that exist between the two countries. Both Austrians and Ethiopians particularly pride themselves on their respective country's great historical past, a fact which, together with the mountainous terrains of the countries, might explain why the countries tend to be generally shut off from the outside world. Both countries were formerly coastal states that became land-locked as they experienced break-up at different points in their history. Perhaps it was fitting that the countries at one point used the Maria Theresa thaler (referred to as "Marteresa" in Ethiopia) as their common currency. At the political level, both Austria and Ethiopia currently practice a federal parliamentary system, in both cases composed of nine states. What sets Austria apart from Ethiopia is its rich democratic culture. I was particularly impressed by the politically active student clubs at Austrian universities, several of which are organized along existing party-political lines.

The course of my doctoral study has not been an easy undertaking, to say the least. It is an understatement to describe the PhD process as a daunting task as it can quite literally make the life of the researcher miserable. Success in undergraduate and master's programmes is generally an easy feat for the perceptive mind. The worst procrastinator endowed with the necessary intellectual acumen can achieve great results in these programmes by simply devoting a portion of his time to prepare for exams or to write short papers within short deadlines. In comparison, the PhD requires the production of a book length original research work over a long period of time. The absence of an immediate incentive of success or threat of failure creates a fertile environment for procrastination during which the researcher can entertain himself into failure through immersion in endless theoretical speculation and frequent conference participations. By the time the necessary threat begins to materialize with the approach of the final deadline, it can be too late to produce a book length of original research work. Ideally, success in doctoral study requires a mix of genius and perseverance, two character traits that don't generally go together (except for amongst a lucky few). As for me, I partly attribute my success to the opportunity I had to undertake my study in the country which gave the world the energy drink Red Bull, a potent source of vigour and perseverance, if not genius.

I am very grateful!

AUTHORS

Chapter 1

Gertraud Findl works in the Themes and Quality Unit of the Austrian Development Agency, the operational unit of Austrian Development Cooperation (ADC). As Advisor for Education and Science, she is mainly responsible for the strategic development of the sector as well as the quality assurance of ADC-financed programmes and projects in the fields of higher education, scientific cooperation and research (including APPEAR) as well as vocational education and training.

Robert Zeiner has more than 30 years of experience in diverse development cooperation organisations and has been, since the beginning of 2004, the Director of Programmes and Projects International for the Austrian Development Agency. Robert Zeiner started his professional career in the Austrian Steel Industry (conducting feasibility studies) and worked from 1983 to 1985 as the director of an SME in Austria. From 1986 to 1991 he was programme coordinator for the Austrian Service for Development Cooperation for Central America, where he was based in Managua, Nicaragua. From 1991 to 2003, Robert Zeiner was director of the Austrian Service for Development Cooperation and HORIZONT3000.

Chapter 2

Andreas J. Obrecht is a social and cultural anthropologist, writer and sociologist; Assistant Professor at the Institute of Sociology, University of Vienna (1988-1993); habilitation in sociology with an emphasis on developmental sociology (1997); head of the Interdisciplinary Research Institute for Development Cooperation (IEZ), Johannes Kepler University Linz (1998-2009); Visiting Professor for the thematic focus Sub-Saharan Africa and South Pacific at the Department for Contemporary History, Karl Franzens University Graz (1998-2013); since 2004 host for science and culture in the ORF-radio broadcast „Von Tag zu Tag"; since 2009 head of the Commission for Development Research (www.kef-research.at) at the Austrian Agency for International Cooperation in Education and Research (OeAD GmbH) and head of the Austrian Partnership Programme in Higher Education and Research for Development (www.appear.at).

Chapter 3

Elfriede Fröschl is a sociologist. Co-founder of Austria's first women's shelter, located in Vienna, and founder of a counselling centre for women in distress in Vienna. Ms. Fröschl has worked as a social worker and as a counsellor and is engaged as a freelance investigator in several social research projects. Currently she coordinates the "Ursachen und Folgen von Gewalt in der Familie" project that analyses the causes and consequences of violence in families. She is FH Professor at the Department of Social Work at the University of Applied Sciences, FH Campus Wien in Vienna and a member of the TECS-team. TECS aims at the improvement of social work education in El Salvador.

Claudia Margarita González López, born 1985 in Managua, Nicaragua; diploma in Technical Chemistry at Universidad Nacional Autónoma de Nicaragua - UNAN-Managua in 2010; research work about precipitation of various substances in milk within the human body; professional experience at UNAN laboratories of Microbiology; collaboration with BIOREM project; focus on bioremediation of heavy metal contaminated soil and water. Since 2012 master's student in Environmental Geology at Vienna University (APPEAR grant), research work on effects of Titaniumdioxide-ultraviolet-systems on humanic acids.

Eva Klawatsch-Treitl is an economist and economic educator. Research focusses are in the areas of heterodox economy and economy of care. Temporarily working as main staff for research and teaching at the Department of Social Work at FH Campus Wien, University of Applied Sciences. She has been actively working in the area of development policy and advocacy both in an honorary capacity and full-time for many years. Adult educator in the area of Economic Literacy. Coordinator of the Association JOAN ROBINSON – Association for the distribution of economic knowledge fair to women, and chairwoman of the development policy network for women's rights and feminist alternatives - WIDE. Coordinator of the academic cooperation TECS - within APPEAR.

Roland Krebs is an Austrian Urban Planning Specialist with experience in strategy planning and urban design and development. He holds a Master of Science in Urban Planning (2001, Vienna University of Technology) and a Master of Business Administration (2007, Universidad de Belgrano, Buenos Aires) and is currently working as planner, designer and project manager in the field of urban development. As a proposal writer and strategy-designer, he has gained experience with international organizations like the URBACT, Austrian Development Agency (ADA), Nordic Development Fund (NDF), the World Bank (WB) and the Inter-American Development Bank (IDB).

Angelika Kreitner, born 1986 in Arequipa, Perú, graduated in International Economy and Business Administration from Vienna University's Faculty of Business, Economics and Statistics, and Media Sciences from the Faculty of Philological and Cultural Studies. Professional experience in documentation and risk analysis of contaminated sites for GeoRisk Environmental Services and various projects regarding ecological research. Beyond that she has worked for Tanzquartier Vienna, Sucht- und Drogenkoordination Vienna and Hochschülerschaft at the University of Vienna. In the area of Gender Studies, she has assisted in various sociological projects with a quantitative as well as a qualitative approach. She currently works as a project manager in the area of advertising.

Gerhard Kreitner was born in Vienna in 1956 and studied Biology, Geography and Regional Sciences at Vienna University, graduating 1983. Professional experience since 1981 at various institutions, e.g. Research Institute for Renewable Energy and Environmental Planning Vienna, Austrian Development Service in Cotahuasi, Peru (advisor of environmental development projects), teaching at Cotahuasi Technical College, Institute for Energy Sciences and Economy Vienna, Institute for Regional Planning of Lower Austria, Environment Agency Austria, research work and field studies on international development, documentation and evaluation of contaminated sites. Various publications focused on bioremediation of contaminated soil and groundwater. Chairman of Institute for Ecological Urban Development Vienna.

Verónica Mora is graduate in Architecture of the National University of Engineering, Nicaragua and completed an MA in Urban Management and Social Vulnerability at the Universidad Centroamericana (UCA) in Managua. She is coordinator of the APPEAR project Urban_Managua. She currently teaches in the UCA's School of Architecture (Faculty of Science, Technology and Environment); her experience is focussed on the social housing sector and the improvement of neighbourhood and housing. She is also a member of the Board of Directors of the Prodel Foundation of Nicaragua that promotes the local development of low-income sectors.

Verena Pflug grew up in Vienna. She studied International Development at the University of Vienna, focussing on Central America as well as Spanish Language Studies. In 2006/07, she spent two semesters as a visiting student at the University of Costa Rica in San José and returned for two months in 2009 to do research for her master's thesis about everyday forms of resistance on United Fruit Company plantations. She graduated in 2010 and worked for the APPEAR project DEPARTIR from 2011 to 2014. In 2013, she finished her part time social work studies and now works as a social worker in Vienna.

Daniel Querol studied Quantitative Biology in Paris and obtained a master's degree in Plant Breeding at McGill, Canada in 1980. He has organized Genetic Resources programmes at state and community level in 6 countries. He has worked on the linking of academic processes with rural realities for the last 25 years. He has been an advisor to the National Agricultural University in Nicaragua since 2007, bridging student and academic staff capabilities with the problems in rural communities through the Integral Participatory Rural Development Program. He coordinated the DEPARTIR-Changing Minds and Structures project, funded through APPEAR.

Maritza Rivas de Romero received her master's in Educational Sciences with a major in Language and Literature. She also has an academic and professional background in journalism, in methodologies and models for online education and in business administration and management in the educational fields. She is Dean of the Faculty of Theology and Humanities, General Administrative Office of the university – Universidad Luterana Salvadoreña (ULS). She participates in the revision of study programmes, develops implementation plans, participates in auto studies for the evaluation of performance processes in higher education, is a member of the project team concerning the partnership in Social Work between Universidad Luterana Salvadoreña and FH Campus Wien and a member of the TECS-Team.

Christoph Stoik is a professional social worker and working as a Lecturer and Academic Associate in the Department of Social Work (master's degree programmes: Social Spatial and Clinical Social Work) at FH Campus Wien. Research foci: community work, community orientation and social space, urban planning, theory and methodology of social work. Counselling of community-based social work projects in Vienna. He is a member of the Austrian TECS-Team.

Eneyda Carolina Arteaga de Valle did her graduate studies in Social Work at the Universidad de El Salvador and at the Universidad Luterana Salvadoreña (ULS) in El Salvador. She has worked in social integrated and protected households for adolescents and teenagers and in counselling institutions of UNICEF in the fields of elementary education and social integration. Coordinator of the Department of Social Work at ULS until October 2014. Currently she works as a Lecturer at ULS, and as an Associated Consultant at the company Desarrollo, Investigación y Consultoría S.A de C.V. (DEICO) San Salvador. DEICO is dedicated to improving the life quality of patients with chronic diseases through healthy nutrition.

Angelika Widowitz, from 2011 to 2014 Social Work degree programme at FH Campus Wien, University of Applied Sciences. Working as a social worker in public service, co-author of the group bachelor thesis "Life thereafter – empowerment strategies of the 'Association of Viennese Women's Centers and their sustainable impacts on concepts of life of former residents", whose main findings have been published in the TECS final publication.

Chapter 4
Samia Al-Botmeh is an Assistant Professor in Economics at Birzeit University, where she has also been the director of the Centre for Development Studies. She completed her PhD at the School of African and Oriental Studies, University of London, in Labour Economics. The title of her thesis was "'Palestinian Women's Labour Supply: Towards an Explanation of Low and Fluctuating Female Labour Force Participation". Areas of interest and publication are gender economics, labour economics, and political economy of development. As part of her directorship, Samia led a number of projects, including the APPEAR project "Conflict, Participation and Development in Palestine". Other projects have included alternatives to neo-liberal development, state formation in Palestine, the macroeconomics of the labour market in Palestine, and gender differentials in labour market outcomes.

Abaher El-Sakka is currently a Professor at the Department of Social and Behavioral Sciences, at Birzeit University, Palestine. He has worked as a Lecturer and Visiting Professor in different French and Belgium universities. Researcher associated to L'institut français du Proche-Orient. He has also published different studies on artistic modes of expressions, social and collective memory, and social identity and protest movements. His most recent publications include *Supporters à distance: les fans du Barça et du Réal en Palestine, La réception populaire de clubs Barça-Real dans la société palestinienne, in Jeunesses arabes. Loisirs, cultures et politique.* Laurent Bonnefoy, François Burgat et Myriam Catusse (dir.), La Découverte septembre 2013; *Les mobilisations protestataires palestiniennes actuelles*, l'iReMMO Institut de Recherche et d'Etudes Méditerranée Moyen- orient, 2013.

Grigor Doytchinov is an architect and has been Professor at the Institute of Urbanism, Graz University of Technology since 1992. He is also a Visiting Professor at RWTH Aachen, STU Bratislava and University of Maribor (2008-date). He studied at the RWTH Aachen and at the UACEG Sofia, and has practiced and researched at SOFPROJEKT and the International Academy of Architecture Sofia. He was a member of the Expert Commission for the Preservation of the Graz Historic Centre and the Jury for the Europa Nostra/European Union Award for Cultural Heritage in The Hague. He has numerous publications on urban design and planning, urban preservation and history of urbanism.

Helmut Krieger is a Lecturer at the Department of Development Studies at the University of Vienna and a consultant to the VIDC/Wiener Institut. He completed his PhD with a thesis on state formation in Palestine from a political economy perspective at the Department of Political Science at the University of Vienna. His main research interests include the Israeli-Palestinian conflict, social movements and the postcolonial state in the Arab world, materialist state theories and the state in the global south as well as international political economy and postcolonial theory. Latest publication: *Umkämpfte Staatlichkeit. Palästina zwischen israelischer Besatzung, neoliberaler Entwicklung und politischem Islam. VS-Verlag: Wiesbaden, 2015.*

Ayman Abdul Majeed is a researcher and survey unit coordinator for the Center for Development Studies at Birzeit University. He has spent nearly 20 years in community research programmes focussed on marginalized groups and areas including remote areas, women, youth, people with disability, children, and Palestinian refugees in Palestine, Jordan and Lebanon. He holds a master's degree in Gender and Development (Birzeit University), and a BA in Sociology (Al-Najah University). Recent publications: *Women with Disability and Access to formal Justice Pillars. Birzeit: CDS, Birzeit University 2013; The Low Participation of Youth in the Labor Market in Palestine: Reasons and Limitations from Gender Perceptions. Population council – Cairo, 2011*

Samar Al Nazer obtained her PhD in Landscape Architecture in January 2009 from the Landscape Department at the University of Life Sciences in Norway, and her Master of Philosophy in Landscape Architecture from the University of Newcastle upon Tyne in the UK in July 1987. Her first degree in Architectural Engineering is from the Faculty of Engineering, University of Jordan in 1980. Currently she is teaching as a Lecturer in the Department of Architecture and on the Landscape Architecture master's programme at Birzeit University.

Dima Yaser is currently an instructor with the Department of Architectural Engineering at Birzeit University. She received her BSc in Architectural Engineering from Birzeit University, where she worked as a teaching assistant for two years. Then she earned a Fulbright scholarship for her master's degree at Pennsylvania State University in the United States. Her research interests are in the fields of urbanism, architectural theory and design, theories of heritage and culture and sustainability. Her teaching areas include architectural theory and design, landscape architecture and visual communication.

Chapter 5
Tri Ratna Bajracharya studied Mechanical Engineering at Tribhuvan University of Kathmandu, Nepal. He graduated in 2007, conducting his doctoral research on "Efficiency Deterioration in Small Pelton Turbines due to Sand-Particles-Led Bucket Erosion". Currently he is director of the Center for Energy Studies at the Institute of Engineering at Tribhuvan University, responsible for energy based projects and various research projects. He also holds membership at the Nepal Engineering Council, the Nepal Engineers Association (NEA), the Society of Mechanical Engineers Nepal (SOMEN) and the Association for Solar Thermal Energy Development Nepal (ASTED).

Eduard Doujak obtained his doctorate in Mechanical Engineering from the Vienna University of Technology in 2000. He is currently working as an Assistant Professor at the Institute for Energy Systems and Thermodynamics (Fluid-Flow Machinery Research Group), also at Vienna University of Technology. His current major research interest is the development of a Small Hydro Pump-turbine for decentralized energy production and storage. He has also investigated the possibility of Small Hydropower Plant pressure pipe desilting by using strongly swirling flow in an Axial Hydro cyclone. In this matter he holds national and international patents and received the national INVENTUM price for the second best invention in 2011. Currently he is also teaching Hydropower Development and Operation at the Tribhuvan University of Kathmandu in Nepal.

Chapter 6
Thomas Grechenig is the head of the Industrial Software (INSO) research group at the Vienna University of Technology and head of the European R&D-provider Research Industrial Systems Engineering (RISE). Professor Grechenig has 25 years of practical experience in industrial software development and IT-planning in general. Current industrial research application fields are Software Engineering, Usability Engineering, IT Security Engineering, Enterprise Information Systems, Health Telematics, Human Resource Management, e-Government and ID-Management Systems. Thomas Grechenig is the project coordinator of ICT4D.

Emílio Mosse is a Professor in the Department for Mathematics and Informatics at the Eduardo Mondlane University (UEM) in Maputo, Mozambique. His research interests are related to communication and work practices within the health sector and health information systems. He was appointed director for the master's programme in Informatics at the Faculty of Sciences in 2005 and head of the Department of Mathematics and Informatics in 2008. Currently he is involved in collaboration with the Faculty of Medicine on the establishment of a health information system.

Andrey Shindyapin works at the Department for Mathematics and Informatics at the Eduardo Mondlane University in Maputo, Mozambique. Areas of scientific interests include functional-differential equations and impulsive systems with applications in mathematical modelling. Professor Andrey Shindyapin has been a member of the academic council of the Faculty of Science since 2007.

Paul Pöltner is currently working on his PhD at the Vienna University of Technology. He is co-founder of the crowd-investing platform "Conda" and directing member of the non-profit organization ict4d.at. His field of research is the future of the internet from a technical and business point of view.

Philipp Schnatter is a student at the Vienna University of Technology. Currently he is writing his master's thesis in the Business Informatics programme. Philipp Schnatter has worked at Vienna University of Technology's INSO research group as project management and scientific assistant since 2012.

Chapter 7
Ekwamu Adipala is a Professor and a graduate of Makerere University and Ohio State University with academic training and specialization in Plant Pathology. He has successfully championed several initiatives in agricultural higher education, making significant contributions to institutional and human-resources capacity building efforts. He is currently the Executive Secretary of the Regional Universities Forum for Capacity Building in Agriculture (RUFORUM).

Grace Akello is a medical anthropologist trained in the Netherlands. She is currently a Senior Lecturer and coordinator for a pioneering Master of Medical Anthropology programme within the Department of Mental Health in the Faculty of Medicine, Gulu University, Uganda. Since November 2012 she has been a research fellow at the African Studies Centre in Leiden, the Netherlands. Her research interests include healthcare service provision for children and adolescents affected by armed conflict and HIV/AIDS in relation to their needs and priorities. She is particularly interested in using qualitative research findings to design major surveys, gendered research and theoretical analyses with the aim of linking evidence to policy-making and project design.

Susanne Dietl studied International Development with a focus on Gender Studies at the University of Vienna, Paris Denis Diderot and the University of Ottawa. Before joining APPEAR's Gender Mainstreaming and Gender Responsive Budgeting Project, she previously worked for the *Deutsche Gesellschaft für Internationale Zusammenarbeit* (GIZ) in their health division for two years. She is currently working as a psycho-social counsellor for unemployed and abused girls and women.

Luise Gubitzer is Professor of Economics at the Institute for Institutional and Heterodox Economics in the Department of Economics at the Vienna University of Economics and Business. Main research areas are topics in alternative economics, with a special emphasis on feminist economics.

Consolata Kabonesa is a Senior Lecturer and dean of the School of Women and Gender Studies, College of Humanities and Social Sciences, Makerere University, Uganda. She has over 20 years of experience as a gender analyst, researcher, trainer and facilitator. Her areas of research interest encompass issues that affect gender relations and human development, including employment, education, technology, health (especially HIV/AIDS), land tenure systems and climate change. She has a PhD in Human and Community Development with a minor in Gender Relations in International Development; an MS in Human Development and Family Studies from the University of Illinois at Urbana-Champaign, USA; an MA in English and American Literature and Higher Diploma in Education from University College Dublin, Ireland; and a BA in Liberal Arts from Stonehill College, Massachusetts, USA.

Elisabeth Klatzer, political economist, PhD from Vienna University of Economics and Business, MA in Public Policy from Harvard University; project leader of the APPEAR project "Gender Mainstreaming and Gender Responsive Budgeting in Uganda"; freelance researcher-activist and consultant; main research areas: feminist economics, gender responsive budgeting, transformation towards human and women's rights based economic integration at global and European level.

Ruth Kutalek, medical anthropologist; Associate Professor at the Centre for Public Health, Medical University of Vienna; Lecturer at the Institute of Cultural and Social Anthropology, University of Vienna and the University of Applied Sciences, Vienna; Visiting Professor at Gulu University, Uganda. She has done research in Tanzania, Uganda, Ethiopia, Liberia and Austria; her main fields of interest are medical anthropology/ethnomedicine, migration and health, global health, medical ethics, ethnopharmacology and ethnobotany. She has been engaged in the development of curricula for medical anthropology at several universities in Austria and Uganda. She has authored and edited numerous book-chapters, articles and several books.

Henry Manyire holds a PhD (Gender Studies), an MA (Women Studies) and a BA (Social Work and Social Administration) all obtained from Makerere University. He is currently a Senior Lecturer in the School of Women and Gender Studies, Makerere University. Teaches postgraduate diploma students of Gender and Local Economic Development courses in Gendered Poverty Analysis and Economic Empowerment and Gender Mainstreaming in Policies, Projects and Institutions. Also teaches a course in Feminist Economics for undergraduates. He further teaches graduate students courses in Gender and Economics of Developing Economies and Foundations of Gender Aware Economic Analysis. In addition, Henry supervises doctoral candidates enrolled at home and abroad.

Tabitha Mulyampiti studied Political Science (PhD, University of Vienna 2000) and Women's Studies (M.A, Makerere University, 1995). She is a Senior Lecturer at the School of Women and Gender Studies, Makerere University. Her published research includes: *"Strategies to Increase the number of Women in Higher Education Leadership"* (2014); *"Politics, the State and Civil Society: the Case of Human Rights Monitoring in Uganda"* (2012); *"Cities on the Move: Assessing Women's Contribution to Economic Growth in the Urban Kampala City"* (2013); *"Donor Power and National Discourse"* (2010); *"ABC approach to HIV/AIDS prevention in Uganda"* and *"The International Aid System and the shaping of the New Aid Modalities in Uganda"* (2011).

Michael Paul Nampala, is an alumnus of Makerere University, Imperial College of London (Wye College) and the University of Liverpool, with academic training in Crop Protection (majoring in Entomology and Crop Pest Ecology) and Public Health. Dr. Nampala is currently engaged in managing grants with a research portfolio that covers multidisciplinary projects implemented by inter- and transdisciplinary research teams with intense university engagement targeting development and deployment of interventions at household levels in 22 countries in Africa, under the auspices of the Regional Universities Forum for Capacity Building in Agriculture (RUFORUM), a network of 46 member universities.

Washington Odongo Ochola holds a PhD in Sustainable Agriculture and Rural Development from the Agricultural University of Athens. He currently works as Policy and Capacity Building Specialist for the USAID Building Capacity for African Agricultural Transformation (Africa Lead II) programme and previously worked as a programme manager for planning, monitoring and evaluation at RUFORUM, and as a sustainable development consultant at International Livestock Research Institute, United Nations Development Programme and Egerton University.

Emmanuel Okalany holds a master's in Geomatics and Natural Resources Evaluation from the University of Florence, Italy. He is currently a climate change policy analysis consultant at International Institute for Tropical Agriculture (Uganda) and previously worked as WATER-CAP project assistant at RUFORUM and assistant tutor on the International Training Course on Organic Agriculture hosted by the Centre for Development Research (CDR) at the University of Natural Resources and Life Sciences, Vienna, (BOKU*)*. His research interests are Soil Sciences, Climate Change and Agricultural Higher Education.

Florian A. Peloschek is a BOKU graduate with academic training in Environment and Bio-resources Management and Organic Agriculture. He has worked in Uganda, Kenya, Ethiopia, Burkina Faso and Bangladesh. His main research interests are sustainable farming, food security and secure livelihoods through inter- and transdisciplinary research approaches and establishing multi-stakeholder engagement through partnerships to sustain research interventions.

Kenneth Senkosi holds a master's in Soil Science from Makerere University and is engaged in rural development as executive director and founder of the Forum for Sustainable Agriculture in Africa. He is also currently working online as a support consultant at a US-based BLB Associates that specializes in developing fertilizer-related investment, policy and strategy instruments. He also works as a business development consultant at the DRC-based Centre for Studies and Actions for Sustainable Development. His main interests are sustainable farming & secure livelihoods through entrepreneurship.

Helmut Spitzer is a Professor of Social Work at the Carinthia University of Applied Sciences, Austria. He has vast research experience in East Africa. His research interests include children in extremely difficult circumstances, international social work, conflict studies, theory and practice of social work, and ageing. He served as the overall coordinator of the PROSOWO project, whose overall aim was to promote professional social work in East Africa. Recent publication (Ed. with J.M. Twikirize and G.G. Wairire): *Professional Social Work in East Africa. Toward Social Development, Poverty Reduction and Gender Equality* (2014)

Janestic Mwende Twikirize is a Lecturer at Makerere University, Department of Social Work and Social Administration, Uganda. Dr. Twikirize is the national coordinator (Uganda) of the PROSOWO project, the vice-president of the Association of Schools of Social Work in Africa (ASSWA) and a board member of the International Association of Schools of Social Work (IASSW). Her research areas and published works focus on a range of contemporary social development issues in her country and the wider African region.

Chapter 8
Philippe Cecchi is a French Senior Scientist at Institut de Recherches pour le Développement (IRD). Prof. Cecchi is a specialist of phytoplankton ecology in shallow waters, and has worked for 20 years in West Africa (Ivory Coast and Burkina Faso mainly) where he has led a succession of interdisciplinary research projects focussed on small reservoirs. He has developed integrated approaches that simultaneously took into account watershed perspectives, anthropogenic influences and ecological interactions in order to provide academic outputs as well as applied recommendations. He has supervised dozens of local students (master's and PhD) and shared the collectively acquired information through numerous scientific outputs. He is currently doing the same with the APPEAR project SUSFISH.

Colette Kabore, engineer for fisheries, holds a master's degree in Civil, Sanitary and Environmental Engineering. She is a specialist in gender and development, and director for standardization and technical support to private promoters at the General Directorate for Fisheries Resources. She owns the Medal of Honor for Forestry. Her main focus in the project SUSFISH was on gender issues.

Gustave B. Kabré is a Professor in the Life and Earth Sciences Training and Research Unit at the University of Ouagadougou (Burkina Faso). He has held the highest positions in his institute and in the University (e.g. Director of Faculty, President of the University). Currently he is the Head of the Laboratory of Animal Biology and Ecology (LBEA) and is a technical advisor to the Minister of Higher and Secondary Education. He is a specialist in fish parasites and diseases and also works on human waterborne diseases such as malaria and schistosomiasis. With LBEA he leads a team that focusses on several aspects of the challenges of water management, waterborne diseases and fisheries.

Martin Kiendrebeogo, biochemist of natural products, is the head of LABIOCA (Laboratoire de Biochimie & Chimie Appliquée) at the University of Ouagadougou, Burkina Faso. Prof. Kiendrebeogo obtained his PhD in 2005 from the University of Ouagadougou. He has benefitted from several doctoral and postdoctoral training programmes in France, Austria and Belgium, where he successfully established successful scientific cooperative projects. His current research interests are focussed on "anti-quorum-sensing" secondary metabolites to overcome bacterial chemoresistance, on natural antimalarial molecules and on the genotoxicity of medicinal plants. Through the MEAMP project, he developed his expertise on quality control assessment of medicinal plants. Prof. Kiendrebeogo also coordinates several other applied and research development projects.

Aline Lamien-Meda is from Burkina Faso, but has lived in Vienna since 2006. Dr. Lamien-Meda has worked as a Research and Project Assistant at the Institute of Animal Nutrition and Functional Plant Compounds, University of Veterinary Medicine, Vienna, Austria since 2007. She was responsible for the coordination of the MEAMP project. In her research activities, she works on active compounds from natural resources as medicinal plants. She did her master's and doctoral degrees at the LABIOCA (Laboratory of Applied Biochemistry and Chemistry), University of Ouagadougou, Burkina Faso.

Andreas Helmut Melcher is a Senior Scientist and Lecturer at the Institute for Hydrobiology and Water Management and partner of the Centre for Development Research at the University of Natural Resources and Life Sciences in Vienna (BOKU). His work is focussed on functional processes and structures of aquatic ecosystems and their environment – in particular ecological assessment methods, fisheries management and climate change effects. He is also interested in education, transformation and applied research bringing together ecology and socio-economy especially in the South (e.g. Burkina Faso, Ethiopia, Kenya, Uganda and Iran). Consequently, his main focus in the SUSFISH project was on overall coordination, education and aquatic ecology.

Otto Moog is a retired Professor of Hydrobiology and former head of the working group on Benthic Ecology and river quality assessment at BOKU's Institute of Hydrobiology and Aquatic Ecosystem Management. He has experience in coordinating EU projects focussing on ecological status assessment methods (AQEM, STAR, ASSESS-HKH), as well as on projects investigating river quality assessment; stream typology; delineation of ecoregions; neobiota; climate change; river restoration; benthic invertebrate taxonomy, faunistic and ecology; assessment and mitigation of environmental stressors with a focus on river engineering, hydropower generation, toxic effluents and organic wastes. Moog has published more than 250 scientific papers (50+ ISI publications). In SUSFISH he was responsible for higher education and the supervision of master's and PhD students.

Aimé J. Nianogo holds a PhD in Animal Science from the University of Georgia in the US (1985-1988). A University Lecturer since 1982, Professor Nianogo has held various positions, including Head of Department at the University of Ouagadougou, Head of Department at the Institute for Environmental and Agricultural Research (INERA), Director of the IUCN country office in Burkina Faso (2000-2008) and Regional Director for IUCN West and Central Africa regional office (since 2008). He has actively participated in several project and programme identification initiatives as well as fundraising efforts and currently supervises a project portfolio totalling more than 18 million Euros per year. Prof Nianogo is the author or co-author of more than 100 papers.

Adama Oueda is Senior Scientist and Lecturer in the Life and Earth Sciences Training and Research Unit at the University of Ouagadougou (Burkina Faso). He teaches ecology and biology at the Institute of Science in Burkina Faso and conducts research on pollution, food web and biodiversity in aquatic environments. He is very active in regional and international projects for collaborative research and education, e.g. BOKU, the Joint Research Unit BOREA of the National Museum of Natural History in Paris, the University Nangui Abrogoua in Côte d'Ivoire and the University of Abomey-Calavi in Benin.

Raymond Ouedraogo worked as a Senior Manager for the Capture Fisheries and Aquaculture section of the Fisheries Department of the Ministry of Environment and Sustainable Development in Burkina Faso from 1995 to 2012. He is currently a researcher at the Institute for Environment and Agriculture Research (INERA). His work is centred on fish ecology, capture fisheries, aquaculture, environmental awareness, aquatic ecosystems and gender. He holds a doctorate from BOKU, Vienna. His main focus in the SUSFISH project was on national project coordination, fisheries management and transformation.

Léon G. Blaise Savadogo, a medical doctor, is currently the head of the Epidemiology and Public Health Department of Bobo Dioulasso University's medical institute, as well as the head of the Laboratory of Nutrition and Health. Professor Savadogos work is centred on mother and child health, nutrition and survival. His main focus in the SUSFISH project was on sustainable fishing to fight hunger.

Moumini Savadogo has headed the IUCN program in Burkina Faso since 2008. In this capacity he coordinates activities covering the areas of biodiversity conservation, environmental governance and deployment of natural solutions to the global challenges of poverty alleviation, food security, climate change, green economy and sustainable development. His areas of interest are the integrated management of natural resources, production systems and environment interactions, climate change and environmental governance. He has been a researcher at the Institute of Environment and Agricultural Research and Wageningen University. From there he holds a doctorate in Animal Science and Sustainable Land Use. His main focus in the SUSFISH project was on biodiversity and endangered species.

Stefan Schmutz is Professor for Aquatic Ecology and head of the Institute of Hydrobiology and Aquatic Ecosystem Management at the BOKU in Vienna. He has experience in coordinating EU projects focussing on fish-based assessment methods biodiversity and multiple environmental stressors. He has published more than 60 scientific publications and has expertise in fish conservation, fish passes, climate change, river restoration and river management, allowing him to work on freshwater ecosystems in Europe, Asia, Africa and Northern America. In SUSFISH he is responsible for higher education and the supervision of master's and PhD students.

Jan Sendzimir is a systems ecologist working on questions of adaptation to and mitigation of the impacts of global change processes in social-ecological systems. He uses conceptual and formal modelling as well as social simulation (role-playing) integrated with field research within participatory science processes, e.g. Action Research or Adaptive Management, to guide scientific research and policy development related to the sustainable development of communities and ecosystems in river systems. He also works on governance issues of agro-forestry in Niger and of fisheries management in Burkina Faso. His scientific focus in the SUSFISH project was to integrate natural and social sciences to support a system analysis of the barriers and bridges to transformation of fisheries to sustainability in Burkina Faso.

Gabriele Slezak is Senior Scientist and Lecturer in the department of African Studies at the University of Vienna. Her work as a sociolinguist is focussed on questions of language awareness, power and ideology, the use of languages in urban contexts in Africa, as well as on their importance in education systems. In her research on linguistic practices in institutional settings she applies a pluri-lingual, speaker-centred approach, which considers languages as communicative resources in social practice. Additionally, she deals with transdisciplinary issues of internationalization policies in higher education systems and development studies. Her main focus in the SUSFISH project was on education and gender issues.

Patrice Toe graduated from the High School for Social Sciences (EHESS) of Paris; he is a Senior Lecturer in Socio-Anthropology of Development at the Institute of Rural Development (IDR), Polytechnic University of Bobo Dioulasso (UPB). A specialist in environmental questions related to development, he is currently the head of the Department of Rural Sociology and Economy and Assistant Editor of the doctoral School of Agronomic Sciences. Nominated as a Knight of the Academic Palms, he has authored three books and several scientific articles. His main focus in the SUSFISH project was on society and fishing.

Herwig Waidbacher has been head of the Department for Water, Atmosphere and Environment at the University of Natural Resources and Life Sciences Vienna since 2004. He has worked in the fields of hydrobiology and tropical limnology, fisheries, fish ecology, and aquaculture in temperate and in tropical water bodies for 30 years. He has led numerous projects on these topics. From 2006-2009 he coordinated the EU-funded project BOMOSA on cage fish farming systems in reservoirs, ponds and temporary water bodies in Eastern Africa (Kenya, Ethiopia, Uganda) and is still cooperating with many African partners, like SUSFISH, in supervising projects and master's/PhD theses.

Henri Zerbo is an engineer in rural development, specialized in forestry, wildlife, fisheries and the environment. He works as head of Fisheries at the General Directorate for Fish Resources in Burkina Faso. His work encompasses the conception, planning, coordination and implementation of undertakings in landscape, environment and forests – especially planning, monitoring and evaluation of policies and legislation in capture fisheries and aquaculture. He works with many national and international partners and has a wealth of experience in participatory approaches for many African countries such as Central African Republic, Ivory Coast, Mali, Niger and Chad. His main focus in the SUSFISH project was on fisheries management and governance.

Chapter 9

Yirgashewa Bekele is an Assistant Professor of Special Needs Education at Addis Ababa University. She received her first degree from Joensuu University, Finland and her PhD in Special Needs Education from Addis Ababa University. She has experience of working at government regional educational offices and has been a volunteer trainer at schools and non-governmental organizations in Ethiopia. Yirgashewa has been involved in various university-based projects in Austria, German, Finland, Norway and America since 2007. She has attended and presented papers at European Education Conferences. Her research interests are in the area of disability in general and barriers to learning and educational achievement of children with disability in particular.

Gottfried Biewer is Professor for Special Needs and Inclusive Education at the University of Vienna (2004-date) and head of the Department of Education. He has worked as teacher in the field of special needs education. After his doctoral degree from the University of Würzburg he became Assistant Professor at the University of Munich, Associate Professor at the University of Koblenz-Landau and Professor at the University of Giessen (all in Germany). His main research interests are inclusive education, comparative research in special needs education, disability issues in developing countries, vocational participation and life course research of persons with disabilities. In these areas he has led several research projects supported by the Austrian Science Fund (FWF) and the European Science Foundation (ESF). From 2011 to 2014, he was the coordinator of the RESPOND-HER project.

Kibrom Mengistu Feleke is an academic member of staff (2004-date) in the Department of Psychology, Faculty of Educational and Behavioral Sciences at Bahir Dar University, Ethiopia. He has an MA in Counselling Psychology from Addis Ababa University in Ethiopia and an MPhil in Administrative Science in Higher Education from the University of Oslo (Norway), the University of Tampere (Finland) and the University of Aveiro (Portugal). His research interests are governance, leadership, management, finance and research policies in higher education as well as themes concerning counselling, educational and social development, and health psychology.

Birgit Habermann works at the Centre for Development Research (CDR) at BOKU University, Vienna. She has studied Ecology and Agroforestry, and has a PhD in Development Studies. She has worked in Pakistan, Kirgistan, Thailand and East Africa, but her main focus is on Ethiopia. Her research interests are critical reflections on knowledge production, participation, and the construction of narratives in natural resource management in East Africa.

Christian Pippan is Assistant Professor at the Institute of International Law and International Relations at the University of Graz (Austria). He has been an Emile Noël Fellow at the New York University School of Law (2002-04), as well as a short-term Visiting Fellow at the Max Planck Institute for Comparative Public Law & International Law in Heidelberg (Germany) and the Lauterpacht Centre for International Law in Cambridge (UK). He has published on various issues of European and public international law, including articles and book chapters on EU development cooperation and human rights, the protection of minorities in Europe, the UN security system, self-determination and statehood, as well as on democratic governance and international law.

Michelle Proyer studied Education and Special Needs Education in Vienna and Berlin. She is currently about to finish her PhD in education (University of Vienna) on the cultural and societal implications of the educational environments of children with disabilities in Greater Bangkok, Thailand. She has been involved in two international projects (CLASDISA and RESPOND HER) during her employment with the Department of Education, Special Needs and Inclusive Education at the University of Vienna. Since September 2014 she has worked as a research associate at Kingston University London. Her research interests focus on disability and its intersections with gender, environment, culture (especially religion), and society.

Tirussew Teferra holds a PhD and is Professor of Special Needs Education at the Department of Special Needs Education, Addis Ababa University. He won the Outstanding Faculty Award for 2013 from Addis Ababa University. He has also earned the prestigious International Medal Award of UNESCO (Jan Amos Comenius) in Recognition of Outstanding Achievements in the field of Educational Research and Innovation. Through the Council for International Exchange Scholars Programme, he was also Fulbright Senior Research Fellow at the University of Indiana in the School of Education, 2003-2004. He is currently the Dean of the College of Education and Behavioral Studies at Addis Ababa University, and was the local project leader of the RESPOND-HER project (2011–2013).

Tadesse Kassa Woldetsadik is Assistant Professor in Public International and Human Rights Law at the College of Law and Governance Studies of Addis Ababa University (Ethiopia) and a Visiting Scholar at Xiangtan University (China). He has previously served as Director of the Center for Human Rights at AAU as well as Dean of the university's Law School. He has published a book on International Watercourses Law in the Nile Basin (2013) as well as articles and book chapters on various issues of public international law, human rights law, labor rights and legal aspects of Ethiopian foreign policy.

Chapter 10
Marie-France Chevron has been a Full Professor since 2008, and affiliated to the Department of Social and Cultural Anthropology, University of Vienna since 2011. Specific research interests: (1) development of urban areas in Africa and Europe (special focus on modernity and globalization, ecology and development, know-how transfer, waste and recycling, and cooperation between social sciences and technical experts) and (2) the theory and history of Social and Cultural Anthropology (in particular: interdisciplinary thinking and historical anthropology, methodology of social sciences, evolution and culture change). Supervision of theses (MA, PhD) on developmental issues in Africa and Europe, and the history of Anthropology. Evaluator and academic reviewer for several research institutions and programmes.

Ronald Luwangula is an Assistant Lecturer at Makerere University, Department of Social Work and Social Administration, Uganda. He is an APPEAR grant holder (2012–2015) under the PROSOWO project framework, pursuing his PhD in Psychology at Alpen Adria Universtät Klagenfurt, Austria. He holds an International Master's in Social Work and Human Rights from Gothenburg University, Sweden and a Bachelor of Social Work and Social Administration from Makerere University Kampala. His research and practice interest areas are child protection, social protection, social development and human rights.

Elijah Macharia Ndung'u is a psychologist, social worker and a doctoral grant holder under the PROSOWO project framework. He holds a Master of Arts degree in Counselling Psychology from United States International University-Nairobi (USIU) and a Bachelor of Arts Degree in Social Work from the University of Nairobi. Currently he is pursuing his PhD in Psychology at Alpen Adria Universtät Klagenfurt, Austria. His areas of research interest are developmental social work, trauma counselling, and trauma of poverty. On PROSOWO, he worked as a research assistant in the social work department at the University of Nairobi.

Kalkidan Negash Obse is a Lecturer of African Union Law and Human Rights at Addis Ababa University (AAU) and a PhD candidate at the University of Graz in Austria. He received his LLB (distinction) from Addis Ababa University and LLM (valedictorian, summa cum laude) from St. Thomas University in Florida, USA. Before starting his doctoral study in Austria, Kalkidan served as Acting Director of the Center for Human Rights at Addis Ababa University and as legal advisor to the University. He was recently awarded a doctoral scholarship by The Hague Academy of International Law which permitted him to complete a research stay at the Academy. Kalkidan has several publications on African Union Law with his most recent publication titled: *"The Arab Spring and the Question of Legality of Democratic Revolution in Theory and Practice", Leiden Journal of International Law.*

Sarah Ayeri Ogalleh is currently a Senior Scientist with CETRAD (Centre for Training and Integrated Research in ASAL Development) as well as a post-doctoral research fellow funded by the Volkswagen Foundation. She holds a PhD in Agriculture and Natural Resources from the University of Natural Resources and Life Sciences, Vienna (BOKU), where her main focus was climate change, agriculture, adaptations and local knowledge. She also holds an MSc in Environmental Science from the Department of Environmental Science at Egerton University and a bachelor's degree in Animal Sciences from Egerton University. Her current research interests revolve around gender, the environment, socioeconomic monitoring systems, integrated approaches and methods for rural development appraisal, Participatory Rural Appraisal (PRA), food security and drought management. She has authored and co-authored many scientific articles, papers and book chapters.

Elke Stinnig started her career as the Programme Manager for the North-South-Dialogue Scholarship Programme at the Austrian Agency for International Cooperation in Education and Research (OeAD) in 2005. She was involved in setting up the Austrian Partnership Programme in Higher Education and Research for Development (APPEAR) and since then has been working as its programme officer, with a focus on the scholarship component and gender issues. She is also the representative of the APPEAR team in the Steering Committee and Donor Harmonization Group. Elke Stinnig obtained a master's degree in Agricultural Sciences from the University of Natural Resources and Life Sciences, Vienna, and is presently undertaking further university education on African Studies at the University of Vienna.

Wossen Argaw Tegegn received a PhD in Social and Cultural Anthropology from the University of Vienna in 2014. Wossen was a resident scholar (2011/12) at the School for Advanced Research, Santa Fe (NM) in USA. In 2003, she got her MPhil degree in English language and linguistics from the University of Trondheim, Norway. She has been a Senior University Lecturer in Ethiopia. She was the founder of the Gender Equity Office at her home university and had long experience in gender issues in the higher education system. Her research interests are in teaching English as a foreign language, early grade literacy education, gender, and female empowerment with a special focus on higher education. She is currently an Assistant Professor in the School of Humanities and Law at Arsi University, Ethiopia.

ANDREAS J. OBRECHT

GESCHICHTEN AUS ANDEREN WELTEN

EINE REISE NACH NEUGUINEA UND INSELMELANESIEN, OSTAFRIKA, NEPAL UND IN DIE KARIBIK

Gute Schuhe, ein schönes Buch, ein Mikrophon und ein Aufnahmegerät – das sind die spärlichen Utensilien aus der modernen Welt, die Andreas J. Obrecht in die Fremde mitnimmt. Auf seiner Reise spürt er den Geschichten und Klängen entlegener Regionen nach, um die Zwischentöne einer beredten und geheimnisvollen Welt aufzufangen und auch am magischen Verständnis dieser Kulturen teilzuhaben – wonach alle Erscheinungen der Natur, des menschlichen Lebens und des sozialen Handelns aufeinander bezogen sind. Dieses Tagebuch einer Weltreise trägt uns von einem Ort zum anderen, von einer Begegnung, von einer Geschichte zur nächsten. Zeit spielt dabei keine Rolle, denn man weiß nie, wie lange die Bewegung, das Zuhören, die Suche, die Reise und mit ihr das Lernen dauern werden.

2006. 352 S. 40 S/W-ABB. GB. 170 X 240 MM | ISBN 978-3-205-77515-7